RACIALIZED CORRECTIONAL GOVERNANCE

Racialized Correctional Governance *provides a thought-provoking analysis of the way correctional policies and practices construct racialized identities. The book traces how older notions of racial inferiority are combined with new technologies of risk and anti-social behaviour to produce a discourse of racialized peoples as criminal populations. The author challenges criminologists to engage in a new way of thinking about race and criminal justice.*

Chris Cunneen, James Cook University, Australia

Advances in Criminology

Series Editor: David Nelken

The full list of series titles can be found at the back of the book.

Racialized Correctional Governance

The Mutual Constructions of Race and Criminal Justice

CLAIRE SPIVAKOVSKY
Monash University, Australia

ASHGATE

Published by
Ashgate Publishing Limited
Wey Court East
Union Road
Farnham
Surrey, GU9 7PT
England

Ashgate Publishing Company
110 Cherry Street
Suite 3-1
Burlington, VT 05401-3818
USA

www.ashgate.com

British Library Cataloguing in Publication Data
Spivakovsky, Claire.
  Racialized correctional governance : the mutual
  constructions of race and criminal justice. -- (Advances in
  criminology)
  1. Discrimination in criminal justice administration.
  2. Racism in criminology. 3. Equality before the law.
  4. Minorities--Legal status, laws, etc. 5. Indigenous
  peoples--Legal status, laws, etc.
  I. Title II. Series
  364'.089-dc23

The Library of Congress has cataloged the printed edition as follows
Spivakovsky, Claire.
  Racialized correctional governance : the mutual constructions of race and criminal justice / by
Claire Spivakovsky.
     pages cm. -- (Advances in criminology)
  Includes bibliographical references and index.
  ISBN 978-1-4094-3751-2 (hardback) -- ISBN 978-1-4094-3752-9 (ebook) -- ISBN 978-1-4094-
8468-4 (epub) 1. Discrimination in criminal justice administration. 2. Corrections--Moral and
ethical aspects. 3. Racism. 4. Criminal justice, Administration of--Moral and ethical aspects. I.
Title.
  HV7419.S65 2013
  365.089--dc23

                                                                                    2013003624

ISBN 9781409437512 (hbk)
ISBN 9781409437529 (ebk – PDF)
ISBN 9781409484684 (ebk – ePUB)

Printed and bound in Great Britain
by MPG PRINTGROUP

Contents

Preface

I want to begin this preface with a brief disclaimer. This preface focuses on the personal and challenging experiences that inspired and shaped the content, orientation, arguments and conclusions of this book. There is therefore potential for this preface to turn into an indulgent and existential discussion about me, the author. This is not my intention. I share these personal and challenging experiences with you, the reader, not simply because they indicate how and why this particular book emerged, but also to invite you to consider how criminology is shaped by the experiences of its scholars.

This book is first and foremost inspired by my experiences in producing criminology. In employing the term 'producing' I refer to two things. First, the content of this book is based on a research project I completed at the University of Melbourne in the late 2000s. The research explored how correctional agencies in the state of Victoria, Australia, and New Zealand approach the offender rehabilitation principle of responsivity in relation to their Indigenous offender populations – what has now become the focus of Chapter 5.

While the focus and content of the project has been significantly transformed in the development of this book, it was only in its production that I began to think about issues of race and criminal justice in a different way. In particular, it was only by thinking about the way correctional agencies engage with the experiences of Indigenous populations as an afterthought or an add-on component to a program when creating and implementing criminal justice practice that drew my attention to the fundamental focus of this book: criminology's problematic treatment of issues of race and criminal justice, and the implications for the way the discipline creates racialized practices and works with racialized peoples. However, it was not the content of the research project that inspired me to write this book. Rather, it was my experiences in producing and delivering conference papers.

Over the past seven years I have presented papers at a variety of criminology and criminal justice conferences. My papers have focused on the use of specific penal tools by criminal justice practitioners, the spaces and orientation of criminal justice systems, the experiences of Indigenous criminal justice staff, and a broad range of other criminal justice issues. Yet regardless of what issue I chose to present at a conference, I encountered the same frustrating problem in the majority I attended. That is, if your conference paper addresses a 'racialized' issue, and by this I mean, if your conference abstract, title or paper mentions a racialized population in any context, the majority of conference convenors will allocate your conference paper to the Indigenous justice, ethnicity, race, or marginalization conference stream. You are put in this stream regardless of whether your paper is about police, courts, corrections, criminal justice, primary prevention, victimology, reintegration or any other aspect of criminology.

While grouping conference papers that address 'racialized' issues is a seemingly logical decision, the reality of the situation is far more complex. Confining my conference papers to the Indigenous justice or ethnicity and race streams meant that I was often the only speaker in the session who would present a paper about penal issues, and that my paper would be presented alongside the only speaker addressing a policing issue, and the only speaker addressing a community or primary prevention issue.

The lack of synergy between our papers was both frustrating and problematic. Unable to find any common threads between our papers other than their engagement with some form of racialized issues, audience members would inevitably respond to our papers in one of two problematic ways. First, an audience member would say, 'this question is for all the speakers, each of your papers show that Indigenous people have problems in the criminal justice system, what do you think is the solution?' Thus conflating all the issues from the various subject matters presented. Second, another audience member would inevitably tell the speakers about an unrelated racialized issue in their life and ask for a response. For example, at the last criminology conference I attended, a white male informed us his daughter had married an Aboriginal man a few years back and that their children seemed to be struggling at school as a result of their 'mixed' heritage. The man wanted to know if we thought his grandchildren's educational problems were related to our discussions of Aboriginal peoples' over-representation in the criminal justice system and, of course, what we thought the solution was.

By placing any criminologist who mentions a racialized population as part of their discussion on penal tools, sentencing, primary prevention or any other diverse criminological topic in the same stream, conference convenors ensure that the actual content of the paper fails to be transferred to the audience members (as is evident in the type of questions elicited from audience members). Moreover, what is transferred is something very different and unintended: an impression that racialized peoples regularly have problems with the criminal justice system and that the problem resides in these peoples' racialized identity.

These repeated experiences have frustrated me immensely. However, they have also inspired me. They have inspired me to think about the different ways criminologists develop their understanding about a topic of interest. They have made me think about the impact on criminologists' understanding of criminal justice issues if papers like mine only ever appear in the race/ethnicity stream of conferences because of their racialized content. Finally, they have made me think about what it means for criminologists' understanding of racialized peoples' experiences if papers like mine are repeatedly met with the same sort of audience response. It is the result of these experiences of producing criminology that have inspired the development of this book.

Claire Spivakovsky,
November 2012

Acknowledgements

This book is based on a large research project which I completed at the University of Melbourne, and I owe a deep debt of gratitude to a number of people who were involved in its completion. In particular I am grateful to Mark Brown. As a supervisor, Mark not only challenged me to go one step further with my analysis, but also provided me the space to independently determine how to take that step, and how to interpret what I found when I arrived. I have used the research skills I gained from Mark's challenges throughout the development of this book. I am also thankful to have shared my time at the University of Melbourne with a number of people who have become good friends along the way. In particular, I am thankful for the unwavering support of Simone Gristwood, the advice and editorial skills of Beejay Silcox and the encouragement of Emma Colvin and Rebecca Hiscock.

I am indebted to the members of staff at the Victorian Department of Justice and the New Zealand Department of Corrections. As this book details, these individuals not only sit at the frontline of contemporary penal practice but also negotiate its operation. I am indebted to these individuals for finding time within their demanding jobs to answer my questions about Indigenous offenders and correctional practice. This book would not have been possible without their words and explanations.

I am grateful to those who have reviewed my work over the years. In particular I am grateful to Kelly Hannah-Moffat, who examined the initial project and provided an engaging and thought provoking examination report. This report enabled me to see how a study about two small jurisdictions in the southern hemisphere may hold greater relevance for criminology's understanding of race and punishment in general. I am also grateful for the expertise of Ashgate Publishing, and in particular for the insightful comments of the anonymous reviewers who challenged me to write a more ambitious book than originally proposed.

While completing this book I have had the opportunity to work in a number of positions in academia, and the community and government sectors. Each of these positions has provided me with new perspectives on what it means to be a criminologist, to produce criminology and to work with criminology's products. There are a number of individuals across these workplaces that I would like to thank for their support over the years. In particular, I thank Sophie Goldingay, Tina Murphy, Tanya King and Joanna Cruickshank of Deakin University, Australia; Sarah Spencer, Kelly Warner and Charles Levy of the Australian Community Support Organisation; Magdalena McGuire and Lois Bedson of the Office of the Public Advocate, Australia; and Lauren Treby and Sara Ferdowsi of Moonee Valley City Council. It has been a privilege to work alongside such inspired, intelligent and genuine individuals.

Finally, I thank my partner Daniel Prior, who, regardless of the choices I make in life, provides unwavering and unconditional support, friendship and love.

List of Abbreviations

AJF	Aboriginal Justice Forum
CBT	Cognitive Behavioural Therapy
CNI	Criminogenic Needs Inventory
GLM	Good Lives Model
IPSU	Indigenous Policy and Services Unit
KJU	Koori Justice Unit
MaCRN	Māori Culture-Related Needs
MFU	Māori Focus Unit
RCIADIC	Royal Commission into Aboriginal Deaths in Custody
RNRM	Risk Need Responsivity Model
RoC	Risk of re-Conviction
SMCA	Specialist Māori Cultural Assessment

Introduction

The Rates of Over-representation

Aboriginal and Torres Strait Islander peoples make up less than three per cent of Australia's population and yet represent almost 24 per cent of Australia's prison population (Joudo 2008). Māori make up 14 per cent of New Zealand's population, but represent over 50 per cent of New Zealand's prison population (Morrison 2009). Only three per cent of Canada's general population is comprised of Aboriginal peoples and yet Aboriginal offenders make up 17 per cent of Canada's federal prison system (Cunneen 2001). In the United States, it is estimated that one in every 25 American Indians over the age of 18 will have contact with a criminal justice system on any given day (Greenfeld and Smith 1999).

For the past two decades, criminologists have used the rates of over-represented racialized peoples[1] in criminal justice systems as a discursive shorthand for discussing issues of race; and why not? These stark and simple figures support several propositions about race and criminal justice:

- over-representation in criminal justice systems is an experience common to and stemming from racialized peoples (see for example Hall, Green, Chambers and Lea 2006: Perreault 2009: Weatherburn 2006);
- over-represented racialized peoples are a feature common to and stemming from Western criminal justice systems (see for example Cunneen 2006: Holdaway 1996: Monture-Angus 1999);
- over-represented racialized peoples in criminal justice systems are a contemporary or historical problem (see for example Finnane and McGuire 2001: Ross 1998); and
- the problem of over-represented racialized peoples spreads across all arms of criminal justice systems – from police, to courts, prisons and reintegration services (see for example Department of Justice 2006: Home Office 2004).

Yet, criminologists rarely look beyond the rates of over-representation to explain why the 'problem' of racialized peoples' over-representation in criminal justice systems only entered criminological discourse in the past two decades. Nor do they

---

1   I use the term 'racialized peoples' to refer to the way that populations such as Aboriginal Australians or Canadians are often identified in terms of their racial status or other socially-constructed identifiers of race.

explain why, after twenty years of acknowledging the problem, a comprehensive theory of race and criminal justice has not developed in criminology.

Accounting for Over-represented Racialized Peoples

This is not to say that criminology is absent of explanations for racialized peoples' over-representation in criminal justice systems. To the contrary, two contrasting explanations are repeated throughout the world. One that implicates racialized peoples as the problem in their over-representation, and one that implicates Western society.

The first explanation challenges the notion of over-representation. It proposes that racialized peoples are imprisoned at a rate *proportionate* to their criminal activity. Those who ascribe to this explanation typically present race as a discrete variable in statistical analyses of prison populations. For example, Weatherburn and colleagues' Australian analyses of prisoner populations conclude that the rates of imprisonment reflect:

- the violent nature of Indigenous offending (Snowball and Weatherburn 2007);
- the greater number of offenders in Indigenous populations when compared to their non-Indigenous counterparts (Weatherburn, Fitzgerald and Hua 2003: Weatherburn, Lind and Hua 2003); and
- the common problematic behaviours of Indigenous populations – such as misusing alcohol and other drugs, or engaging in family violence (Weatherburn 2006: Weatherburn, Snowball and Hunter 2006).

Similar arguments have been presented in New Zealand in relation to Māori offenders. For example, a group of researchers from the Institute of Environmental Science and Research recently disseminated controversial findings about what they termed, the Māori 'warrior gene' (Hall, Green, Chambers and Lea 2006; Lea and Chambers 2007). The researchers claim Māori have a unique genetic sequence causing them to have higher levels of an enzyme associated with risk-taking and aggressive behaviour. The researchers propose this 'warrior gene' could explain why Māori are 'more aggressive and violent and more likely to get involved in risk-taking behaviour like gambling' (One News 2006).

The second common explanation for racialized peoples' over-representation challenges the notion that over-representation is a 'problem' with racialized peoples. It proposes that over-represented racialized peoples in criminal justice systems are a *symptom* of Western colonization. Proponents of this explanation typically draw on a combination of interviews, archival documents and other historic artefacts about government relations with racialized peoples. Beginning again with Australian examples, Broadhurst (1997) concludes that the States and Territories of Australia that most demonstrate qualities of 'frontier culture' – perceiving Aboriginal peoples as a threat to 'vulnerable' settler societies – are more likely to exhibit a punitive attitude towards sentencing Aboriginal offenders. Similarly, Cunneen's body of work (2001, 2006, 2011; Cunneen and McDonald 1997) concludes that historical factors such as colonization are responsible for embedding Aboriginal over-representation in Australia's criminal justice systems.

Similar arguments regarding the symptomatic nature of over-representation can be found in other jurisdictions (see for example Holdaway 1996; Ross 1998). For example, in the Canadian context, Monture-Angus (1999: 25) argues that Aboriginal offending is fundamentally tied to the impact of colonization. Monture-Angus proposes that current risk assessment processes do not account for this impact and, as a result, they ensure that Aboriginal offenders enter prison systems more often than their non-Aboriginal counterparts.

Reducing criminology's interpretation of race and criminal justice to these two, opposing explanations is deeply problematic. Not only does this binary fall short of a comprehensive criminological theory, but its repeated presence appears to have impeded criminologists from developing one. What has filled criminological discussions instead is a debate about the methodological rigour of these studies of over-representation (for an example of this debate see Cunneen 2006 and the rejoinder, Weatherburn and Fitzgerald 2007; see Phillips and Bowling 2003; and Cheliotis and Liebling 2006 for commentary on the repetitive, dead-end nature of this debate in other parts of the world).

Engaging with racialized peoples' over-representation in this way is seemingly out of character for criminology. Criminology is a rendezvous discipline. It proposes that most, if not all, criminological issues take form among a broader range of socio-economic and political factors. It therefore borrows and blends concepts from law, sociology, anthropology, politics, journalism, psychology, urban planning, economics, social work and a range of other disciplines in order to account for these complex issues. Yet, this fundamental feature of criminology is largely absent from the discipline's attempts to account for over-represented racialized peoples in criminal justice systems. This issue has simply been interpreted with two contrasting and limited explanations. I propose this seemingly out of character response is symptomatic of a broader problem in criminology.

The Process of Excising Race from Criminology

Criminology treats the topic of race as if it was the offal of the discipline. By this I mean that criminology has largely excised issues of race from broader discussions of police, courts or corrections. It relegates these disjointed pieces of racialized criminology to a small corner of the discipline. It then interacts with this disjointed pile of racialized issues as if they have always been separate from mainstream criminology – as if they have no prior, current or future connection to criminological thought or practice.

This is not to suggest that criminologists have played a malicious role in the discipline's problematic treatment of race. Rather, the process of excising race from criminology has occurred in subtle and diffuse ways. For example, criminology students and their academics work with textbooks that either omit discussions of racialized peoples, or constrain them to a single chapter on race, crime and criminal justice (see for example Findlay, Odgers and Yeo 2005; Hale, Hayward, Wahidin and Wincup 2009; Hucklesby and Wahidin 2009; Newburn 2007). Within this chapter, a diverse array of criminal justice issues relating to racialized peoples are presented, regardless of the relevance of one issue to the next. Consequently, students are left with the impression:

- racialized peoples present with numerous problems across criminal justice systems; and
- these problems are not associated with those raised and discussed in previous chapters of their textbook.

Similarly, annual criminological conferences, such as those of the American, British, Australian and New Zealand Societies of Criminology, typically categorize their conference sessions according to key criminological issues. There are sessions to discuss 'drugs', 'policing culture', 'sentencing' and 'punishment' (see for example Deakin University, Australia and the Australian and New Zealand Society of Criminology 2011; British Society of Criminology 2011). Yet, racialized peoples' 'drug' issues are rarely heard in the 'drugs' session; and racialized peoples' experiences of criminal justice systems are rarely heard in the context of 'policing culture', 'sentencing' or 'punishment' in practice. Instead, these accounts are typically aired within streams focusing on Indigenous populations or ethnicity, with titles such as 'Indigenous offending and imprisonment', 'trafficking and ethnicity', or 'criminal justice and ethnicity'. They are relegated to these *population-based* sessions where they can be heard alongside a series of other unrelated criminological *issues*.

Confining the issues of racialized peoples to population-based streams ensures these issues and the broader experiences of racialized peoples:

- do not enter broader criminological discussions;
- are only heard in the context of other 'racialized' criminal justice issues; and
- can be missed altogether when, for example, criminologists presume the 'criminal justice and ethnicity' session will not contain discussions relevant to their research on 'drugs'.

The Effects of Excising Race from Criminology

The process of excising race from criminology affects the way criminologists *engage* with racialized issues. It affects both the way criminologists identify solutions to criminological problems, and how they construct these problems and solutions.

Identifying homogenous problems and solutions in criminal justice

The criminological literature on culturally appropriate practice exemplifies how criminologists' capacity to identify solutions to criminological problems is affected. This body of literature acts as a container for some of the disjointed racialized issues extracted from mainstream criminological discussions (for example, issues about over-policing, sentencing circles, over-representation in custody and so on). It also acts as a forum within which the histories and experiences of diverse racialized populations are presented as interrelated through the commonality of 'race'. As a result, the solutions scholars generate from this literature to problems such as over-representation are distorted.

'Culturally appropriate' solutions to criminological problems often homogenize the experiences of diverse racialized and marginalized groups. For example, Jones, Masters, Griffiths and Moulday (2002) use disconnected experiences of diverse racialized populations in a range of criminal justice systems to generate principles for culturally relevant assessment with Aboriginal offenders in Australia. Similarly, Lum (2011) devises a 'cultural competence framework' which is presented as suitable to use in relation to a diverse range of racialized and marginalized populations – from First Nations Peoples and Latino Americans, to lesbian, gay, bisexual and transgender persons.

Homogenizing the experiences of diverse racialized and marginalized populations in these ways is problematic. Waldram (1997) provides an apt account of how 'solutions' such as these encourage criminal justice practitioners to develop inappropriate cultural practices when working with racialized populations. Using Canadian Prison Spirituality Programs as an example, Waldram details how homogenous 'culturally appropriate' programs are capable of:

- *redefining* individuals' perceptions of their culture – by providing them with a generic account based on a range of different cultures; and
- *creating* connections to culture for individuals who were raised without this connection.

Debating the right to speak about racialized problems and solutions

The process of excising race from criminology also affects the way criminologists construct racialized problems and solutions. That is, some criminologists have begun to ask, who *has* identified problems like over-representation and who *should* identify solutions like culturally appropriate practice?

Emerging bodies of texts such as the 'new minorities' contend that only minority researchers have the right to explain other minorities' experiences in the criminal justice system (see for example Phillips and Bowling 2003; Phillips 2005). Scholars such as Phillips and colleagues argue that solutions for racialized peoples' over-representation in criminal justice systems can not be found until criminology deconstructs how it problematizes over-representation. Phillips and Bowling (2003) contend it is minority researchers who are best placed to deconstruct the process of criminological knowledge production surrounding their populations' over-representation, because minority researchers are best placed in the inherent power relationship between researcher and (minority) research participant.

While I agree with Phillips and Bowling's contention, I am concerned about the ramifications of their proposal. In a discipline that has already largely excised race from mainstream criminological thought, I am concerned that a proposal to further relegate racialized issues to the domain of minority researchers will be co-opted by the discipline. I am concerned that proposals like this will be used by criminology to abrogate its role in engaging with issues of race and criminal justice altogether.

The impact on criminology
As it currently stands, engaging with racialized issues in the ways described above has removed any sense of proportionality. There is no sense within the discipline of:

- the full nature of the problems facing racialized peoples;
- how big racialized problems are in criminal justice systems,
- the parts of criminal justice systems where these problems present;
- what changes, developments or tensions occur alongside these problems in other areas of criminal justice; and
- the similarities or differences between the problems facing racialized peoples and those facing other populations in criminal justice systems.

What is provided instead is an impression that racialized peoples are a particular problem within criminal justice systems, and two very limited ways to account for this.

Establishing a Different Relationship between Criminology and Racialized Issues

This book seeks to break this tradition in criminology. It aims to provide criminology with tools to engage with issues of race and criminal justice in their 'proper dispersion' (Foucault 2000a: 374). Foucault used the term 'proper dispersion' to describe one of the core features of genealogy – where researchers pay attention to all mutations, deviations and errors that occur in the history of a practice, in order to question the practice's self-evidence. I use the term 'proper dispersion' in a slightly different way. I use it to:

1. describe what has largely been absent from criminology – engaging with issues of race at the numerous points that they are dispersed across criminal justice systems, and paying attention to the deviations and errors that occur when race is taken into account at these points; and

2. indicate how criminology can remedy this problem – engaging with constructions of race, the practice of criminal justice and the orientation of criminological discourse by drawing attention to the mutations that have occurred in their interrelated formation.

I am not the first to invite criminology to engage with issues of race and criminal justice in a different way. Over the past decade, several penal scholars have moved towards exploring the logics, tools, technologies and practices that allow problems like racialized peoples' over-representation to take shape. These scholars encourage other criminologists to follow suit. Two vital insights can be found in these scholars' work.

Constructing Racial Identities through Criminal Justice

First, a collection of Canadian and United Kingdom scholars illuminates the intersections, collisions and crossovers between constructions of racialized identities and the technologies of criminal justice (Hannah-Moffat and Maurutto 2010; Hudson and Bramhall 2005; Maurutto and Hannah-Moffat 2007). These scholars draw attention to the role and manner by which penal tools construct racial identities and the consequences of this construction for racialized peoples. They draw particular attention to the role of risk assessment tools in the construction process.

For instance, Maurutto and Hannah-Moffat (2007) discuss the markers used in Canadian risk assessment tools to identify and classify offenders' risk of reoffending. They show how risk markers are typically based on aggregate data of common factors in offender populations and, as a result, these markers are proxy measures of lower socio-economic status. Consequently, groups who are socio-economically marginalized, such as Aboriginal peoples of Canada, may be assessed as posing a high risk of reoffending. This assessment occurs not because Aboriginal peoples have a greater propensity to engage in offending behaviour, but because Aboriginal peoples are more likely to present with a range of factors associated with low socio-economic status.

Yet, even when factors associated with Aboriginal peoples' marginalization are recognized as distinct from those of 'risk', incorrect associations can occur. Later work by Hannah-Moffat and Maurutto (2010) shows how factors associated with Aboriginal peoples' marginalization – such as dislocation from communities, acculturation and disadvantage – are treated in culturally appropriate pre-sentence reports (Gladue reports) as non-criminological variables. However, when these variables are incorporated into risk-based pre-sentence reports, this association is distorted. In risk-based reports, these factors either appear as something akin to 'risk of reoffending' factors, or as unprocessable factors that hold no relevance for calculating risk or targeting criminogenic need.[2]

Hudson and Bramhall (2005) further contribute to this emerging body of work on risk assessment tools in their study of probation in north-west England. Hudson and Bramhall illuminate a different problematic feature of risk assessment processes: racialized interpretations of risk markers. They demonstrate how risk factors such as 'having a problematic relationship with family', are interpreted in different ways by probation services, depending on localized constructions of race. Accordingly, 'White' offenders are assessed as posing a risk of reoffending because they *lack* a relationship with their family, whereas Asian offenders are assessed as posing a risk of reoffending because they possess *too close* a relationship with their family. Hudson and Bramhall argue that these interpretations reflect an insidious national construction of 'Asianness' in English culture, in which associations with 'over-close' or 'controlling' Asian families are perceived as problematic.

Hudson and Bramhall (2005) also comment on the unprocessable nature of some racialized issues in risk assessment tools. They illustrate how Asian offenders' claims of racial provocation are not processed as part of their risk assessment. This omission occurs because there is no clear space in current risk assessment tools to either transcribe these issues of race, or to measure their impact on offending behaviour. They argue this omission is problematic because information about racial provocation could aid assessment of the offender's attitude towards offending behaviour – a key dynamic risk factor.

While the collection of findings presented above is small, it provides a vital insight into the dispersion of race and criminal justice issues in criminological thought and practice. These studies show how social constructions of race are propagated through the technologies, techniques and logics of the criminal justice system, while experiences of racialization remain unprocessable. They suggest the problem of over-representation may have less to do with whether or not racialized peoples or Western institutions behave problematically, and more to do with the way either of these explanations for over-representation are positioned, co-opted or discarded when identifying criminality and risk.

Shaping Criminal Justice through Constructions of Race

The intersection of racial and penal constructs is not a modern development. Bosworth (2004) indicates that racial constructions have informed and shaped the emergence of criminal justice tools and logics across the world. Using the development and trajectory of punishment in France, England and the United States over the past few centuries as examples, Bosworth (2004) illustrates how

---

2   'Criminogenic needs' are defined as 'dynamic risk factors'. That is, they are risk factors which have a direct relationship with a person's offending behaviour (hence the term 'criminogenic'), and which are capable of changing through targeted treatment (hence the term 'dynamic').

factors and behaviours deemed anti-social or punishable in each country are linked to notions of nationhood and otherness. In France, for example – where the issue of French citizenship is fundamental to the notion of nationhood – non-citizens and foreigners are over-represented in prison. Similarly, in England – where British notions of nationhood rest on the traditional identity of British subjects as White subjects – British Asians and Afro-Caribbean people are over-represented. Finally, in the United States – where differences and differentiation between ethnic groups is paramount – an array of ethnic populations is over-represented, including African Americans, Latinos and American Indians. In light of these findings, Bosworth (2004: 237) encourages criminologists to consider the ways by which 'notions of race have simply been written into the entire notion of punishment itself'.

A range of scholars from the United States have taken up this task. In this vein, Wacquant (2001, 2009, 2010a, 2010b, 2010c) repeatedly draws attention to how major shifts in United States' penal systems have been based on issues of class, race and the workforce in America. In particular, Wacquant (2010a, 2010b) illuminates how the trend towards the 'hyperincarceration' of class and race in the United States is fundamentally tied to the decay and implosion of the traditional ghetto. He argues that over the second half of the twentieth century the ghetto was 'prisonized' and the prison was 'ghettoized'. That is, both the ghetto and the prison took on the characteristics, populations and operations of the other. His work shows how this role reversal 'ensnares' lower class African American men in the prison system and redeploys the prison as a container for poverty.

Davis (2003) takes a step further back in the history of construction. Davis ties the development of the United States' penal system to the decay and implosion of slavery in its southern States. She observes how African American men's inclusion and regulation in legal sanctions for punishment came into effect at the same time and in the same proportions as their removal from legal sanctions of slavery. Her work illuminates how legal sanctions were generated in response to southern States' desire to maintain control over African American people when other forms of regulation were abolished.

Viewed together, the findings of Bosworth, Wacquant and Davis illuminate the vital role racialized issues have played in the formation and orientation of criminal justice. They show how constructions and regulations of racialized identities are intimately linked to the historical formations of criminal justice systems, not simply propagated by modern penal techniques such as risk assessments. These scholars show how notions of nationhood and otherness are instrumental to both the development of criminal justice systems and the techniques that will see specific populations more often appear within them.

Exploring the Mutual Constructions of Race and Criminal Justice

What has been started by the small collection of works presented above is an account of the two ends of the relationship of race and criminal justice: the construction of race through penal tools and logics, and the role of racialized issues in the formation and orientation of criminal justice. What is still missing is an account of the middle – of the places where these processes of construction intersect and support one another, and of the places where these processes of construction intersect and are supported by criminological discourse. What is largely absent from criminology is an account of the collision, negotiation and transference that takes place through the mutual constructions of race, criminal justice and criminology.[3] This book provides an account of this missing middle ground.

The Structure of the Book

This book invites criminology to address its history of excising race from the discipline by engaging with issues of race and criminal justice in their proper dispersion. Its purpose is therefore to provide criminologists with a set of tools to engage with the mutual constructions of race, criminal justice and criminology. To address this purpose, this book performs three tasks. First, it develops a set of rules for engaging with issues of race and criminal justice in their proper dispersion. Second, it applies these rules to a series of case studies of race, criminal justice and criminology's mutual construction. Finally, it uses the findings arising from these case studies to propose a method of approach for criminologists when they engage with issues of race and criminal justice in the future. Consequently, the book is divided into three sections.

Section 1: Criminology's role in the proper dispersion of race and criminal justice
The first section, covering two chapters, addresses criminology's role in the proper dispersion of race and criminal justice. Chapter 1, *The 'Infallible Science' of Offending Behaviour*, addresses the role criminology *has played* in the dispersion of race and criminal justice. I argue criminology's correctional literature has become a medium for practice over the past two decades. It has become the domain for works written expressly for the purpose of informing, documenting and legitimizing principles, techniques and approaches used in practice. I contend criminology has used this medium to generate an 'infallible science' of offending behaviour which both bears and continues the legacy of criminology's treatment of race as offal into the field of practice.

To evince this argument, I employ the case example of the emergence and sustained appeal of the Risk Need Responsivity Model of offender rehabilitation. This Model emerged in the early 1990s criminology literature, claiming to provide

---

3   An exception to this statement is Gomez (2010). Gomez looked at the mutually constitutive nature of law and race through a series of monographs. Gomez (2010: 488) provides a review of a dozen monographs on law and race in society and concludes that 'law and race construct each other in an ongoing, dialectic process that ultimately reproduces and transforms racial inequality'.

correctional agencies with actuarial based tools and risk management approaches for effective offender classification and treatment. These tools and approaches have since become the staple for many correctional agencies across the world. I argue that criminology's problematic treatment of racialized issues plays a key role in the way these tools and approaches were developed in criminological literature, and used in correctional practice. I trace how these tools and approaches deploy a figure of the offender who is: (1) founded in age-old notions of innate, racialized deficiency; (2) regulated by modern notions of risk and anti-social behaviour; (3) produced by rituals of penal practice; (4) presented as transferable across criminal justice jurisdictions, regardless of population differences; and (5) capable of propagating the notions of an innately criminal racialized population. In doing so, this chapter reveals the role criminology plays in *distorting* the dispersion of race and criminal justice.

Next, Chapter 2, *The Rules of Engagement*, proposes a different way for criminology to engage with the dispersion of race and criminal justice. As the title suggests, I use this Chapter to present a set of rules of engagement that criminology can use to *maintain* the proper dispersion of race and criminal justice.

To do this, I draw on a range of theoretical constructs and lenses which bring awareness to particular operations and processes in practice without predetermining their intentions or direction. In particular, I engage with Foucault's oeuvre. I contend that Foucault's constructs of power, discourse and genealogy can be used to understand both the position of racialized peoples in the criminal justice system, and the frameworks of knowledge that explain these positions.

I also address the limitations of Foucault's constructs when accounting for racialized issues. I do this by supplementing Foucault's work with a range of theoretical lenses developed by other scholars, including Butler, Bosworth, Carrabine, Spivak, and Miller and Rose. I use this integrated work to provide three key rules of engagement for criminology that are then applied within the next section of this book.

Section 2: The mutual constructions of race, criminal justice and criminology

The second section of the book applies the rules of engagement in a series of case studies of the mutual constructions of race, criminal justice and criminology. The section comprises three chapters.

The first two chapters, chapters 3 and 4, consider the application of the rules of engagement in the context of the complex relationship between national identity, racialized subjectivity and criminal justice. These chapters explore the role that this complex relationship has played in the formation, transformation and reconfiguration of criminal justice in different jurisdictions. Each chapter provides a jurisdiction-specific case study of the mutual construction process.

Chapter 3, *Unavoidable and Undeniable History*, provides a case study of the complex relationship between national identity, racialized subjectivity and criminal justice in the formation, transformation and reconfiguration of the criminal justice system in the Australian State of Victoria.[4]

Australia has a unique history of settler colonization[5] which began when the first British settlers claimed that Australia was *terra nullius* – it belonged to no one. This history has been continued by successive Australian Federal Government policies which continue to remove Aboriginal peoples from their land through a variety of means (for example, assimilation and decreased life expectancy). Over the past two decades, the Victorian State Government has produced a series of criminal justice initiatives, agreements and programs with Aboriginal communities that seek to respond to this history of colonization and the Australian Federal Government's role in it. Chapter 3 explores these responses in detail.

Chapter 3 reveals the messy relationship that has formed between Victoria's criminal justice system and Victorian Aboriginal communities. I argue that a constellation of location-specific factors have forced open Victoria's criminal justice system to Aboriginal peoples' authority. I propose Aboriginal peoples have used this position of authority to rewrite Western offender management frameworks and practices with Aboriginal knowledge and perspectives on population management. I show how this messy relationship plays a fundamental role in the formation and orientation of Victoria's criminal justice processes and practice.

Chapter 4, *Biculturalism: Struggling to Maintain Dual Histories*, also provides a case study of the relationship between national identity, racialized subjectivity and criminal justice and the role of this relationship in the mutual constructions of race and criminal justice. This study focuses on the formation, transformation and reconfiguration of New Zealand's criminal justice system.

New Zealand also has a unique history of settler colonization, one which is vastly different to that of Australia. New Zealand's history is hinged on a Treaty, the Treaty of Waitangi. This Treaty was signed in 1840 by the British Crown and some (but not all) Māori Chiefs. It provides the founding principles on which any interaction between the New Zealand Government and its Māori population should be built; including which rights Māori are entitled to share with New Zealand's non-Māori population, and which they are entitled in addition.

Chapter 4 reveals how this very different history of colonization in New Zealand led to the emergence of a 'bicultural' New Zealand Department of Corrections, where Māori and non-Māori staff provide different types of authority about Māori offending behaviour. I illuminate how this 'bicultural' institution has

---

4   The Commonwealth of Australia is made up of six States (Victoria, New South Wales, Queensland, South Australia, Tasmania and Western Australia), two mainland territories (the Australian Capital Territory and the Northern Territory) and eight external territories (principally smaller islands and the Australian Antarctic Territory).

5   The term settler colonization is used to describe situations in colonized societies where the purpose of colonization was to settle land, not exploit labour (see Wolfe 1999 for a detailed account of Australia's settler colonial history).

struggled to locate Māori offenders somewhere between the Western world and the Māori world. I argue this struggle has allowed for criminology's 'infallible science' of offending behaviour to co-opt the Department of Corrections' attempts at bicultural practice with Māori. I show how this struggle plays a fundamental role in the formation and orientation of New Zealand's criminal justice processes and practice.

The final chapter in section two, Chapter 5, *Diverse History, Common Practice*, considers the application of the rules of engagement from a different angle of the mutual construction process. It explores the way penal logics and technologies contribute to the construction of racialized identity. It does so by re-engaging with the Victorian and New Zealand case studies presented in chapters 3 and 4. It explores how the principle of responsivity, a penal technology that emerged from criminology's 'infallible science' of offending behaviour (presented in Chapter 1), has been approached by the Victorian Department of Justice and the New Zealand Department of Corrections in relation to Aboriginal and Māori offenders. The chapter focuses on the logics, technologies and tools used in the practice of responsivity, and the subject positions Aboriginal and Māori offenders are expected to occupy in relation to this practice. I argue that the location-specific constellation of factors informing and transforming the Victorian Department of Justice and the New Zealand Department of Corrections also transforms the logics, technologies and tools of this principle. I further illuminate how this process of mutual construction ties into the process of constructing racialized peoples' futures through location and population-specific responsibilization strategies.[6]

In performing this set of three explorations, this book not only sheds some light on the missing middle account of the mutual constructions of race, criminal justice and criminology, but also provides one of the first accounts of the messy and complex ways that racialized peoples within settler-colonial societies have been encouraged to enter the correctional sphere. It reveals how racialized peoples are made responsible for the management of racialized offenders. It also shows how racialized peoples use this position of authority to rewrite Western criminology's conceptions of offending behaviour, race and the relationship between the two.

Section 3: Charting a new method for engaging in the mutual construction process
The final section of the book comprises the Conclusion. The Conclusion addresses the final task of the book: to propose a method of approach for criminologists when engaging with issues of race and criminal justice in the future.

---

6   Rose (2000) refers to 'responsibilization strategies' as the process through which citizens are encouraged to take responsibility for their past, and directed to become responsible for their future according to neo-liberal norms and values.

The Orientation of the Book

Having outlined what this book will do, it is necessary to briefly indicate two things it will not. First, this book does not draw on the voices of Aboriginal or Māori offenders. Instead, it draws on the voices of Aboriginal and Māori staff at criminal justice institutions who act as authorities in these offenders' management.

This decision reflects a personal belief and choice. As a person of Eastern European and Australian descent, educated through the mainstream systems of Australia and the United States, I have been raised to view the world through Western 'norms'. I am therefore capable, as Linda Tuhiwai Smith (1999: 42) wrote, of bringing to bear on 'any study of Aboriginal peoples, a cultural orientation, a set of values, a different conceptualization of such things as time, space and subjectivity'. I believe I am therefore equally capable of bringing this Western conglomeration of tools, knowledge and orientations to a study of Western knowledge, discourse and institutional practice, and those who choose to engage in their formation, operation and direction. It is in the latter way that I choose to conduct myself.

Second, this book does not evaluate the programs and practices it presents. Nor does it engage in discussions and judgements about their 'cultural appropriateness'. Doing so would mean going back to the simple lens of reading racialized issues from the binary previously described (that is, programs and practices do or don't 'work' because of the problematic nature of racialized offenders or the problematic nature of Western criminal justice systems). Instead, this book uses programs and practices to illustrate inscriptions of power and resistance on institutional and offenders' bodies. By this I mean the book uses programs and practices to show:

- how positions like 'authoritative racialized staff' and 'over-represented racialized offenders' have been mobilized in criminal justice systems;
- how and in what ways individuals and institutions negotiate these positions; and
- the effects mobilizing and negotiating these positions have on the mutual constructions of race and criminal justice.

Having shared my decisions about how this book will engage with issues of race, criminal justice and criminology, I once again implore criminologists to consider: how do we, as criminologists, shape the orientation of criminology and the broader field of criminal justice, and how have we let this orientation take the form it has? This is the focus of the next chapter.

Chapter 1
The 'Infallible Science' of Offending Behaviour

The evolution of the Risk Need Responsivity Model of offender classification and treatment in criminology has inadvertently extended criminology's legacy of treating issues of race as criminological offal into the field of practice.

For the last two decades, correctional agencies in Canada, Australia, New Zealand and parts of the United Kingdom and United States of America, have invested in offender rehabilitation as the primary means to reduce their exploding prison population. For the majority of these agencies, this investment has focused on the actuarial-based tools and risk management approaches of the Risk Need Responsivity Model (RNRM); and why not? For the last two decades, the correctional literature has repeatedly proclaimed that effective offender rehabilitation only occurs when these tools and approaches are followed. There have been whole journal issues (see for example *Crime and Delinquency* 2006 52(1) or *Psychology, Crime and Law* 10(3)), text books (Andrews and Bonta 2010) and other documents (Bonta 1997) dedicated to the success of the RNRM.

Yet, offender rehabilitation has not always occupied such a prominent space in correctional practice. From the mid 1970s to the early 1990s, offender rehabilitation was sidelined for more punitive approaches to offenders' behaviour (Andrews et al. 1990c). Correctional agencies were disillusioned about the effectiveness of offender rehabilitation; they, like Martinson (1974: 25), were willing to believe that 'with few and isolated exceptions, the rehabilitative efforts ... have had no appreciable effects on recidivism'. So what changed? Or, more precisely, what allowed offender rehabilitation to re-enter the correctional sphere as a legitimate option for practice after two decades of silence? How did it come to take this particular form? And, what does this mean for the figures of the racialized and non-racialized offender located in this practice?

This chapter answers these questions over four key sections. The first traces the reappearance of offender rehabilitation in correctional practice. It draws particular attention to the criminological literature's role in both the reappearance of offender rehabilitation and establishing the RNRM as the preferred approach. The second section traces the appeal of the RNRM in correctional practice. It presents the core provisions of the RNRM, illuminates their long history in criminology, and demonstrates the process of modernization that allows these age-old provisions to be reconstituted as novel and necessary parts of contemporary practice. The third section explores the products of the RNRM's combination of old and new criminology. It exposes the markings on institutional and individual bodies and reveals the production of an 'infallible science' of offending behaviour. The final section discusses the impact of this 'production' on the figures of the racialized and non-racialized offender. Together these sections provide an account of criminology's role in the mutual constructions of race and criminal justice.

The Reappearance of Offender Rehabilitation

Offender rehabilitation's reappearance in correctional practice can largely be attributed to two key developments in the 1990s correctional literature.

Making 'Nothing Works' Pejorative

First, a body of work emerged which aggressively undermined the conclusion 'nothing works' in offender rehabilitation. This body of text not only discredited the arguments supporting the conclusion, but also attacked those who provided the arguments, and those who believed them. For example, Bonta (1997) presents the 'nothing works' conclusion as 'anti-rehabilitation rhetoric' or a 'rehabilitation myth'. Andrews and colleagues accuse those who developed work contributing to the 'nothing works' conclusion as lacking 'a rational appreciation of evidence' (Andrews et al. 1990b: 370), and as incapable of contributing anything to the correctional field other than incorrect, 'sweeping conclusions' about the effectiveness of offender rehabilitation (Andrews et al. 1990b: 372). Finally, Gendreau (1996a) proposes practitioners and politicians only support the 'nothing works' conclusion for personal gain. Gendreau argues that practitioners and politicians 'eagerly embraced 'nothing works' to help justify abandoning rehabilitation and redirecting American correctional philosophy and practice to the new epoch of deterrence and 'doing justice'' (Gendreau 1996a: 145).

The effects of this multi-faceted attack on the 'nothing works' movement were varied. The works of Andrews, Gendreau and their colleagues did not affect broader correctional practice of the time. However, their aggressive rebuttals made 'nothing works' pejorative. In doing so, Andrews, Gendreau and their colleagues created a very small space for the prospects of offender rehabilitation to be reconsidered and discussed in correctional discourse. It is in this reopened space that a second key development was allowed to take shape.

The Principles of Effective Classification and Treatment

In the mid 1990s, a set of principles for effective classification and treatment of offenders emerged from the correctional literature. As correctional agencies were not practicing offender rehabilitation at this time, these principles were not based on contemporary practice. Rather, the data originally collected to demonstrate 'nothing works' was reanalysed to identify 'what works' in offender treatment and classification.

Reusing this seemingly contradictory data had two benefits for proponents of offender rehabilitation. First, proponents strengthened their contention that 'nothing works' scholars lacked 'a rational appreciation of evidence' by drawing an opposite, supporting set of findings about offender rehabilitation from their data. Second, using new found tools such as meta-analysis, proponents of offender rehabilitation were able to approach the seemingly contradictory data in a different way. They were able to identify from a collection of disparate studies the common factors related to offending behaviour and its effective treatment. These factors were used as the foundation for a set of principles for effective classification and treatment, entitled: risk, need, responsivity, professional discretion and program integrity.

Risk
The risk principle provides correctional agencies with two instructions:

1. Correctional agencies must assess and classify their offender population in terms of the risk of reoffending they pose to the community (Andrews and Bonta 2010). This process is achieved by assessing the number of 'static risk factors' an offender possesses. Static risk factors are those factors which rarely change once accumulated, and which are associated with offending behaviour. For example, does the offender have a history of offending behaviour and if so, how many previous offences have they committed? Depending on the number, type and severity of risk factors, the offender will be classified as low, medium or high risk.
2. Correctional agencies need to provide offenders with a level of treatment that reflects their risk classification (Andrews and Bonta 2010). Accordingly, 'low-risk' offenders should receive little to no treatment, while 'high-risk' offenders should receive the most intense forms available.

Need
The need principle provides correctional agencies with instructions about the type of treatment offenders require. According to this principle, offenders require treatment that targets their 'criminogenic needs'. Criminogenic needs are defined as 'dynamic risk factors'. Dynamic risk factors are factors which have a direct relationship with a person's offending behaviour (hence the term 'criminogenic'), and which are capable of change through targeted treatment (hence the term 'dynamic'). Some of the core criminogenic needs identified by the RNRM include anti-social attitudes, anti-social associates or anti-social values (Andrews, Bonta and Hoge 1990).

Responsivity
The responsivity principle provides correctional agencies with instructions for delivering effective offender treatment. The principle indicates correctional agencies must acknowledge and identify variances that may exist in offenders'

personality and cognitive-behavioural characteristics (Andrews and Bonta 2010). Variances amongst and between offender populations may be the result of internal factors, such as an offender's level of intellectual functioning, or external factors, such as inappropriately designed or delivered treatment programs (Ogloff and Davis 2004).

Professional discretion and program integrity

The professional discretion principle (also referred to as the 'override' principle) instructs correctional staff to use professional discretion at specific times in the classification process. In particular, staff are told to use discretion to 'override' a classification level if they believe it will not result in the most appropriate treatment (Andrews, Bonta and Hoge 1990). However, staff are cautioned to use this principle sparingly. It is proposed that professional override is only likely to be necessary in less than ten per cent of cases (Andrews and Bonta 1995). In fact, the program integrity principle indicates that too much, or the wrong type of, involvement by professional staff can lead to problems in risk assessment and classification.

The program integrity principle instructs correctional agencies to monitor how their staff use each of the risk, need, responsivity and professional discretion principles, in order to maintain the integrity of the approach. In particular, correctional agencies are instructed to check for factors such as 'staff resistance' or 'inadequate training' which could undermine the approach (Andrews and Bonta 2010; Ogloff and Davis 2004).

The Promise of a New Relationship between Criminology and Corrections

Thus, after 20 years in the wilderness, correctional practitioners were provided with a prescriptive promise: follow these simple instructions and your work with offenders *will* be effective. And it worked. In the two decades since the 1990s, little has changed in the practice of offender rehabilitation. The RNRM is still the staple of many correctional agencies across the Western world (for example, Australia and Canada). Moreover, where the RNRM is not practiced, its trademark focus on targeting static and dynamic risk factors is still evident in correctional agencies' practice (for example New Zealand, the United Kingdom and some states of the United States of America). And, the practice of this form of offender rehabilitation has repeatedly been shown to be more effective than punishment alone (McGuire 2000, 2002a, 2002b).

As a result of this comprehensive uptake, the RNRM changed the relationship between criminological thought and practice. Or, more precisely, the emergence of the RNRM formalized what Foucault (1985) would call a 'practical' relationship between them. The emergence of the RNRM in correctional literature allowed the literature to become the domain for texts that provide correctional agencies with principles, techniques and approaches to use in the development of practice (see for example Andrews, Bonta and Hoge 1990). It also paved the way for these principles and techniques to be considered, applied, tested and eventually constituted by correctional agencies as practice (see for example Birgden and McLachlan 2004). The resilience, longevity and facilitative effects of the RNRM beg the question: what is so appealing about this particular form of offender rehabilitation?

The Appeal of the Risk Need Responsivity Model

The appeal of the RNRM lies largely in the three key things it provides correctional agencies:

1. a set of attributes for identifying and classifying offenders;
2. a complementary set of prescriptive guidelines for addressing offending behaviour; and
3. the promise of an attainable goal – risk management.

What is fascinating about these provisions, however, is the way practitioners and scholars discuss them. The RNRM is touted as one of the most invigorating developments in contemporary correctional practice. Gendreau (1996a: 147) proposes that scholars and practitioners should be nothing less than 'indebted' to the RNRM's developers for providing such a novel approach to offender classification and treatment.

Yet, the novelty of the RNRM is questionable. There is nothing inherently new about the three conceptual provisions of the RNRM outlined above. Rather, as it will now be shown, what is novel is the way that old and new criminological discourses have been combined within these three provisions to correctional agencies, and the curious and concerning effects this combination produces in correctional practice.

A Universal Set of Offender Attributes

The first provision of the RNRM are the categorical and predictable attributes of offenders. Anti-social attitudes, anti-social values, anti-social associates, family dysfunction, poor problem-solving skills, substance abuse, a lack of employment or employment skills; these attributes are presented within RNRM literature as the defining features of all offending populations (Andrews, Bonta and Hoge 1990). It follows therefore, that if correctional agencies arm themselves with tools to correctly identify these attributes, they can not only determine who may constitute an offender within their population, but also predict the likelihood of recidivist behaviour.

Criminology's history of identifying categorical and predictable offender attributes
This is not the first time criminology has presented correctional practitioners with propositions about offenders' categorical or predictable attributes. As far back as Lombroso (1876), criminology entertained the notion that there was a distinct category of individuals in society who could be identified and classified as 'criminal' (as opposed to 'healthy' or 'insane'). 'Criminal man' could be identified by his possession of certain physiologically deficient attributes, such as the size and shape of their head. Accordingly, practitioners in Lombroso's time were instructed to use their knowledge of physiologically manifesting criminality, to divide and separate the criminal population from the rest of society.

Similar ideas about 'criminal man' and his categorical and predictable attributes have appeared in later criminological texts. For example, they have appeared in the works of:

- proponents of early twentieth century eugenics – where the case for sterilizing inherently deficient criminals was argued so effectively that several states of the United States of America passed sterilization statutes (see Lombardo 2011 for a comprehensive account of the eugenics movement in the United States);
- Sheldon (1949) – whose work on 'somatotyping' proposed a link between the behaviour of a person and their body shape, and identified that delinquents typically have 'mesomorphic' body types that are hard, muscular and athletic; and
- modern racialized genetic arguments, such as those presented in the Introduction of this book – where the over-representation of racialized peoples in criminal justice systems is explained by things like a Māori 'warrior gene' which supposedly makes Māori more aggressive and more likely to engage in risk taking behaviour (Hall, Green, Chambers and Lea 2006; Lea and Chambers 2007).

The critical distinctions between old and new criminology
Yet, there are three key distinctions between the RNRM's claims of categorical and predictable offender attributes and those of early positivist criminologists.

1.   Attribute type

There is a distinction in the *type* of attributes identified. It is the anti-social behaviour of offenders that is categorically problematic in the RNRM, not the heritage or appearance of offenders.

Anti-social behaviour is a modern concern. It is a concern that rarely appears before the 1990s, but since this time, has increasingly captured the attention of practitioners in a range of fields (see Millie 2008). In particular, it has captured the attention of politicians in the United Kingdom and as a result, the United Kingdom has introduced the *Anti-Social Behaviour Act 2003* and Anti-Social Behaviour

Orders.[1] Anti-Social Behaviour Orders are civil orders which aim to 'protect the public from behaviour that causes or is likely to cause harassment, alarm or distress' (Home Office 2006).

While the RNRM shares the same focus on anti-social behaviour as other interventions and approaches around the world, it does not share their problems. One of the core criticisms of the laws surrounding anti-social behaviour in the United Kingdom is that they are too broad in application (see Squires 2008). In the RNRM, the definition of anti-social behaviour is discrete. The anti-social behaviour of offenders only refers to: anti-social attitudes, anti-social values, anti-social associates, family dysfunction, poor problem-solving skills, substance abuse, and a lack of employment or employment skills.

2.   Approach to attributes

There is also a distinction in the *approach* the RNRM takes to identifying offender attributes, and that of early positivist criminologists. Lombroso and colleagues present 'criminal man's' physiologically deficient attributes as evolutionary remnants. For these scholars, the unusual size or shape of a criminal's head was seen as a marker from an earlier, unsophisticated point in human evolution. Thus, in an effort to build their theory about offending behaviour, Lombroso and colleagues dedicated much time to tracing the evolution of human development and its markings on the appearance of man (Lombroso 1876; Sergi 1901; Niceforo 1901).

Yet, these early criminologists' approach to tracing the evolution of human development was subjective. Lombroso and colleagues presented white Europeans as the pinnacle of evolution, and relegated all non-white European populations to a location somewhere earlier along the evolutionary timeline. As a result, the figure of the offender that emerged at the birth of criminology was a racialized offender. It was a racialized offender whose categorical and predictable attributes of offending behaviour changed according to the different points on the evolutionary timeline that racial populations were located.

The developers of the RNRM did not provide race with such a 'privileged' position in their account of offending behaviour. At numerous points in the development of the RNRM, the developers explained that there was no need to prioritize or even acknowledge variances in racial backgrounds amongst offenders because, race was '_not_ regarded as a major factor' in offending behaviour (Bonta LaPrairie and Wallace-Capretta 1997: 131, original emphasis).

The choice to exclude race as a variable in accounting for offending behaviour is not surprising. As it was noted in the Introduction of this book, criminology has long presented racialized issues as separate and inconsequential to the past, present and future of criminological thought and practice. Nor is the choice to

---

1   Anti-Social Behaviour Orders were first introduced under the United Kingdom's Crime and Disorder Act 1998 and later extended under the Anti-Social Behaviour Act 2003.

exclude race inherently problematic. Lombroso's and other early criminologists' creation of racialized criminal man illustrates what happens when race is presented as a major factor in offending behaviour.

However, the exclusion of race as a variable in accounting for offending behaviour has had a significant impact on the way the RNRM presents offender attributes. Because race and other markers of difference were explicitly excluded in the design of the RNRM, the anti-social, categorical and predictable offender attributes identified are propagated as universal. That is, they are presented as being present within any offender population across the world, regardless of differences between those populations.

3.   Capacity for uptake

Herein lies the final critical distinction between the old and new figure of the offender: the capacity for uptake. The traditional figure of the offender identified by Lombroso and colleagues had a limited capacity for uptake outside Italy (where it was first constructed). By placing race as the major factor in offending behaviour, Lombroso and colleagues ensured that any practitioner outside Italy would need to undertake the painstaking process of identifying the specific evolutionary remnants present in their populations (see for example Lombroso's later works on criminality in the United States of America such as Lombroso 1898).

In contrast, by removing race and difference from consideration, the developers of the RNRM ensured the free transportation of a constructed figure of the anti-social offender. Contemporary practitioners, instructed that the *only* history they ever need to take into account is the universally common history of anti-social offending behaviour, were given the tools to transport this construction of the offender across the world regardless of age, gender or cultural differences within their offender population. This is the appeal of the RNRM, a universally applicable theory of offending behaviour.

A Prescriptive Set of Principles

The anti-social attributes of offenders are not the only transportable provision of the RNRM. In fact, these attributes serve little function without the RNRM's core prescriptive guidelines for their use: the risk, need and responsivity principles.

As indicated earlier, these principles address three purposes. First, they advise correctional agencies who should receive the most attention – high-risk offenders with the greatest number of offender attributes. Second, they instruct correctional agencies how this attention should manifest – as treatment that targets offender attributes. Finally, they suggest how correctional agencies should deliver this targeted treatment – through approaches that are responsive to offenders' variances. In other words, these prescriptive guidelines provide correctional agencies with a framework for assessing and addressing difference within their anti-social offender population. In doing so, these guidelines provide correctional agencies with the expertise necessary to affect offenders' propensity for offending behaviour.

Criminology's history of affecting offenders' behaviour
This 'expertise' is not new to correctional practitioners. One of the core arguments of Foucault's (1991a) *Discipline and Punish*, is that the birth of the prison prompted the correctional gaze to shift from punishing the offender's body for the crime committed, and refocus on disciplining, identifying, classifying, dividing and targeting the individual's internal attributes and capabilities. In fact, Foucault (1991a) proposes it was only when the attributes of the offender came into focus in this way (as calculable and malleable), that the prison was able to move from its traditional role of punishing past behaviour, to the contemporary role of disciplining current and future behaviour so as to realign the individual with an ideal notion of the norm.

Yet, once again, while there are ancient foundations for the RNRM's approaches, something new has been built on them. The RNRM does not simply define the degree of deviation of any given individual from the norm, nor does it contribute to a process that aligns individuals with this ideal. Rather, the anti-social attributes listed by the RNRM attest to the levels of *risk* offenders pose to society. This is why the RNRM texts repeatedly inform correctional agencies their most important task is to identify, classify and divide their offender population in relation to the level of risk they pose – low, medium or high (Andrews 1999; Andrews and Bonta 2010; Andrews, Bonta and Hoge 1990; Andrews et al. 1990b; Andrews et al. 2006; Bonta 1996, 1997, 2002; Bonta and Cormier 1999; Gendreau 1996a, 1996b; Gendreau and Andrews 1990; Ogloff 2002; Ogloff and Davis 2004). Thus, in the RNRM, the fundamental issue is the degree of risk the individual poses to society, not the degree to which they have deviated from an ideal norm.

To understand the implications of this change in focus it is necessary to consider the final appealing feature of the RNRM: an attainable goal.

An Attainable Goal

When the attributes of the offender attest to risk and not (ab)normality, the goal of correctional practice shifts from treating the deficiency of an offender to managing their risk. Correctional agencies are in fact warned by RNRM texts that if they view their offender population as uniformly abnormal – and ignore the fact low risk offenders are substantially different from high risk offenders – they will exacerbate the problem of offending behaviour, and increase the levels of risk offenders pose (see for example Andrews, Bonta and Hoge 1990; Andrews and Bonta 2010; Andrews 1999). Consequently, the task of correctional agencies is not just to locate the figure of the anti-social offender on the continuum of risk, but also to chart their movement from one end to the other as their risk is managed.

Criminology's history of risk management

Once again, the priority placed on risk management is not unique to the RNRM. Around the time the RNRM began to gain traction in correctional practice, Feeley and Simon (1992) proposed that a 'new penology' was emerging in the correctional field. The 'new penology' was characterized by three changes within corrections:

1. an emerging discourse of probability and risk;
2. prioritizing internal objectives, such as the efficiency of the penal system, over external goals, such as offenders' rehabilitation; and
3. a move towards penal techniques which aggregate offender populations, rather than focus on each individual.

This is not to suggest the emphasis on risk management is unique to the penal system either. Both Beck (1992, 1998, 2000; Beck, Giddens and Lanash 1994) and Giddens (1990, 1994 and 1998) are renowned for their work on the recent shift to a 'risk society'. These scholars draw attention to the way that risks have become 'manufactured' in society through technological advances, and how these advances have brought with them a new emphasis on uncertainty, and a new need for governments to manage and reduce largely incalculable risks. Thus, it is not that the 'new penology' or the RNRM represent new developments in the way society conceptualizes and works with risks. Rather, as Garland (1995: 201) argues, the penal system's shift towards risk management in the 1990s was a change in management which had 'long been taken for granted elsewhere'.

Thus, at the time that the RNRM began to gain traction, penology and broader society was developing the discourse, technologies, frameworks of knowledge and language that could accept the RNRM's age-old claims of categorical and predictable characteristics of offenders on the one hand, and modernize their appearance and notarize their nature on the other.

Producing the Modern-day Offender

This is not to suggest the RNRM's novelty lies solely in its capacity to hide age-old notions of offending behaviour within new criminological constructs. Rather, the RNRM's combination of old and new criminology has provided the conditions for two novel developments to occur in the production of the offender.

Single Factor Prediction

For the first time in criminology's production of the figure of the offender, the notion of single factor prediction has emerged. To explain, on a scale of normality, the position of an individual is determined in reference to an ideal. Accordingly, if an individual possesses a single offender attribute they will be seen as having moved slightly away from this ideal (although perhaps still within an acceptable normal range). With the introduction of risk management and the continuum of risk, this norm becomes irrelevant. The continuum of risk is a continuum only intended for use with offender populations, or in other words, the 'abnormal'. It is a continuum whose only reference points are low, medium or high risk. Accordingly, while Lombroso's 'criminal man' required several distorted features and unpleasant characteristics before he moved far enough down the scale of normality to be considered abnormal, a single anti-social attribute is enough for a correctional agency to locate the modern-day offender on the continuum of risk.

The irrelevance of the norm in contemporary criminology has implications for the goals of correctional practice. Formerly, the goal when working with biologically or psychologically deficient offenders was to cure or rid them of deficiencies so they could return to a normal, acceptable range. The correctional field was instructed to be pragmatic about their potential to affect change. They were told to focus their attention on targeting offenders who possess the least deficiencies, because these offenders would be most amenable to change (Lombroso 1876). Now the contrary is true.

Correctional agencies must reverse their attention to make the largest difference. When the offender population are understood as posing an ongoing risk to society, the correctional field must focus their attention on offenders who present with the greatest amount of 'risk' factors (that is, anti-social attributes). It is only by focusing attention in this way that correctional agencies can, in time, reduce the risk of reoffending in their offender population, and manage their offenders at a lower level of risk.

What correctional practitioners and scholars have therefore gained from the development and sustained appeal of the RNRM is not simply the redeployment of some foundational beliefs about offending behaviour couched in modern concerns. Rather, they have gained a belief that offenders who come before them are not only abnormal, but are a category of society that will, regardless of any intervention, pose some level of risk to the rest of society and its norms.

The Rituals of Risk

Of course correctional practitioners and scholars were not expected to take the RNRM's propositions about offending behaviour at face value. They were not asked to accept that offenders standing before them posed an ongoing risk to society, or that there were differences in risk between an offender with one or two anti-social attributes and an offender with several more. Rather, correctional agencies were encouraged to become part of an assessment process that proved to both themselves and the wider correctional audience the 'truth' about offending behaviour. This is the second key development of the RNRM, the creation of a specifically designed assessment tool, the Level of Service Inventory, and all its versions and updates (for example, Level of Service Inventory – Revised, Level of Service Inventory – Revised: Screening Version, The Level of Service/Case Management Inventory, Youth Level of Service Inventory and so on).

Through the use of this assessment tool both offenders and correctional agents enter something akin to what Foucault (1998: 61) terms a 'ritual of discourse'. During the assessment process both offenders and correctional agents enter a predefined discussion about offending behaviour that comes complete with prescribed responses.

What is interesting about the prescribed words of the assessment ritual, however, is the minimal dialogue necessary to complete it. Foucault (1998) spoke of rituals of discourse as emerging from the religious confession. Here the speaking subject is implored to narrate the full nature of their sins and behaviours within the confines and constructs of religious discourse ('forgive me father for I have sinned ...'). The offender is not expected to provide the same level of information during their assessment.

In the Level of Service Inventory Revised – Screening Version, it is important for the offender to admit if any of their friends have been involved in crime. Yet, it is not necessary for the offender to discuss at length: how the friendship formed, how they perceive their friend's behaviour, if they have undertaken any actions to distance themselves from this behaviour and so on. Even if the offender chooses to respond to questions about their lifestyle and friendship group with a thorough discussion of their experiences and their feelings, this information is only entertained to the extent that it can indicate a 'yes' or 'no' answer.

Consequently, all offenders need to do to complete the ritual of assessment is respond in the most basic ways to the prescribed questions and, in doing so, have no choice but to constitute themselves as being anti-social in character and risky in nature. Are you currently unemployed? Yes. Do you have any prior adult convictions? Yes. Do you rely upon social assistance? Yes. You are a risk to the community.

Similar rituals have been observed outside of the penal sphere. Lash (2002: 216) suggests that in the move to an information society and technological culture, there has been a shift 'from a register of meaning to one of *operationality*'. Lash contends the development of new forms of communication through technology has changed the way we seek and understand information. In particular, our need to know *why* something occurs has been displaced by our capacity to understand *how* it operates. This is the essence of what is occurring in contemporary risk assessments. The need to know why offenders associate with people who have been involved in crime, or why they came to rely upon social assistance, has been displaced by the capacity of risk assessment tools to document how risk operates in relation to their anti-social behaviour.

Changing the nature of authority
But the offender is not the only subject in this ritualistic assessment. Rather, the ritual requires a correctional agent who can read the prescribed questions, listen to the answers provided, write the words 'yes' or 'no' in the appropriate space, and make a final judgement about risk. Yet, the judgement correctional agents provide is also prescribed.

The Level of Service Inventory prescribes two judgements for correctional agents. First, when something more than a 'yes' or 'no' response is required, the correctional agent is expected to listen to the answers provided and either document the narratives of the offender, or determine if the offender's situation is, or is not, 'a relatively unsatisfactory situation in need for improvement' (Andrews and Bonta 2001). Second, when all answers have been collected from the offender, the correctional agent is provided with a set of statistical tools that can perform the ultimate judgement for them: the level of risk that the offender poses to the community. All that correctional agents need to do is enter the offender's responses into the computer program provided, and what is generated for them is the location of each attribute of the offender on the continuum of risk, and the overall location of the offender on the continuum.

Thus, it is not just the way correctional agencies seek and understand information about offenders that has changed through the RNRM and its tools for assessment, but also the nature of correctional authority. The capacity of correctional agencies to judge and respond to their offender population no longer resides in the inherent expertise of criminal justice professionals. Instead, it resides in their capacity to follow the instructions of an externally developed tool. In this way, it is both the offender *and* the correctional agent that has been silenced through the addition of the RNRM and its tools for assessment. Both the offender and the correctional agent are placed in such a position that nothing other than the 'truth' about anti-social offenders' risk can be spoken, heard or charted. This is an 'infallible science' of offending behaviour.

The Effects of the 'Infallible Science' of Offending Behaviour on Criminology

Given the limiting features of this 'infallible science', it should come as little surprise some correctional scholars have raised concerns about the effects of viewing offenders myopically in terms of their risk (see for example Brown 2000; Hannah-Moffat 2005; Turnbull and Hannah-Moffat 2009). Yet, as stated at the beginning of this chapter, almost all correctional agencies that prioritize offender rehabilitation at the present either employ the RNRM or something very similar (that is, something equally focused on managing risk). It is therefore necessary to ask, what is the enduring appeal of this 'science' of offending behaviour that outweighs any countervailing concerns?

Previously it was argued that the emergence of the RNRM provided the conditions for the correctional literature to take on a 'practical' function (Foucault 1985). The correctional literature has become the domain for texts that provide correctional agencies with principles, techniques and approaches to be used in the development of practice (see for example Andrews, Bonta and Hoge 1990); and these principles are considered, applied, tested and eventually constituted by correctional agencies as practice (see for example Birgden and McLachlan 2004).

I now propose that the reciprocal relationship between correctional literature and practice has transformed the correctional literature from having a 'practical' function to being a *medium for practice*.

The correctional literature has become the medium through which any attempts to change practice are voiced, heard and judged. In particular, it has become the medium through which any alternatives to the RNRM's science of offending behaviour are disqualified, and any attempts to colonize on the RNRM's success are undermined. What is in fact enduring about this science of offending behaviour is therefore its capacity to remain untouched within correctional practice, not its inherent appeal. Illustrating this point is the failed emergence within correctional literature and practice of what is termed here, 'the normalized offender'.

The Failed Emergence of the Normalized Offender

The figure of the normalized offender emerged in the early 2000s, predominantly through the texts of the Good Lives Model (GLM) of rehabilitation (see for example Ward 2002a, 2002b; Ward and Stewart 2003b). The GLM contends all individuals seek three basic human needs: autonomy, relatedness and competence. These needs are facilitated by a series of primary human goods, such as knowledge or excellence in agency or at work. Primary goods are in turn facilitated by a set of secondary goods. These goods are associated with individual's specific circumstances (for example, employment as an electrician).

The GLM proposes offending behaviour occurs when an individual seeks to develop or enhance one of their primary human goods through an inappropriate secondary means. For example, a person seeking intimacy may pursue a sexual relationship with a child because they are unable to form an intimate relationship with another adult. Their inability may be due to limited social opportunities, or perhaps due to the type of work they perform (Ward 2002b). According to the GLM, these are the telltale actions of the 'normalized offender'; an individual who is born without any incorrigible deficiencies marking them as distinct from the rest of the population; who seeks to pursue the same life goals as all other members of society; but who may choose an inappropriate and illegal means for pursuing this goal if they feel unable to do so in other ways. The normalized offender is, unlike their anti-social counterpart, capable of being returned to the norm.

Criminology's history of constituting offenders as normal members of society
There are two important things to note about the figure of the normalized offender. First, like the anti-social offender, the normalized offender is by no means new to criminology. Also around the birth of the discipline, Beccaria (1775) and Bentham (1780) argued that if the justice system hoped to create effective laws and punishments for managing criminal behaviour, then the system would need to recognize the figure of the offender was actually just the figure of man. The offender was a rational and free-willed individual whose criminal behaviour, like all other human behaviours, was hedonistic.

The heritage of the normalized offender in criminology raises a second interesting point. The normalized offender has traditionally stood in contrast to the anti-social offender and its predecessor, 'criminal man'. Criminology has typically been split between those who take a classical view of the offender – as a wayward but normal member of the population – and those who take a positivist view of the offender – as an entity fundamentally distinct from the norm. Yet, in this modern day incarnation of the age-old divide, the normalized offender is not presented as the direct alternative to the anti-social offender. In fact, the normalized offender that returned in the early 2000s GLM literature was represented as a better developed version of the anti-social offender. It was presented as something within which the anti-social behaviours of offenders could be embedded (see for example Ward 2002a, 2002b; Ward and Brown 2003).

The machinery of production
Changing the appearance of the anti-social and normalized offenders in this way was not an easy task. Whole production lines of machinery were employed to both reposition the 'facts' about anti-social offending behaviour under a new light, and introduce new elements to already accepted 'truths' about offenders and their behaviour. The GLM literature was tasked with performing this Trojan horse manoeuvre.

First, almost every GLM text began by praising the developers of the RNRM for their contributions to the correctional field. It was not uncommon for these texts to acknowledge how grateful the correctional field should be for finally having an approach to offender rehabilitation that targeted the problematic attributes of offenders (Ward 2002a, 2002b; Ward and Brown 2003, 2004; Ward et al. 2004; Ward and Eccleston 2004; Ward and Gannon 2005; Ward, Laws and Hudson 2003; Ward, Mann and Gannon 2007; Ward and Maruna 2007; Ward and Stewart 2003a, 2003b).

Second, these praiseworthy contributions of the RNRM were subtly shifted from being the *only* relevant factors in offending behaviour to *one key set* of factors within a broader theory about human behaviour, life goals and the factors that frustrate individuals from achieving good lives. For example, many GLM texts confirmed that individuals who chooses to engage in sexual relationships with children may have the anti-social attitudes, anti-social values or poor problem-solving skills correctional agencies have been able to tick on their checklist for offending behaviour for the past decade (Ward 2002b; Ward and Brown 2003, 2004; Ward and Maruna 2007). However, these texts would also state that anti-social attributes are only indicators of the issues 'frustrating' individuals from pursuing sexual relationships in pro-social ways (that is, with someone their own age).

Finally, a new form of practice was proposed. The GLM texts argue correctional agencies must consider offenders' anti-social attributes in perspective. Correctional agencies were told they needed to take into account: the life goals of individuals, the factors that hinder them from achieving these goals (the attributes of the anti-social offender) and the possible pro-social and attainable means by which the individual can return to pursuing their life goals (Ward and Stewart 2003b; Ward, Mann and Gannon 2007; Ward and Gannon 2005).

Despite these efforts, the GLM literature was not successful in its production of the normalized offender. Nor was it successful in repositioning the anti-social attributes of offenders as only one element of what is known about offending and human behaviour. Consequently, the figure of the normalized offender now appears before correctional audiences only infrequently, embodied within publications focused on the GLM (see for example Ward and Gannon 2005; Ward, Mann and Gannon 2007; Langlands, Ward and Gilchrist 2009; Purvis, Ward and Willis 2011).

Breaching the rules of risk management
The problem with the production of the normalized offender was that it held no ground in contemporary correctional practice. The GLM texts, while disguising the figure of the normalized offender in the more palatable discourse of anti-social behaviour, did not submit their chameleon figure to the practice of risk and risk management. The GLM texts made no contribution to correctional agencies' understanding of *how* anti-social behaviour operates in relation to risk. Rather, it asked them to return to the painstaking practice of tracing *why* offending behaviour occurs.

However, it was not just the nature of the GLM's request that saw the normalized offender fail to hold ground in contemporary correctional practice. Rather, it was also the threats made by proponents of the RNRM in the correctional literature. In the same way the correctional field was warned in the 1990s that they would exacerbate the risk of offenders if they were foolish enough to consider offenders as posing equal levels of risk to the community, the RNRM texts of the 2000s warned correctional agencies that the risk to the community would increase if they mistook the GLM's chameleon figure for the real thing. Correctional agencies, viewing their offending population as only needing someone to steer them back onto the right track towards the norm, would not only fail to manage risk, but also contribute to its growth. As Ogloff (2002: 249) states, looking at anything beyond the management of the RNRM's specified risk factors would achieve nothing more than reinforcing 'offenders' pro-criminal thoughts and beliefs'. With the stakes so high, how in good conscience could correctional agencies choose to accept the propositions of the GLM?

This is the enduring appeal of the RNRM, or more precisely, the enduring effect of its dominance in criminological thought and practice. Through the medium of the correctional literature, the RNRM has the capacity to not only deploy specific 'truths' about offending behaviour (that is, the 'truth' about anti-social behaviour and predictable risks), but also to work with various practices aimed at creating and validating these 'truths' (that is, specifically designed risk assessment tools). In doing so it has gained the ability to render other formulations seemingly naïve, simplistic, retrograde, or even dangerous. Thus, capitalizing on the medium it created, the RNRM now has the capacity to both encourage correctional agencies to work with risk, and to threaten them with the consequences of getting it wrong. What does this mean for the figure of the racialized offender located in this practice?

Co-opting the History of Race

The enduring effect of the RNRM on criminological thought and practice dovetails perfectly with criminology's binary explanation for over-representation.

By the 1990s the over-representation of racialized offenders in all aspects of criminal justice systems became such an obvious problem within the correctional sphere that it could not be ignored or denied by correctional agencies. This is not to suggest that racialized offenders suddenly committed a disproportionate number of crimes in the one to two decades prior to this time. Rather, it was not until the 1970s that many jurisdictions began to collect data about racialized peoples' birth or identity (Finnane and Richards 2010). Moreover, it was not until the late 1980s and early 1990s that this data was used to support the call for Royal Commissions into the situations of several racialized peoples (see for example, Australia's Royal Commission into Aboriginal Deaths in Custody 1991 and Canada's Royal Commission on Aboriginal Peoples 1996). It was for these reasons that racialized peoples' over-representation only emerged as an undeniable problem in the 1990s.

Consequently, much of the 1990s and 2000s literature focused on how this 'problem' could be rationalized and addressed. There were a variety of ways this issue could be problematized. Day (2003) indicates the prescriptive guidelines of the RNRM were not as appropriate for measuring the characteristics of Indigenous offenders as they were for their non-Indigenous counterparts. Allan and Dawson (2004), argue the tools used by correctional agencies to measure risk provide inaccurate assessments for Indigenous offenders, leading to incorrect classifications as high-risk offenders.

While each of these explanations for racialized peoples' over-representation is plausible, neither gained much ground in broader discussions of imprisonment and rehabilitation. This is because the problem of racialized peoples' over-representation, much like the topic of race in general, was considered as a separate and separated issue. It was considered to be separate from problems with offender rehabilitation theory and practice, and as needing to be discussed only in reference to other racialized issues in criminology (for example, culturally appropriate practice).

Accordingly, the research undertaken to explore over-representation was extremely limited in scope. Abiding by the guiding practice of separating race from criminological issues, scholars repeatedly used race as a discrete variable to explain incarceration rates. For example, Wijesekere (2004) charts the trends and differences between Australian Indigenous and non-Indigenous adult incarceration from 1991–2001. Walker and McDonald (1995) chart the differences in the Australian rates of incarceration and the reasons behind them. Carach, Grant and Conroy (1999) chart the Australian imprisonment data from 1988–1998. Roberts and Melchers (2003) chart the trends in Canadian incarceration statistics from 1978 to 2001. Snowball and Weatherburn (2007) perform a logistic regression analysis of the sentencing of Australian Indigenous offenders. The list goes on (see La Prairie 2002; Latimer and Foss 2005).

Each of these studies came to the same limited conclusion as a result of engaging with the problem of over-represented racialized peoples in the same, limited way. Racialized peoples' over-representation occurred because racialized offender populations were growing at an increased rate in comparison to other members of the offender population. Racialized peoples' over-representation was both a *problem* and a *symptom* of the different nature of racialized offenders.

From documenting over-representation to producing a criminal race
Presenting over-representation as a problem and symptom of the different nature of racialized offenders has had some troubling impacts on criminology. In particular, scholars have slipped from discussing racial status as the only variable they chose to compare in a study of incarceration rates, to presenting racial status as a variable of criminality. For example, Weatherburn and colleagues produced a series of studies using Indigenous status as a discrete variable. As a result, these scholars promulgate a variety of disturbing causal relationships between Indigenous populations and crime. They indicate that over-representation of Indigenous peoples in the criminal justice system occurs because of the violent nature of Indigenous offending (Snowball and Weatherburn 2007), the common problematic behaviours of Indigenous populations (Weatherburn 2006; Weatherburn, Snowball and Hunter 2006) and the greater number of Indigenous offenders in the population (Weathburn, Fitzgerald and Hua 2003; Weatherburn, Lind and Hua 2003). This collection of findings has lead to their recent conclusion that 'Indigenous defendants are more often sent to prison because they commit more serious offences, acquire longer criminal records, and more frequently breach non-custodial sanctions' (Snowball and Weatherburn 2007: 287).

Thus, the figure of the racialized offender emerged in the post-1990s criminological literature as unlike any other. Racialized offenders are different not simply because they have different racial status, nor even because they experience an increased rate of incarceration in comparison to non-racialized offender populations. Rather, they are unlike any other offending population because their 'race' makes them more criminal. Race is constructed as the reason behind increased offending and incarceration. Therefore, over-representation is rationalized as nothing more than a symptom of the racially different nature of these offenders.

Of course, as with a number of other 'new' theories presented so far, constituting racialized peoples as dangerous or inherently different is not a recent development. This process has been repeatedly documented in the post-colonial literature, with many theorists arguing that the dichotomy between the 'savage' racialized person and the 'civilized' westerner is a fundamental feature of western societies constituting their authority over racialized peoples (see for example Ashcroft

2001; During 1995; Fee 1995; Goldie 1995; and see Bhabha 1994 for an account of hybrid savage/civilized identities). The constituted nature of racial difference is also a key feature in the associated fields of settler-colonial studies (see for example Wolfe 1991, 1994, 1997, 1999, 2002), and investigations of 'whiteness' (see for example Aveling 2004; Berger 1999; Duster 2001; Frankenberg 2001; Elder, Ellis and Pratt 2004; Giroux 1999; Moreton-Robinson 2004).

These varied bodies of text illustrate in multiple contexts how the figure of the racialized person has always been constructed as different from both normal and abnormal members of the population. They collectively show how 'difference' is always constituted as negative, dangerous and fundamentally tied to race.

From a criminal race to decimated protective cultures
Not all members of the correctional field were willing to accept the criminological literature's depiction of racialized offenders and their racially different nature. Around the world, academics and Indigenous activists began to question the relevance of statistically presented racial differences in offending. In Australia, for example, Cunneen (2006) proposes using data without proper conceptualization, and grounding of the issues surrounding Indigenous offenders does not prove the inherent criminality of Indigenous people, but the inherently simplistic and superficial nature of research undertaken. In New Zealand, Jackson (1988) argues that the Western staple of empirical research that presents statistical differences between populations is simply not capable of presenting facts about Māori or other indigenous populations. Ross (1998), writing on the situation of Native Americans, took this argument one step further. She argues that imprisonment and all the laws and regulations that support it are not just Western in assumption, but colonial in nature. For Ross, racialized peoples' over-representation, and the ways that Western science accounts for it, are nothing more than the continuation of colonization.

By deconstructing and reconstituting the previous findings about over-representation as illegitimate and irrelevant, these authors re-posed the question of how to rationalize racialized peoples' over-representation. This time, the response provided comprised two interconnected arguments about history, culture and identity. First, as Davis (1999: 12) put it, 'the real issues' in relation to the over-representation of Indigenous peoples was not the problem of their 'race', but rather the fact that Indigenous peoples had a long and complex history of being treated poorly because of their racial status. Second, many Indigenous peoples have lost or decreased contact with their culture because of the ways they have been treated, and as a result, many racialized peoples have been forcibly separated from the protective nature of their cultural identity (Cunneen 2006; Cunneen and McDonald 1997; Jackson 1988, 1995).

Thus, in this second account of racialized offenders, racialized offenders are not different because they are a more dangerous 'race' of offender. They are different because they have different experiences than other offender populations. Racialized offenders have been colonized, dispossessed of land, assimilated into an alien culture and have been discriminated against on both individual and structural levels. Moreover, racialized offenders were not over-represented in comparison to non- racialized offenders because their 'race' is a criminal trait. Rather, different historical events such as colonization, dispossession and assimilation have disassociated racialized offenders from the protective nature of their culture. Thus, the removal of culture, not the fact of race, has become the 'problem' in over-representation.

A definitive and extending science of offending behaviour
These two arguments about over-representation have largely stood in place of a comprehensive theory about race in criminology. However, while criminology as a whole has wavered between these two lines of reading racialized issues, the correctional sphere were told what was 'true' about racialized offenders. When the discussion shifts from, 'why are there more racialized people in prison?' to, 'how should correctional agencies address and reduce racialized offending?' the discourse of risk and risk management appears. Indeed, what is most striking about the racialized offender rehabilitation literature is how easily these readings of protective culture are co-opted by the discourse of risk and risk management. A good example of this process can be seen in Day, Howells and Casey's (2003) work on Aboriginal offenders and the effects of colonization in Australia, but similar examples can be found in both Canada (see for example the Public Works and Government Services Canada 1996) and New Zealand (in particular Durie 1996, 1998a, 1998b, 2001, 2003, 2005).

For over a decade, Day, Howells and Casey have rejected the idea that race is a criminal trait. Instead they contend that Aboriginal offenders are marked by their historical and cultural differences and their loss of culture (Day, Howells and Casey 2003; Day et al. 2004; Howells and Day 1999, 2003; Howells et al. 2004; Howells, Day and Davey 2005). Accordingly, in their article *The Rehabilitation of Indigenous Prisoners: An Australian Perspective,* Day, Howells and Casey propose that the factors associated with Aboriginal offending are: 'acculturation/ deculturation (loss of connection to one's culture), separation, displacement and abandonment, coping with discrimination, identity issues and being bicultural, reconnecting with spirituality and Aboriginal heritage' (Day, Howells and Casey 2003: 126). While these propositions about historical or cultural differences have found space and support in the culturally appropriate literature (see for example Jones, Loredo, Johnson and McFarlane-Nathan 1999; Jones, Masters, Griffiths and Moulday 2002), they have been co-opted in the practical domain of the offender rehabilitation literature to support a different contention.

In this domain, the only way these alternative conceptualizations can be operationalized is if they are made to fit within the existing framework for managing and rehabilitating offenders. Accordingly, although the words of historical and cultural difference that were meant to be associated with the removal of protective Aboriginal culture still appear within contemporary correctional practice, the meaning behind them has changed. What is presented within correctional literature is no longer the story of *why* these different experiences have challenged the protective nature of Aboriginal culture, but *how* these experiences are to be understood as the calculable and predictable traits of Aboriginal offenders. The protective nature of Aboriginal culture and the effects of its removal are repositioned, identified and targeted in the same ways as the other anti-social attributes of risk offenders. This is the irony of the RNRM: what started out as an attempt to remove race from accounts of offending behaviour has become a powerful tool for criminalizing its appearance in offenders.

These findings on co-opting and criminalizing race are reminiscent of those of Hannah-Moffat, Maurutto, Hudson and Bramhall, presented in the Introduction of this book. Across their works, these scholars illuminate the way contemporary technologies of risk and risk management:

- conflate markers of risk with those of lower socio-economic status (Maurutto and Hannah-Moffat 2007);
- use and redeploy social constructions of race when assessing the presence of risk factors (Hudson and Bramhall 2005); and
- present actual accounts of racialized peoples experiences as unprocessable factors that hold no bearing on risk assessment or management (Hudson and Bramhall 2005; Hannah-Moffat and Maurutto 2010).

However, these authors present these findings as exemplars of how criminal justice constructs race. I propose something different. Hannah-Moffat, Maurutto, Hudson and Bramhall's findings about co-opting and criminalizing race are exemplars of the emergence of the 'infallible science' of offending behaviour in criminology and its effects on criminal justice. They are examples of the way that this 'science' co-opts and disqualifies any propositions about offending behaviour that do not fall in line with its own. Moreover, they are examples of the way that this science demands correctional practice does not divert its attention from the goal of managing risk.

Locating the findings of these scholars within the broader discursive practice traced by this chapter signifies some final conclusion about the role of criminology in the process of mutual construction.

The Role of Criminology in the Process of Mutual Constructions

What allows the 'science' of offending behaviour to disqualify some notions of race while co-opting others is criminology's 'excessive historicity' (Butler 1997). Butler uses the term 'excessive historicity' to describe how 'autonomy in speech, to the extent that it exists, is conditioned by a radical and originary dependency on a language whose historicity exceeds in all directions the historicity of the subject' (Butler 1997: 28). I use the term 'excessive historicity' here to refer to three things:

1. The excessive historicity of the figure of the anti-social offender and their risky behaviour in criminology – as this chapter shows, this figure of the offender can be traced back to the birth of the discipline, with its appearance mutating and transforming to align with criminological developments as they emerge.

2. Criminology's excessive history of engaging with issues of race outside their proper dispersion – as this chapter shows, criminology has a long history of positioning race as either the major factor in offending behaviour or, more recently, as something irrelevant to it. It is this excessive history which provides the conditions for the figure of the anti-social offender to be presented as transportable between jurisdictions, regardless of location-specific histories or populations.

3. Criminology's excessive 'practical' history – as this chapter establishes, the criminological literature has the capacity to transform and transfer the conversations of criminologists to the practice of criminal justice agencies. It is this excessive history, with the aid of the tools and technologies of risk management, which sees the figure of the anti-social offender produced in the practice of each jurisdiction regardless of location-specific differences.

I propose that it is the combination of criminology's excessive histories that allows for the 'science' of offending behaviour to disqualify some experiences of racialized peoples while co-opting others. Specifically, it is this combination that ensures that the experiences of being a racialized person – of being colonized, of living in a settler-colonial society, of being vilified because of racial status – are disqualified because there is no space in criminology (not just risk assessment tools) for these experiences to be 'processed'. Moreover, it is this combination that ensures that the socio-economic markers of racialized peoples' experiences – being unemployed, in poor health, having a problematic relationship with family and community – are co-opted to support the continued transportation of this practice because this is the only space criminology has provided for these experiences.

Thus, I propose that there is a much broader, far reaching and older process of mutual construction taking place than that brought to light by Hannah-Moffat, Maurutto, Hudson and Bramhall's work. I contend that contemporary tactics of criminal justice are not simply capable of constructing and criminalizing racialized identities, but that the construction of racialized identities plays a role in the formation and propagation of these tactics. Moreover, I propose that it is *criminology's* construction of race that plays this role, and it does so because criminology has formed a practical relationship with criminal justice – one which both bears and continues the legacy of criminology's abuse of race. Finally, I argue that criminology's legacy affects *all* offender populations, not just racialized offender populations. What has been created through the medium of the criminological literature is a highly transportable figure of the offender that is used with all populations, regardless of any variances in populations (that is, race, age, gender and so on).

Thus, the question becomes: how can criminology engage with issues of race and criminal justice in their proper dispersion, when its legacy of misappropriation is intimately tied to the mutual constructions of race and punishment? This is the focus of the next chapter.

Chapter 2
The Rules of Engagement

Criminology needs rules for engaging with issues of race and criminal justice in their proper dispersion. This chapter develops these rules. It approaches this task by engaging with Foucault's oeuvre. It pays particular attention to Foucault's constructs of power, discourse and genealogy. It also supplements these constructs with a range of theoretical lenses developed by other scholars, including Butler, Bosworth, Carrabine, Spivak, and Miller and Rose.

The chapter comprises five core sections. The first outlines the key competing forces criminology must recognize and engage with in order to maintain the proper dispersion of race and criminal justice. This section also explains how and why Foucault's theoretical work provides the best foundation from which to navigate this process of engagement. The second, third and fourth sections work with three of Foucault's core concepts: power, discourse and genealogy. These sections are substantial and outline a number of guidelines for criminology scholars. The final section draws on these guidelines to devise three key rules of engagement. The section demonstrates how to apply these rules to determine the phases, focus and nature of analysis needed in scholarly research.

The Difficulties of Working with Issues in Their Proper Dispersion

Maintaining the proper dispersion of race and criminal justice is a difficult task. It requires criminology to explore the messy relationship between contemporary penal practice, racial constructions and criminological discourse. It further requires the discipline to entertain a variety of disparate and conflicting elements colliding with this relationship. Criminology will need to balance the competing forces of:

1. the local and global – to understand how local laws, legislation, and notions of nationhood intersect with global trends towards things like a 'culture of control' (see Garland 2001b), and universal principles for best practice with offenders (see Andrews and Bonta 2010);
2. the specific and general – to recognize how criminal justice systems are responsible for developing targeted programs, geared towards the specific risk/need factors of some sub-offender populations (for example, women and racialized groups), as well as creating strategic goals to manage the behaviour of their entire offender population;

3. the silenced and propagated – to acknowledge how criminology simultaneously excises issues of race from mainstream discourse, and propagates a disjointed collection of discussions about diverse racialized and criminological issues in one corner of the discipline;

4. the instructive and documentative – to recognize how criminological literature has become a medium for practice. The literature is capable of both informing the emergence of penal techniques, and subsequently documenting, evaluating and legitimizing their formation; and

5. the historical and contemporary – to understand how the experiences of racialized peoples are marked by their relationship with governments, past and present.

Maintaining the proper dispersion of these disparate and contradictory elements requires a sophisticated set of theoretical tools. Criminology offers a range of tools and lenses to this end. The 'new penology' (Feeley and Simon 1992), the 'new punitiveness' (Pratt et al. 2005) and the 'culture of control' (Garland 2001a) are just three examples of theoretical perspectives that emerged in the past two decades from criminology. Each of these perspectives provides vital insight into the formation and operation of contemporary penal practice. However, these perspectives have limited utility in the context of this book. As the previous chapter indicated, these developments have taken form in a discipline that has largely excised race from its thought. Consequently, while Feeley and Simon's work on the 'new penology' helps us understand the conditions within which logics of risk emerged in penal practice (as discussed in the previous chapter), this work sheds little light on the impact of this emergence on racialized offenders. Nor does this work illuminate the role of criminology's constructions of racialized and 'de'racialized figures of the offender in the formation of the 'new penology'.

The situation is not better if the issue of racialization is placed at the forefront of theoretical engagements. Post-colonial, settler-colonial, whiteness and critical race theories provide important insight into the historical and contemporary experiences of racialized peoples. These theories provide compelling evidence of the socially constructed nature of race. Yet, as I have argued elsewhere (Spivakovsky 2007), these theories limit readings of practice to their preferred constructions of race. They often bind the experiences of racialized peoples to the referent of colonization and in doing so, invite scholars to give space and voice to subjects whose ways of being are understood *only* in reference to the actions of the West. The utility of such tools is limited – they help to illuminate the processes of colonization embedded in contemporary penal practices, but no more.

What is needed therefore, are not theories for reading racialized criminal justice issues from one side or the other (that is, a criminal justice issue or a racialized issue), but tools that account for these readings amongst the numerous other disparate and conflicting elements colliding in the proper dispersion of race and criminal justice.

Using Foucault's Cautionary Prescriptions

The work of Michel Foucault provides an excellent foundation from which the required tools can be established. This is because Foucault developed his work from the following central premise: 'I write precisely because I don't yet know what to think about a subject that attracts my interest' (Foucault 1991d: 27). Accordingly, Foucault generated a set of 'cautionary prescriptions' to guide his explorations of subjects, but not predetermine the results of his studies (Foucault 1998: 98). Consequently, what Foucault's work provides are *dynamic* theoretical tools that are both capable of opening up a field of research and transforming in response to that field.

This chapter engages with three of Foucault's dynamic theoretical tools: power, discourse and genealogy. It approaches these tools as cautionary prescriptions, not as static rules that must be applied in criminology. It supplements and transforms their epistemological emphasis to better meet this book's focus on the mutual constructions of race and criminal justice. It then uses these transformed tools to propose key rules of engagement that criminology scholars can use to open up their field of research into the proper dispersion of race and criminal justice.

The Operation of Power

One only has to look to the number of interviews, chapters and books Foucault dedicates to conceptualizing power to understand how central this concept is to his methodology (see for example Foucault 1980b, 1990, 2000b). Only three core principles of power's operation are relevant here. These are: power is neither possessed nor personalized; there are resistances to power; and power has dynamic strategies and tactics.

Power is Neither Possessed nor Personalized

Foucault does not view power as an oppressive force that could be held by one person or group over another. Power could not be 'acquired, seized, or shared, something that one holds on to or allows to slip away' (Foucault 1998: 94). Rather, Foucault proposes that power operates in an intangible and mobile manner. For example, in *The History of Sexuality One*, Foucault (1998) shows how it would be foolish to presume that the power of the bourgeoisie silenced discussions of sex in the nineteenth century. Rather, this century was marked by a whole conglomeration of emerging discourses about sexuality and life. These discourses regulated what it means to have sexuality; how, when and by whom sexual acts could be performed; and, where, in what context and to whom sex could be discussed. This is why Foucault (1980d: 36) further argues that 'individuals are the vehicles of power, not its points of application', because power takes form between individuals and across changing social relationships.

Foucault's propositions about power are difficult to reconcile with the histories of racial discrimination and oppression that have taken shape across the world. How is it possible that we repeatedly see racialized peoples over-represented in every aspect of criminal justice systems if power is not an oppressive force?

An answer to this question can be found in Foucault's discussion of the subtle nature of power. Foucault argues certain groups, institutions or governments are allowed to appear 'in power' while others appear 'disempowered' because power invests itself in subtle but consistent ways. As he explains, 'I would say that the State consists in the codification of a whole number of power relations which render its functioning possible' (Foucault 1980c: 122). That is, the State is supported by a whole number of institutions, organizations, advertising campaigns and individuals whose actions, attitudes and ways of being are aligned with those of the State. But what does this mean for racialized peoples?

According to this understanding, a criminal justice system that arrests racialized peoples at greater rates than their counterparts, or ensures that racialized peoples are 'x' times more likely to serve a custodial sentence, does not have power over these racialized groups. Rather, this criminal justice system, as a particular apparatus of the State, has been allowed to appear within a privileged position of power. It appears in this privileged position because of the multiple and minute ways that power has invested itself in things like the attitudes of the population towards law and order issues, the social construction of race, and the regulatory practices of government policies.

What is still unclear, however, is how being in a place of privilege is different from possessing power. How is it possible that the prison, which holds a disproportionate amount of racialized people in comparison to the general population, does not have power over this group?

How power became depersonalized

There are two interrelated arguments in Foucault's work that clarify this point of confusion. First, Foucault states individuals remain the 'vehicles of power' even when they appear to possess it or act as its target, because power is nothing more than 'actions upon actions'. As Foucault (2002: 341) explains, 'in effect, what defines a relationship of power is that it is a mode of action that does not act directly and immediately on others. Instead, it acts upon their actions: an action upon an action, on possible or actual future or present actions'. Foucault's (1991a) account of the prisoner in *Discipline and Punish* provides an excellent example of power operating through 'actions upon actions'.

In *Discipline and Punish,* Foucault (1991a) argues that the birth of the prison changed power relationships between the State and society. By moving criminals behind prison walls, the State lost its capacity to display its sovereign power through public exhibits of torture and death. As a result, the State changed its tactics for engaging and managing the behaviours of its subjects. Instead of continuing to engage with prisoners through brutality, the actions of prisoners were influenced through a variety of *depersonalized* actions. For example, the spaces of the prison were redistributed so only particular behaviours or actions could comfortably take form within them. The timing of certain activities was controlled so particular sequences of behaviour were learnt by the prisoner. In other words, the actions of prisoners were affected by the changed conditions within which prisoners could operate and react.

The machinery of power

Further building on this notion of depersonalized power is Foucault's proposition about the machinery of power. Foucault argues that while individuals and institutions can occupy privileged positions of power (for example, the prison administrator who manages redistributed spaces, or facilitates the timing and nature of certain activities), power is in fact its own 'machinery', it is something that 'is no longer substantially identified with an individual who possesses or exercises it by right of birth' (Foucault 1980a: 156).

This contention is also made evident in *Discipline and Punish*, this time through the description of the Panopticon. Here, Foucault explains that the capacity of the observation tower to make prisoners feel under constant observation operates regardless of whether there is a prison warden, prison officer, or no one standing in the centre of it. Thus, the actions of prisoners change not by force or repression, but by the actions and expressions of this machinery of power.

Yet, even with this additional information, it is still difficult to fathom how a racialized prisoner, sitting in their cell alongside a disproportionate number of other racialized prisoners, would not feel or appear powerless because of their *racialized* identity, even if their status as a prisoner did not render them as such. Judith Butler's work on identity performance helps to reconcile this concern.

Crossing a boundary in Foucault's account of depersonalized power

Butler's (1990, 1997) work on identity performance is based on three interrelated arguments about gender. In general, I have concerns about scholars using feminist and gender theories to explain the experiences of racialized peoples. In particular, I worry the use of these theories allows for the commonality of being 'othered' by a white male society to appear as a more significant factor in the experience of racialized peoples than any of the unique character, history and experiences of these vastly different and differing populations. Butler's work does not present with this problem. This is because Butler's theory of identity performance offers important insight into the ways that groups who have traditionally been constituted as disempowered are able to displace the codification of power relations that sees groups 'othered'.

As previously stated, Butler provides three interrelated insights. First, Butler (1990: 25) contends 'identity is performatively constituted by the very "expressions" that are said to be its result'. Second, Butler clarifies, identity is a 'copy of a copy', not a replica of some 'original' way of being (1990: 31). Accordingly, what is performed in each copy is something which 'expands the boundaries of what is, in fact, culturally intelligible' about that form of identity

(1990: 29). Finally, Butler (1990) proposes that the process of performing identity *displaces* positions of privilege that have been codified, it does not *consolidate* them (1990: 30). This final point is better explained in Butler's (1997) work, *Excitable Speech*. In this book Butler proposes that: (1) 'we sometimes cling to the terms that pain us because at a minimum, they offer us some form of social and discursive existence' (Butler 1997: 26); and (2) 'autonomy in speech, to the extent that it exists, is conditioned by a radical and originary dependency on a language whose historicity exceeds in all directions the historicity of the subject' (Butler 1997: 28).

These arguments provide insight into the position of racialized prisoners. They indicate that:

1. The identity of racialized prisoners is performatively constituted by expressions such as their over-representation or marginalization, or their occupation of a less privileged position of power within prison and society.
2. Over-represented, marginalized or disempowered appearances have developed from years of construction and performance, with each performance changing and extending what is and can be known about racialized peoples.
3. Racialized prisoners may seek to move away from a position or marginalization in society. They may object to the over-representation of their people in criminal justice systems. Yet, they may continue to form their identity in terms of over-representation, marginalization and disempowerment because of the 'excessive historicity' of these identities.
4. By performing over-representation, marginalization or disempowerment in their own way, racialized prisoners change the boundaries of what is known about these positions. By performing these seemingly inescapable positions, racialized prisoners displace these positions' structures.

Guideline One:

Criminology's engagement with issues of race and criminal justice should be narrow in focus, but broad in scope. Scholars should bring attention to the ways individuals perform specific identities in relation to a broad range of power relations. Scholars should ask: how and in what ways are racialized prisoners marked by excessive racial, penal and other histories? And, how and in what ways do individual racialized prisoners shift the boundaries of these histories as they negotiate their place within and beyond them?

Thus, there is constant movement taking place in power relations' formation and operation. The racialized prisoner, imprisoned alongside a disproportionate number of other racialized prisoners, is capable of shifting, mobilizing and displacing the racialized position that has been reinforced by their imprisonment. Herein lies the first guideline for engaging with issues of race and criminal justice in their proper dispersion.

There are Resistances to Power's Investments

This guideline illuminates something important about Foucault's concept of power. Largely missing from Foucault's account of power is an indication of how individuals negotiate their position in power relationships. Indeed, one of the most common critiques of Foucault's work is that it does not provide a sufficient account of agency and the role of the individual, especially in relation to gendered or racialized power relations (see for example Bernstein 1994).

Foucault did not omit an account of agency from his work. Rather, in all discussions about power, Foucault stresses there are resistances, where individuals negotiate their position in power relationships. For example, in *The History of Sexuality One,* Foucault encourages us to see how:

> … there is a plurality of resistances that are possible, necessary, improbable; others that are spontaneous, savage, solitary, concerted, rampant, or violent; still others that are quick to compromise, interested, or sacrificial; … [and] just as the network of power relations ends by forming a dense web that passes through apparatuses and institutions, without being exactly localized in them, so too the swarm of points of resistance traverses social stratifications and individual unities. (Foucault 1998: 95–6)

The problem with this account of resistance however, is that much remains unclear about the role of individuals in its formation and operation. How, for example, is it possible for there to be a plurality of resistances? How and why does one form of resistance take shape over another? What determines if resistances are possible or improbable? Bosworth and Carrabine's work, both separately and combined (Bosworth 1996, 1999; Bosworth and Carrabine 2001; Carrabine 2004), can be used to provide some answers to these questions.

Crossing a boundary in Foucault's account of resistance
First, some explanation for the plurality of resistances can be found in Bosworth and Carrabine's (2004: 513) proposition that resistances are about 'subjective identity'. Resistances, they argue, are inextricably linked to how the individual understands and performs their position in power relationships. For example, one individual may take ownership of certain racialized roles. Another may fail to perform a gendered role. Yet another may only perform their gendered role, but ignore their racialized role. For these scholars, each of these actions represents resistances to power, because resistances occur when individuals mobilize

their identity through their performance of self. Thus, it is through individuals' mobilizations of identity that it becomes possible for there to be a plurality of resistances.

The subjective nature of resistances also explains how it is possible for one version of resistance to take form over another. For example, Bosworth's (1996) work shows how a woman who complies with a request from a male prison guard, bowing to their authority, may appear complicit to the hierarchies of the institution they are in, or subservient to the gendered and racialized positions they have been allotted within broader society. Bosworth also shows how another woman, refusing to perform this same request, may appear resistant. Yet, Bosworth argues, each of these women are expressing resistances to power. This is because the actions of each woman are based on their understanding of their position in their immediate situation and broader society. Thus, regardless of if these women's actions result in them completing a requested task, delaying its progress, or stopping it altogether, each action is a resistance to power's investment. Multiple expressions of resistance can take form in a single environment, because each formation of resistance is based on the way each individual negotiates and performs their identity in that environment.

Carrabine's (2004) work enhances this account of multiple forms of resistance in a single environment. Carrabine illuminates how individuals negotiate multiple elements of their identity in a single environment and how their simultaneous negotiations produce a variety of different actions. Using the Strangeways prison riots as a lens, Carrabine shows how men involved in the riots simultaneously negotiated their identity in relation to the prison hierarchy, and their gender. The men negotiated what it meant for them to be 'strong men' in a hierarchized prison environment. As a result, the prison riots were comprised of men who became overt contributors, as well as men who played the roles of bystanders and opportunists. What allowed one man to perform resistance through overt actions while another performed it through overt inaction was the individual's understanding of themselves, their immediate situation and their multiple positions in broader society.

Providing an answer for the final question about possible and improbable resistances is Bosworth's (1996) work. Bosworth shows how the resistant actions of an individual are influenced by the individual's immediate and impending circumstances, not just shaped by their subjective identity. For example, Bosworth illustrates how some women in prison choose to comply with orders they have previously refused when they are approaching a parole hearing. She also shows how some women change their behaviours and decisions when they become concerned about their family's situation outside of the prison. Bosworth encourages us to see how even in these seemingly coercive circumstances (where some forms of resistance seem improbable) there are still resistances. These women are still choosing to comply with the rules of the prison, rather than being forced. Moreover, they are making choices based on how they understand themselves and their position both inside and outside of the prison.

Engaging with Foucault, Bosworth and Carrabine's accounts of resistance in this way allows this chapter to shed light on an important feature of resistances. Resistances operate in terms of the ability of the individual to be exactly who they understand themselves to be, and to think and act in the way that they do at a given moment. Accordingly, resistances are capable of changing form from one individual to the next, from one moment in the lifecycle to another and so forth. This insight provides a second important guideline for engaging with race and criminal justice in their proper dispersion.

Guideline Two:

Turning attention to the individual's performance of identity is only a first step. Criminology scholars should explore how individuals negotiate their identity within their immediate situation and their broader social situation. Scholars should ask, how and in what ways an individual's actions within a prison environment embodies both the way the individual understands their role in the prison and their role in society (as mother, father, income provider and so on). Moreover, scholars should remain aware of the multiple levels of identity negotiation that may be taking place within any given context. That is, scholars should trace the dynamic and evolving ways individuals negotiate their identity, paying attention to the moments of change and the reasons for it.

The Dynamic Tactics and Strategies of Power

This chapter has suggested that power is neither possessed nor wholly oppressive. Yet, the machinery of power clearly moves towards particular ends, allowing some ways of being to take form while restricting the appearances of others (for example, over-represented racialized peoples in criminal justice systems). What then, is the strategy or purpose of this depersonalized machinery of power? An answer to this question can be derived from Foucault's discussion of power's directions.

In outlining his 'cautionary prescriptions' for how to conduct a study of sexuality without viewing power as a possession, Foucault (1998: 99) provides the following two qualifications about the directions of power:

> No "local centre", no "pattern of transformation" could function if, through a series of sequences, it did not eventually enter into an overall strategy. And inversely, no strategy could achieve comprehensive effects if it did not gain support from precise and tenuous relations serving, not as its points of application or final outcome, but as its prop and anchor point;

and thus, Foucault continues, 'one must conceive of the double conditioning of a strategy by the specificity of possible tactics, and of tactics by the strategic envelope that makes them work' (Foucault 1998: 100). These qualifications about the directions of power provide two insights. First, the operation of power, which uses individuals as anchorage points, could not function if it did not ultimately become part of a strategy. Second, a strategy of power only exists where there are specific tactics that invest in individuals. In other words, power has tactics and strategies and these are interdependent.

Disciplinary power
How these interdependent elements of power operate is illuminated in Foucault's (2007) description of disciplinary power in his 1977–78 lectures at the Collège de France. Foucault (2007: 56) states, 'I think it is indisputable, or hardly disputable, that discipline normalizes'. In other words, the strategy of disciplinary power is normalization. How does disciplinary power achieve this aim? Through a very specific set of tactics which Foucault (2007: 56–7) proceeds to list:

> Discipline, of course, analyzes and breaks down; individuals, places, time, movements, actions and operations. It breaks them down into components such that they can be seen, on the one hand, and modified on the other ... Second, discipline classifies the components thus identified according to definite objectives. What are the best actions for achieving a particular result ... Third, discipline establishes optimal sequences or co-ordinations ... Fourth, discipline fixes the process of progressive training and permanent control, and finally, on the basis of this ... it divides the normal from the abnormal.

Thus, the ability for disciplinary power's strategy of normalization to come into effect is bound to the appearance and support of specific tactics. Disciplinary power requires the tactics of: judgement, classification, modification and the establishment of an optimal model. Inversely, each of these tactics serve no purpose, unless they eventually enter into this overall strategy of normalization, where each tactic provides an important development in understanding the population and their relation to an optimal model of 'normal'.

Security
Disciplinary power's strategy of normalization is not the only strategy power takes. Later in the same lecture, Foucault presents a description of the operation of security[1] and its different strategy of normalization. Unlike disciplinary power's prescriptive strategy of normalization, security's strategy moves the individual towards a 'norm' that reflects an account of what is 'normal' and 'abnormal' in the population. This approach requires a different set of tactics, as Foucault (2007:

---

1   Within a year of the 1977–78 lecture series, Foucault linked the operation of security to the operation of biopolitics (see Foucault 2008).

63) explains, '… we have a plotting of the normal and the abnormal, of different curves of normality, and the operation of normalization consists in establishing an interplay between these different distributions of normality and [in] acting to bring the most unfavourable in line with the more favourable'.

Again, this description of security illustrates the interdependence between tactics and strategies of power. Security's strategy of normalization takes shape through the specific tactics of plotting the distribution of the population; recognizing the natural variations of normality; and setting a 'realistic' (as opposed to optimal) model. This model is then used as a base for facilitating movement in the population towards the most favourable ways of being realistically 'normal'.

These discussions about the operation of disciplinary power and security illuminate two fundamental features of power. First, power is not simply the machinery that operates between people – facilitating changes in a person's actions in an ad hoc fashion. Rather, there is a strategy to power's operation. Second, the strategy of power will change over time. Yet, regardless of its focus, the machinery of power will always include tactics that facilitate the individual changing or moving towards a purposeful end. This suggests that the current positions of racialized people in society – as marginalized, over-represented, disempowered and so on – are related to the tactics and strategies of power. The question is, however, which strategy and tactics produce these effects in the populations?

Governmentality

At a later point in the same lecture series, Foucault contends that from the nineteenth century onwards, the strategy and tactics of power have moved ever so slowly towards 'governmentality'. He uses this term to describe a rationality of how to govern the population and oneself, when governing and government are understood as a form of power. Foucault proposes that from the nineteenth century onwards, governmentality has operated on a binary of power relations. On the one hand we have elements of sovereign and disciplinary power acting together towards one common goal: 'police'. Accordingly, we have elements of the 'king working directly on his subjects' (Foucault 2007: 339), alongside elements that are working towards regulation and prescription, all with the purpose of 'preventing the occurrence of certain disorder' (Foucault 2007: 354). On the other hand, we have elements of the apparatus of security working towards a different goal: the economy and management of the population. Here we have tactics for understanding the population – forecasting and regularizing its growth – working alongside tactics of managing population growth, with both tactics eventually tying into the overall strategy of directing the economy and management of the population towards the strength of the State.

Miller and Rose (2009) propose a simpler account of governmentality. Drawing on Foucault's foundations, these scholars contend that diffuse investments of power mobilize certain ways of being and align them with the aspirations of authorities. Miller and Rose (2009: 55) propose these investments can be traced through the *political rationalities* of how to govern a population – which includes who should be governed, in what ways and by whom – and the *governmental technologies* that 'give effect to governmental ambitions' through a range of calculative and documentative techniques. This is why Rose, O'Malley and Valverde (2006), also emphasize that when exploring the strategy of power, the objective is to address two sets of questions: (1) 'who or what is to be governed?' and (2) 'who governs what?' (Rose, O'Malley and Valverde 2006: 84–5). In light of these discussions of the changing strategies and tactics of power, this chapter now proposes a third guideline.

Guideline Three:

The individual's performance of identity is only one element of a power relationship. Criminology scholars should also focus on the technologies, logics, experts and institutions that encompass and feed into this performance. Scholars should ask: who or what is being governed? How are they being governed? Who governs what? And why has this particular operation of governance taken shape?

How exactly criminology scholars can undertake this task can be discerned from Foucault's discussions of discourse.

The Operation of Discourse

The function of discourse was paramount to Foucault's presentation of power relationships. Foucault dedicated books (for example Foucault 1969), lectures (for example Foucault 1981) and interviews (for example Foucault 1991c) to develop this concept; emphasizing different facets of discourse between works. Only three elements of Foucault's work are relevant here: the regulated nature of discourse, the operation of discursive practice and the symbiotic relationship of discourse with power.

For Foucault, discourse demarcates the various 'positions of subjectivity' and establishes the 'field of regularity' that facilitates such subjectivity. But what do these functions of discourse entail?

Regulating the Subject and Object of Power

Foucault's work draws attention to the regulated practice that surrounds and supports different discourses. For example, Foucault's (1981) inaugural lecture at the Collège de France, *The Order of Discourse*, illuminates a series of procedures and rules which regulate how certain statements appear instead of others. Foucault refers to these procedures as: exclusion, rarefaction and application.

The procedure of exclusion

As the name suggests, the procedure of exclusion acts to allow some words, ideas and statements to be said, while others are rejected and excluded. What determines if a statement or idea will be allowed or excluded from discourse is its inherent 'truth'. Or, more precisely, the fate of a statement or idea resides in its capacity to align with what is considered 'true'. The connection between discourse and 'truth' is revealing of Foucault's line of thought.

For Foucault (1980c), the 'truth' represents an indicator of what knowledge and practices are deemed acceptable at the time, and by implication, what knowledge and practices are deemed irrational, unacceptable, illogical and false. Accordingly, the discursive process of exclusion's focus is not just on allowing the 'truth' to be heard, but equally about demonstrating the illegitimacy, irrationality and completely unacceptable nature of alternative words, ideas and statements. The process is about identifying and demonizing 'false' claims such that they can never enter a 'rational' discussion again.

The offender rehabilitation practice of cognitive behavioural therapy (CBT) offers an ideal example of how the procedure of exclusion manifests. CBT emerged from the discipline of psychology in the 1950s. The practice aims to change the effect a person's cognition has on their behaviour. This aim is achieved when psychologists and their patients perform two sequential tasks. First, the psychologist and patient identify the patient's 'erroneous thought processes' – that is, those cognitions that lead to unwanted feelings and behaviours. Second, the psychologist and patient develop alternative, positive thought processes for the same situations, which the patient can use in place of the negative. If successful, the replacement thought processes will break the connection to unwanted feeling and behaviour and allow the patient to lead a pro-social life. In the late 1980s and early 1990s, correctional psychologists transformed this process to the practice of offender rehabilitation.

When correctional agencies employ this psychological approach to rehabilitate offenders, the two tasks of CBT are reoriented to target offending behaviour. Here, the offender's statements, ideas and words are subject to a procedure of exclusion:

- The offender's discourse concerning the events of the offence is provided to the correctional psychologist – 'she was asking for it'.
- The offender's discourse is then reflected back to them by the psychologist as erroneous and irrational ways of thinking – 'can you see how your feelings of hurt and anger made it appear as if she was antagonizing you when in fact she was not?'
- The psychologist then offers new ways of thinking and speaking about the offence and future situations where offences may occur – 'I am feeling hurt

and angry, I know that this affects my judgement, have they really said "xyz" because they knew it would upset me?'
- This new discourse is then presented to the offender as a rational response to the offence situation, and one they should learn to have instead.

As a result of this procedure, the offender is encouraged to recognize the 'truth' of their situation and discontinue their erroneous thought processes (for examples of the techniques used by psychologists during CBT sessions see Moster, Wnuk and Jeglic 2008).

The procedure of rarefaction

Further aiding the procedure of exclusion in the production of discourse is the procedure of rarefaction. Again, as the name suggests, this procedure is focused on limiting or making rare the opportunities where new discourses can emerge and present alternative 'truths'. This procedure is aided by two processes. The first limits opportunities for alternative discourses through association. Here, discourses are associated with foundational ideas, narratives or words, such as traditional or religious beliefs. This process clarifies that the idea or statement in question has *always* been the correct approach, not just what is acceptable by current standards. This process associates contemporary statements with transcending 'truths'.

Once associated with transcending 'truths', contemporary discourses use these 'truths' to further limit opportunities for alternatives to arise. Foucault refers to this process as becoming established with a broader discipline. Here, the word 'discipline' refers to a collective corpus of statements with a common purpose. That is, statements that are unified by specific measures of objectivity and criteria for inclusion and exclusion (Foucault 1981: 56–8). Accordingly, disciplines determine the conditions and criteria by which any statement will be accepted within a particular discourse.

The failed emergence of the figure of the normalized offender in criminological thought and practice illuminates how the procedure of rarefaction operates. As the previous chapter detailed, the GLM literature attempted a Trojan horse manoeuvre – to disguise the figure of the offender in the more palatable discourse of anti-social behaviour. In doing this, the GLM literature (inadvertently) followed the procedure of rarefaction. It attempted to limit the possibility for scholars and practitioners to associate anti-social behaviour with contemporary concerns of risk. It did this by relocating the discourse of anti-social behaviour to a foundational idea about human nature and behaviour. The literature attempted to associate the discourse of anti-social behaviour with the transcending 'truth' of primary and secondary goods, and mankind's pursuit of good lives.

These attempts failed. As previously argued, the GLM failed to submit their chameleon figure to the broader discipline of risk and risk management that had gained traction in the broader political sphere. As a result, the propositions of the GLM about mankind's pursuit of good lives held no ground under the specific measures of objectivity and criteria for inclusion and exclusion of the broader discipline of risk. The GLM's chameleon figure was evaluated as risky, and the claims of the GLM literature judged as false.

The procedure of application

Finishing the trio in the production of discourse is the procedure of application. This procedure ensures that individuals who choose to speak within one discourse are subsequently excluded from speaking in alternative discourses. This procedure is facilitated through a process that sees alternative discourses, and those who choose to speak them, characterized as irrational.

The enduring 'appeal' of the infallible science of offending behaviour exemplifies the procedure of application. That is, through capitalizing on the medium of the practical literature it created, the RNRM has ensured any practitioner or scholar who chooses to speak about anti-social offenders and their ongoing risks to society cannot change their minds. As argued in the previous chapter, the RNRM's dominance in criminological thought and practice ensures that correctional agencies are encouraged to work with risk management, and threatened with the consequences of getting it wrong once they submit. Thus, the procedure of application *applies* both the rules of the discipline and the consequences for breaking them.

Together, this three-part production of discourse acts as a process of systematic exclusion. All alternative systems of knowledge and practice that exist or may come to exist, are either directly or implicitly excluded. They are either excluded through negative characterization, or left without space to establish support and acceptance. This is the field of regularity of which Foucault speaks. A fourth guideline is now apparent.

Guideline Four:

Criminology scholars should consider what is and is not said about racialized problems in the discipline and practice. They should consider *who* voices particular statements about racialized problems, *how* they are voiced, and *what* do they say.

But, before scholars can do this, it is necessary to consider how this regulatory system actually relates to the 'positions of subjectivity'.

Regulating the positions of subjectivity

In relation to the 'positions of subjectivity', Foucault emphasizes the necessity to move beyond viewing certain ways of being as natural, or as self-evident. Instead, he encourages us to consider how certain ways of being are *constituted* through discourse. For example, when reflecting on the constitution of madness, Foucault (1969: 35) states:

> ... mental illness was constituted by all that was said in all the statements that named it, divided it up, described it, explained it, traced its developments, indicated its various correlations, judged it, and possibly gave it speech by articulating, in its name, discourse that were to be taken as its own.

Therefore, it is not that there is a natural formation of madness in society. It is not that we have simply stumbled upon mental illness over the years and through frameworks of knowledge have been able to correctly identify it. Rather, madness or mental illness is a creation. It is something that emerged from the 'field of regularity' that named it, divided it, judged it and so on (see Foucault 1967 for greater discussion of the creation of madness). Madness, as one way of being in society, is constituted by discourse.

The same can be said about the anti-social offender and their categorically risky behaviour. This figure of the offender was created by all the statements the RNRM made in the practical literature. It was created by all the RNRM's attempts to name anti-social offending behaviour, describe its risk and explain its presence in society. This figure was further sustained by all the ritualistic assessments correctional agencies undertook that judged this figure and 'gave it speech' by operationalizing its appearance; documenting how risk operates in relation to the figure's anti-social nature. The relationship between the field of regularity and the positions of subjectivity indicates a fifth guideline.

Guideline Five:

When exploring what is and is not said about racialized problems in the discipline, criminology scholars should also consider *who* or *what* is constructed as: the problem, the solution and the authority on these matters; and, *how* are their positions operationalized in practice.

The Role of Discursive Practice

Notably, in his later work on *The Order of Discourse*, Foucault (1981) further indicates that the creation of ways of being, such as madness, are not simply constituted through the words and statements of individuals, but rather through a whole discursive practice. Foucault (1981: 53) explains:

> You have only to think of the whole framework of knowledge through which we decipher that speech [of madness], and of the whole network of institutions

which permit someone – a doctor or a psychoanalyst – to listen to it, and which at the same time permit the patient to bring along his poor words or, in desperation, to withhold them.

Thus, the discourse of madness and thinking errors is not simply a regulated practice, but a practice which demarcates the objects and subjects of power. For example, madness, as an *object* of power, is constituted as a way of being that requires a 'framework of knowledge' that can name, divide, describe and explain it. It is also constituted as a way of being that requires specific *subjects* to perform it. On the one hand, it needs the networks of authorities who can listen to and judge its presence. On the other, it needs the individual who personifies it and is expected to articulate it (that is, the madman).

This is why Foucault calls discourse 'a space of differentiated subject-positions and subject-functions' (Foucault 1991b: 58). It is through the tight web of constituting ways of being, of creating a means for understanding and interpreting ways of being (scientific knowledge), and of asserting the authority of those who are deemed capable of listening and judging these ways of being (institutions or persons of authority), that the individual person will be invested by power towards a particular end. But what does this mean in the context of racialized peoples and criminal justice systems? To an extent, the work of Gayatri Spivak clarifies this point.

The practice of racialized discourse

Spivak's work (see in particular 1985, 1990) draws attention to a further layer of discursive practice. Spivak shows how objects and subjects of power are enveloped by a broader way of understanding the world. Thus, for Spivak, the madman is not simply constructed through the therapy of the psychoanalyst, who listens to their irrational speech and makes judgement on their progress through a psychological framework of knowledge. Rather, it is a *Western* madman and psychoanalyst who are constituted by a *Western* psychological framework of knowledge.

Much of Spivak's work documents the process by which the West (and in particular Europe) draws on Western knowledge and notions of the world to constitute certain ways of being. Her work shows how Western knowledge is used to interpret, understand and document the ways of being of non-Western populations. Spivak (1985, 1990) refers to this process as the dual actions of 'worlding' and 'epistemic violence'. Here, the West engages with non-Western populations from the assumption that they are encountering 'empty earth' on which they are entitled to write the inscriptions of the Western world. The West further inscribes this earth with Western knowledge and epistemologies, which render non-Western populations as knowable, understandable and definable according to Western terms and concepts.

In light of Spivak's and Foucault's discussions of discursive regulation, a sixth guideline is necessary.

Guideline Six:

Criminology scholars should not simply trace the performativity of the individual and technologies in the operation of power. They should also consider the discursive practice that has in part facilitated this. Specifically, they should address three tasks:

1. Scholars should trace the frameworks of knowledge that can name, divide, describe and explain racialized peoples, correctional approaches, offending behaviour and so on. They should pay particular attention to the epistemological foundations of these frameworks.
2. Scholars should also map the institutions or persons of authority that have been deemed capable of judging what is or is not to be considered 'true' about racialized offenders and their management. They should pay particular attention to the ways that these authorities engage with non-Western knowledge.
3. Scholars should illuminate the subject-positions provided for the discipline of criminology, correctional agents and racialized offenders to take-up. They should focus on how various subjects are expected to articulate the self-evidence of racialized peoples' position in prison and society.

The Rituals of Power and Discourse

The above discussions indicate some of the ways that discourse is related to power: discourse demarcates the objects and subjects of power. However, Foucault did not see discourse as subservient to power, or power as subservient to discourse. Rather, he proposed them as existing within a symbiotic relationship. As he explains in *The History of Sexuality One*, the question that must be posed is:

> In a specific type of discourse on sex, in a specific form of extortion on truth … what were the most immediate, the most local power relations at work? How did they make possible these kinds of discourses and conversely, how were these discourses used to support power relations? (Foucault 1998: 97)

Therefore, there is a discourse-truth-power relationship. On the one side, discursive practice demarcates the objects and subjects of power. It establishes the 'truth' of the object of madness, and positions the madman and psychoanalyst as its interlocutors. On the other side, however, the operation of power relations allows discursive practice to gain foundation. Power invests in particular institutions. It allows these institutions to appear in a privileged position. In doing so, it provides foundation for these institutions' frameworks of knowledge, their claims of truth, and their authority.

Illustrating how the discourse-truth-power relationship operates is Foucault's example of the confession in *The History of Sexuality One*. In this example, Foucault claims that:

> The confession is a complex ritual. It is a ritual of discourse in which the speaking subject is also the subject of the statement. It is also a ritual that unfolds within a power relationship, for one does not confess without the presence (or virtual presence) of a partner who is not simply the interlocutor but the authority who requires the confession, prescribes and appreciates it and intervenes in order to judge, punish, forgive, console and reconcile. Moreover, the confession is a ritual in which the truth is corroborated by the obstacles and resistances it has had to surmount in order to be formulated. Finally, it is a ritual which the expression alone, independently of its external consequences, produces intrinsic modifications in the person who articulates it: it exonerates, redeems and purifies him; it unburdens him of his wrongs, liberates him, and promises him salvation. (Foucault 1998: 61–2)

This example of the confession illuminates the dual sides of the discourse-truth-power relationship. First, the ritual of confession exemplifies how the rules of discourse allow for investments in objects and subjects towards particular ends. Thus, the speaking subject must not only confess their sins according to the language and structure of the religion, but in doing so must also become the subject of the statement whose behaviour transforms from the very act of speaking in this prescribed way. Second, the ritual of confession further illustrates how power's investments allow for particular discourses to appear and not others. The only reason the speaking subject undergoes this transformation is because of investments such as: the creation of apparatuses and people of authority, or the opening of confessional spaces which must be filled with proscribed words and interactions. Finally, it is because of the relationship between discourse and power that the individual reveals both the 'true' nature of their conduct and the unquestionable need for this whole system of regulation to operate.

The previous chapter traced a similar ritual of discourse operating in the correctional sphere: the ritualistic assessment of the anti-social offender and their categorical risk. In this ritual, the offender confessed their anti-social attributes according to the register of risk management's operationality, and in doing so, became the subject of their responses about anti-social behaviour and its relationship to risk. Moreover, the only reason the offender underwent this transformation is because of investments like: the creation of a logic of risk, the tools of risk management and their authorizing nature, the opening of risk assessment rooms, and the hiring of 'authorities' who can use the inherent expertise of risk assessment tools without jeopardizing their operationality. It is the combination of all of these things that both constituted the anti-social offender with their categorical risk, and made the whole system of risk management fundamental to correctional practice.

The operation of the discourse-truth-power relationship in the correctional field illuminates a final guideline.

Guideline Seven:

Criminology scholars should trace the interrelationship between the investments of power and discursive practices. They should pay attention to the specific formation of racialized issues in criminological discourse and practice. Scholars should explore the different performances that subjects demarcated by this relationship are *expected* and *allowed* to play. That is, scholars should not only consider who or what is constructed as the problem, solution and authority on these matters, but also what ritualistic investments of power (for example, purpose built spaces and technologies) allow for these constructions to manifest easily while others struggle to gain footing.

Exactly how scholars can do this is indicated in Foucault's work on genealogy.

Genealogy: The History of Power, Discourse and the Body

In *Nietzsche, Genealogy, History*, Foucault (2000a) explains that the concerns of the genealogical approach are descent and emergence. Here the term descent refers to the 'stock' or heritage of an idea, practice or way of being. For Foucault, a practice's heritage is complex and can never be traced back to a single transcending 'truth' or a point of origin. This is why Foucault (2000a: 374) proposes we must 'maintain passing events in their proper dispersion', in order to pay attention to all the mutations and deviations that have occurred in the formation of ideas, practices and ways of being, and not ignore or hide dead-end or undesired events in order to present a neat line of continuity between 'The Origin' of a practice and now.

The question is, why do this? Or, more precisely, how does it help to pay attention to all the mutations that have occurred in positioning racialized peoples as over-represented or disempowered? Foucault argues that when we maintain the proper dispersion of things we are able to realize the disparity of our beginnings. That is, we are able to realize 'the errors, the false appraisals, and the faulty calculations that gave birth to those things which continue to exist and have value for us' (Foucault 2000a: 374). Yet, even with this additional information the genealogical approach seems odd. How does realizing the errors that gave birth to formations, such as over-represented racialized peoples, help if in the end they are still over-represented or disempowered? Foucault's complementary work on emergence clarifies this point.

By realizing the errors and mutations that give birth to practices or positions such as over-represented racialized peoples, we are able to illuminate how those practices or positions have been constructed to appear as something more – as natural ways of being. Accordingly, the focus of emergence is on illustrating how, through excluding, ignoring and disqualifying the messiness of descent, certain ways of being emerged as natural and self-evident – for example, how the anti-social offender with categorical risks has emerged as a 'true' depiction of the figure of the offender because of the exclusionary tactics of the infallible science of offending behaviour.

Foucault refers to this two part process of tracing descent and emergence as exposing 'a body totally imprinted by history and the process of history's destruction of the body' (Foucault 2000a: 376). In doing so, Foucault prompts yet another set of questions, namely: what exactly does this mean? Who or what constitutes a body? What does it mean to have a body imprinted by history? And what does exposing this process achieve? Each of these questions has already been answered in the development of this chapter.

First, the two 'bodies' that need to be exposed are an individual's body and an institutional body. The previous sections of this chapter establish that at the intersection of discourse and power, certain subject and object positions are mobilized. They show that these positions always include the individual as a vehicle of power (for example, the madman, the anti-social offender or the racially different offender) and the person or institution of authority who acts as another anchorage point of power, whose role it is to listen, judge, and analyse the individual's account (for example, the psychologist, the risk assessor or the prison authority). It is each of these 'bodies' that are of concern.

Second, the process of transforming a body totally imprinted by history and the process of history's destruction of the body is the process of performing and displacing identity. The previous sections of this chapter showed how individuals will continue to carry out roles that appear counterintuitive primarily because these roles have 'excessive historicity'. For example, racialized prisoners may continue to perform the roles of over-represented, marginalized or disempowered peoples. However, in doing so, these individuals displace the structures of these positions.

Finally, what is achieved by exposing these bodies and the ways that they have been marked by history is movement. By allowing doubt to surface around the certainty that things are the way they are for a specific, transcending, reason, we are able to think and act in new ways. The Introduction to this book exemplifies the significance of this process.

The Introduction brought attention to both the ways that the 'problem' of over-represented racialized peoples has been constructed and explained in criminology, and the process that allowed for this construction and explanation to appear acceptable and self-evident – the excise of race from its proper dispersion in criminology. In doing so, the Introduction illuminated how the piecemeal nature of criminological explanations of issues such as over-representation are not simply problematic, but are also *symptomatic* of the disparity in criminology's approach to racialized issues. It was only in exposing how the bodies of racialized peoples and criminology (as a discipline comprised of texts, conversations, teachings, and presentations) had been marked by this history that this book could now ask criminology to move away from this process. How exactly criminology can do this is outlined below through three key rules of engagement.

The Rules of Engagement

This chapter has identified a series of guidelines for engaging with race and criminal justice in their proper dispersion. It is now time to use these guidelines to construct a framework for analysis that maintains the proper distribution of the five disparate and conflicting elements presented at the beginning of this chapter (local and global; specific and general; silenced and propagated; instructive and documentative; and, historical and contemporary). This framework comprises three cautionary rules of engagement.

1. Rule of Scope – balancing the local and global with the specific and general

The task of engaging with race and criminal justice in their proper dispersion is quite broad. The guidelines identified in this chapter indicate that criminology scholars can approach this task by bringing attention to a much narrower point of focus: the bodies of individuals and institutions. Criminology scholars should therefore focus on the performance of identity that takes place both in relation to the immediate circumstances of individuals, and the excessive historicity of those circumstances. How scholars can do this in practice is exemplified by the structure and orientation of this book.

Applying the Rule of Scope
This book engages with the proper dispersion of: global criminological discourses about race and criminal justice, localized constructions of race and nationhood, and contemporary criminal justice practices with racialized populations. In applying the 'Rule of Scope', this book approaches these intersecting elements of mutual construction through two phases of analysis.

The first phase of analysis focuses on the institutional body and its markings. This phase explores the ways that racialized identity is performed within criminal justice systems in location-specific ways. It draws attention to: the ways that racialized peoples are positioned in criminal justice systems by official discourses, how racialized peoples negotiate this position performatively, and the role of immediate factors (for example, growing rates of over-representation), global factors (for example, the infallible science of offending behaviour) and historical factors (for example, notions of nationhood) in each of these positioning processes.

The second phase of analysis focuses on the body of the individual and its markings. The phase explores the ways that contemporary criminal justice processes intersect with location-specific constructions of race. It exposes the circumstances within which racialized offenders are expected and allowed to perform and negotiate their identity.

2. Rule of Investment – balancing the strategies and tactics of power with the historic and contemporary

When criminology scholars engage with race and criminal justice in their proper dispersion, they are likely to observe numerous investments of power. It is important that these investments are not viewed as wholly oppressive (that is, interpreting racialized peoples' over-representation and marginalization as an ongoing process of colonization in which the West always holds power over racialized peoples). Instead, criminology scholars must also observe the *productive* nature of power – the ways in which power facilitates change in the actions and attitudes of the population. To do this, criminology scholars must observe the resistances to power's investments in all their various formations. How scholars can do this in practice is also exemplified by this book, this time through the method of approach taken in the two phases of analysis.

Applying the Rule of Investment
While the phases of analysis developed under the 'Rule of Scope' bring this book's attention to two different points of focus from which it can engage with the mutual constructions of race and punishment (the institutional body and the individual's body), a single method of approach is needed across these phases. In applying the 'Rule of Investment', this book must ensure that seven questions are addressed across these two phases:

1. Who or what is being governed in a specific criminal justice issue, process or practice?
2. How does the machinery of power operate to facilitate this issue, process or practice (for example, opening of functional spaces where only particular activities can take place comfortably)?
3. How has this machinery of power been met with resistances, and by whom?
4. What circumstances or events appear to shape the way resistances have manifested?
5. What do these resistances to power produce?
6. Have these various investments of power and resistances changed tactics and strategy over time?
7. How has this process of change contributed to the markings on institutional and individual bodies?

3. The Rule of Regulated Practice – balancing the silenced and the propagated with the instructive and the documentative

In asking the seven questions outlined above in their own work, criminology scholars will not only trace the investments of power, but further illuminate the symbiotic relationship that these investments have with discursive practice. When this occurs, criminology scholars should consider how statements presented on racialized peoples and criminal justice are regulated by the operation of a power-truth-discourse matrix. They should trace the different subject positions that are *invested* by power and *regulated* by discourse. How scholars can do this is once again exemplified by the approach taken in this book.

Applying the Rule of Regulated Practice

To apply the 'Rule of Regulated Practice' this book will use the information gleaned from the previous seven questions to bring attention to the following three points of focus:

1. The framework of knowledge presented as capable of naming, describing and explaining offending behaviour and the experiences of racialized peoples.
2. The 'speaking' subjects who are expected to share their experiences of offending behaviour or racialization, and subsequently validate what has been named, described and explained about offending behaviour and racialized peoples.
3. The 'experts' who are presented as being capable of listening to, or judging what others say about these experiences.

Read together, these three rules provide guidance for the orientation of the remainder of this book. This book should use these rules to open up the field of research into race and criminal justice and transform these rules in response to the field.

Opening Up and Transforming the Field of Research

As indicated in the Introduction, this book will open up the field of research into race and criminal justice across its second section. This section will apply the rules of engagement in a series of case studies of the mutual constructions of race, criminal justice and criminology. The section is comprised of three chapters.

Chapter 3, *Unavoidable and Undeniable History*, and Chapter 4, *Biculturalism: Struggling to Maintain Dual Histories*, focus on the complex relationship between national identity, racialized subjectivity and criminal justice. These chapters explore the role this complex relationship has played in the formation, transformation and reconfiguration of criminal justice in different jurisdictions. Each chapter provides a separate case study of the mutual construction process, with Chapter 3 focusing on the mutual construction process in the Australian State of Victoria, and Chapter 4 focusing on the process in New Zealand.

In applying the rules of engagement, these chapters will bring attention to the location-specific power-truth-discourse grids operating in the Victorian Department of Justice and the New Zealand Department of Corrections. Each chapter will explore how institutional and individual bodies are marked by the history of investments in their specific grid. The chapters will also explore how these bodies perform, displace and resist this history, and the transformations that these actions produce. Together, these two chapters will provide reference points from which to determine the *nuances* of location-specific grids in operation.

Chapter 5, *Diverse History, Common Practice* applies the rules of engagement from another angle of the mutual construction process. As explained in the Introduction, Chapter 5 explores the way that penal logics and technologies contribute to the construction of racialized identity. It does so by exploring how the principle of responsivity, a penal technology that emerged from criminology's infallible science of offending behaviour (presented in Chapter 1), has been approached by the Victorian Department of Justice and the New Zealand Department of Corrections in relation to Aboriginal and Māori offenders.

In applying the rules of engagement, Chapter 5 will bring attention to the intersection of global (that is, the science of offending behaviour) and location-specific power-truth-discourse grids. The chapter will focus on the ways that institutional and individual identity are negotiated in and amongst this complex intersection. It will also explore the strategies of government that emerge from this messy constellation of factors. To do this, the chapter will consider both the logics, technologies and tools used in the practice of responsivity, and the subject positions Aboriginal and Māori offenders are expected to occupy in relation to this practice.

Together these three chapters will open up the field of research into race and criminal justice by applying the rules of engagement. They will also transform these rules in response to this field when necessary.

The Conclusion to this book will present the key transformations that have taken place across these three chapters. It will also illuminate the key features of the mutual constructions of race and criminal justice, and the constellation of factors that allow these features to emerge. It will then use all of this information to propose a method of approach for criminologists when engaging with issues of race and criminal justice in the future.

Chapter 3
Unavoidable and Undeniable History

The Victorian Department of Justice's practice in relation to Aboriginal offenders represents one of the first breaks in correctional history from the increasingly extending regulation of the science of offending behaviour and its discourse of anti-social offenders and categorical risks.

This chapter explores the mutual construction of race and criminal justice from the local, institutional level. It explores how localized constructions of nationhood and racialized identity contribute to the formation, transformation and orientation of criminal justice. It uses the Victorian Department of Justice (located in the Australian State of Victoria) as its case example. The Victorian criminal justice system was selected for the following four reasons:

1. *Australia's colonial history.* As will be explained in detail in a moment, Australia has a unique history of settler-colonization.[1] The first settlers claimed that Australia was *'terra nullius'* – it belonged to no one. As a result, many Australian Federal Government policies over the past century have attempted to remove Aboriginal peoples from the land in one way or another – for example, through assimilation, unequal rights to education, and restrictions on opportunities for work. It was not until 1992 in a judgement of the Australian High Court that the claim of *'terra nullius'* was overturned. This judgement, in Mabo v Queensland (No. 2),[2] marked an opportunity for new relationships to form between the Australian Federal Government and Australia's Aboriginal population. However, notwithstanding the findings against the claim of *'terra nullius'*, the High Court held that Australia remains under the sovereignty of the British Crown, and that there is only one system of law in Australia. It is this history of colonization that provides the foundations upon which any interaction between Australian Governments and Aboriginal peoples is built.

2. *The tension between State and Federal Governments.* Australia is a federation. Under Australia's federal system, the Federal Government holds legislative power over taxation, defence, foreign affairs and postal and telecommunications services, whereas the six State Governments of

---

1   As noted in the Introduction, the term settler colonization is used to describe situations in colonized societies where the purpose of colonization was to settle land not exploit labour (see Wolfe 1999 for a detailed account of Australia's settler colonial history).

2   Mabo v Queensland (No. 2) (1992) 175 CLR 1.

Australia retain legislative power over all other matters occurring within their borders, including police, hospitals, education and public transport. As such, the State Government of Victoria must balance its population's interests with those of the Federal Government on behalf of the Australian population as a whole. It must also balance Government and Aboriginal relations in Victoria with the Government and Aboriginal relations that have been established by past and present Federal Governments. Over the past two decades, the State Government of Victoria has approached these tasks by producing a series of criminal justice initiatives, agreements and programs with Aboriginal communities in Victoria, which respond to the Australian Federal Government's role in colonization and its ongoing structures and effects.

3. *The relationship between the State Government of Victoria and Victoria's Aboriginal peoples.* Each State Government of Australia is required to develop responses to their Aboriginal population. Yet, there are a range of jurisdictional specific factors that appear to play a role in each response, including: the proportion of Aboriginal people in the State, the specific problems faced by Aboriginal communities in that State, and the history of past State Government responses to these problems. Victoria has a comparatively small Aboriginal community and small, albeit over-represented Aboriginal offender population. Yet, Victoria's State Government is the only Government in Australia's Federation to develop multiple, evolving, agreements with Aboriginal communities in relation to criminal justice initiatives. Victoria's unique approach to Aboriginal populations has had significant impacts upon the nature and direction of the mutual constructions of race and criminal justice in Victoria.

4. *The approach of Victoria's Department of Justice towards the tools, tactics and logics of the global criminological literature.* Chapter 1 showed how an infallible science of offending behaviour has captured the attention of the correctional sphere. From the pervasiveness of this finding it would be reasonable to expect that any correctional agency claiming to prioritize risk management would bear the markings of this science. This is certainly true of the Victorian Department of Justice's approach to non-Aboriginal offenders. The *Reducing Re-offending Framework* (Birgden and McLachlan 2004), which acts as the foundation of Victoria's approach to offender and prisoner management, repeats the discursive props and tactics that support the production of an anti-social offender and their categorical risks in the correctional literature. However, when attention is turned to the approach to Aboriginal offenders, this expectation no longer holds true. The Victorian Department of Justice has placed Aboriginal offenders beyond the grip of the ever extending science of offending behaviour and its construction of offenders. It has repositioned the Aboriginal offender in a location-specific discourse of 'difference'.

These four factors illuminate the range of Government and Aboriginal relationships operating in Victoria, and the role assumed by the Victorian Department of Justice in responding to them. This chapter applies the Rules of Scope, Investment and Regulated Practice, previously developed in Chapter 2, in order to capture the proper dispersion of these four elements in the formation and orientation of the Victorian Department of Justice. Accordingly, the chapter focuses on the markings of the history of mutual construction on institutional and individuals' bodies. It does this by asking: who or what is being governed in the Victorian Department of Justice's approach to Aboriginal offenders? Using what authority, logics, and frameworks of knowledge? Supported by which tactics, tools and investments of power? To what ends? And, with what role played by resistances to power?

In order to answer these questions, the chapter draws on the official documents of the Victorian Department of Justice and interviews with Aboriginal and non-Aboriginal staff working in the area of Aboriginal offending. It uses this information across five key sections. The first section provides a brief history of Government and Aboriginal relations in Australia. It draws particular attention to the role of Australia's history of settler-colonization in the orientation of Victoria's criminal justice system. The second section explores who or what is being governed in the Victorian Department of Justice's approach to Aboriginal offenders. This second section draws attention to the way that Aboriginal offenders are positioned in official documents and the genealogy of these positions in Victoria and Australia more broadly. The third section furthers the exploration of governance by drawing attention to who and what the Victorian Department of Justice has been authorized to govern and who and what have become *governable* about the Department of Justice's institutional body. The fourth section traces the tools and tactics that have been invested in the institutional body, exploring the products of power's investment. This section considers the question, to what end has the Victorian Department of Justice been invested and transformed by the tactics of power? The final section focuses on the role of resistance in the governing process. It explores the ways that Aboriginal staff members negotiate their roles in a justice agency responsible for governing and managing an over-represented Aboriginal offender population.

A Brief Correctional History of Government and Aboriginal Relations

Australia has a short and violent history. The first settlers landed in the Australian State of New South Wales on 26 January 1788. These settlers took a variety of approaches to dealing with the presence of Aboriginal peoples. Some settlers forcibly removed Aboriginal peoples from the land, while others came to informal agreements with Aboriginal peoples on how the land could be shared or sold. In 1835, the *Proclamation of Governor Bourke* ended any informal agreements. The *Proclamation* claimed that Australia was empty, that it belonged to nobody (*terra nullius*). The *Proclamation* declared that Aboriginal peoples 'roamed' the land, but did not tend to it in 'civilized' ways, nor protect its ownership with 'civilized' laws (Buchan and Heath 2006).

The consequences of these claims were overwhelmingly detrimental for Aboriginal peoples of Australia. To highlight but a few examples, these claims allowed for Aboriginal peoples to be located outside British law; they justified the use of Australia as a penal colony by the British; and gave licence to British settlers removing Aboriginal peoples from their land by any means necessary (see Finnane and McGuire 2001; Hogg and Carrington 2001). This is the starting point of Australia's Western history.

This starting point has been followed by a number of discriminatory Government policies; policies that have, in one way or another, continued to remove Aboriginal peoples from the land. For example, in 1961 the Australian Government passed the *Policy of Assimilation*. This policy sought to erase the Aboriginal 'race' over generations (see Armitage 1995). It denied Aboriginal peoples their basic human rights, paving the way for Aboriginal peoples to develop the greatest number of health and other lifestyle issues in Australia (see the annual Social Justice Reports published by the Australian Human Rights Commission, for a detailed account of the impact of the policies and actions of past and present Australian Government's on the health of Aboriginal and Torres Strait Islander peoples). It is this history of colonization and settlement that was brought to the forefront in Australia's first detailed account of the experiences of Aboriginal peoples in criminal justice systems: the Royal Commission into Aboriginal Deaths in Custody (RCIADIC).

The Royal Commission into Aboriginal Deaths in Custody

In 1987, the then Prime Minister of Australia, Bob Hawke, announced the formation of the RCIADIC. The RCIADIC was established to examine the deaths of Aboriginal peoples in police, juvenile and prison custody over the period 1 January 1980 to 31 May 1989. This equated to 99 deaths across Australia. Amongst other conclusions, the RCIADIC states:

> Aboriginal people die in custody at a rate relevant to their proportion of the whole population which is totally unacceptable and which would not be tolerated if it occurred in the non-Aboriginal community. But this occurs not because Aboriginal people in custody are more likely to die than others in custody, but because the Aboriginal population is grossly over-represented in custody. Too many Aboriginal people are in custody too often. (Royal Commission into Aboriginal Deaths in Custody 1991, vol 1: 6)

In doing so, the RCIADIC not only provided one of the first official accounts of Aboriginal peoples' disadvantage in society, but also one of the first accounts of their over-representation in Australia's criminal justice systems.

These damning accounts led the RCIADIC to provide Australia's State and Territory Governments with 339 recommendations in a *Final Report* (Royal Commission into Aboriginal Deaths in Custody 1991). These recommendations both demonstrated the need for Australian Governments to redress past and present disadvantages experienced by Aboriginal peoples and provided guidelines for doing this.

For six years, Australia's State and Territory Governments considered the findings and recommendations of the RCIADIC. They met in 1997, at the Australian National Summit on Aboriginal Deaths in Custody, to discuss their approach. At the conclusion of the Summit, each State and Territory committed to address disadvantage and over-representation in their jurisdiction by forming agreements with their Aboriginal communities.

In response to this commitment, the State Government of Victoria negotiated and entered into an agreement with Victoria's Koori[3] community. This agreement was entitled, *The Victorian Aboriginal Justice Agreement: Phase One (VAJA1)* (Department of Justice and Department of Human Services 2004) and was launched by the Department of Justice in 2000.

Victoria's response to the Royal Commission into Aboriginal Deaths in Custody
The *VAJA1* aimed to reduce Aboriginal peoples' over-representation in Victoria's criminal justice system. To do this, it sought to address the underlying issues facing Aboriginal peoples.[4] The Agreement outlined a set of principles and objectives to guide 'the working relationship' between the Koori community and the Victorian

---

3   The terms Koori, Koories, Aboriginal people(s) and Indigenous will be used throughout this chapter reflecting and respecting such broad usage within and across Victoria's Aboriginal communities. In general, the terms Koori or Koories will only be used when the Department of Justice makes specific reference to this Aboriginal population, the term Aboriginal peoples will be used to refer to all Aboriginal populations in Australia and the term Aboriginal people will be used to refer to specific Aboriginal people discussed in this chapter.

4   Addressing the underlying issues facing Aboriginal peoples was a common focus for all Justice Agreements developed in Australia at this time (see for example the Western Australian Aboriginal Justice Agreement (Department of Justice et al. 2004) and the New South Wales Aboriginal Justice Agreement (New South Wales Aboriginal Justice Advisory Council 2003). However, each State adopted a different way to address this focus. For example, both the Victorian Aboriginal Justice Agreement: Phase Two (Department of Justice 2006) and the New South Wales Aboriginal Justice Plan (New South Wales Aboriginal Justice Advisory Council 2003) indicate that Aboriginal community safety is a key concern for these States. However, the Victorian Department of Justice (2006) constructs this concern in terms of ensuring Koori communities have the same rights and experiences as non-Aboriginal communities, while the New South Wales Justice Advisory Council (2003) constructs this in terms of recognizing the desires of Aboriginal people and communities in New South Wales to work together to resolve the crime and offending problems of Aboriginal peoples.

Department of Justice (Department of Justice and Department of Human Services 2004: 5). These principles and objectives included tasks such as:

- increasing community participation;
- developing culturally appropriate programs and services;
- developing a co-ordinated and strategic approach;
- delivering fair and equitable justice services for Aboriginal peoples; and
- recognizing the impact of Aboriginal peoples being dispossessed of traditional lands, separated from children or families, and experiencing other devastating outcomes from past government policies.

The *VAJA1* also outlined several smaller initiatives for the Department of Justice. One such initiative involved conducting a review to identify if, how and when the Department of Justice implemented the recommendations of the RCIADIC. This review began in 2003 and was completed in 2005 with the publication of *The Victorian Implementation Review of the Recommendations of the Royal Commission into Aboriginal Deaths in Custody (Implementation Review)* (Implementation Review Team 2004).

The *Implementation Review* was conducted through a 'partnership approach'. It therefore drew both 'on the perspectives of government agencies with their self-assessment reports on implementation and on the views and experiences of Indigenous peoples' (Implementation Review Team 2004: 88). The *Implementation Review* spanned more than 700 pages and addressed several purposes, including:

- outlining the main findings and recommendations of the *Final Report*;
- considering how these findings and recommendations were implemented by the Department of Justice through the *VAJA1*;
- determining what issues remained unresolved; and
- presenting a new set of recommendations for the Department of Justice.

Around the same time as releasing the *Implementation Review* (2004), the Department of Justice also published the *Victorian Government Response to the Implementation Review of the Recommendation of the Royal Commission into Aboriginal Deaths in Custody (Victorian Government Response)* (Jackomos 2005). The purpose of this document was to provide a way forward for the Department of Justice, building on the findings of the *Implementation Review*. *The Victorian Government Response* recommended a new phase of the Victorian Aboriginal Justice Agreement. This phase was realized the following year with the launch of *the Victorian Aboriginal Justice Agreement: Phase Two* (Department of Justice 2006).

The Victorian Aboriginal Justice Agreement: Phase Two (VAJA2) was created for two purposes: to respond to the progress and limitations of *VAJA1*, and to renew the commitment between Government and the Koori community.[5] Like *VAJA1*, *VAJA2* comprised several principles and objectives aimed at reducing Aboriginal over-representation in Victoria's criminal justice system. In *VAJA2*, these principles and objectives included:

- making mainstream services more responsive and inclusive of the Koori community's needs;
- providing crime prevention and early intervention techniques; and
- reducing the level of victimization experienced by the Koori community.

VAJA2 is the final document (to date)[6] in this series of publications about Victoria's past and present relationship, commitment and partnership with the Koori community.

Together, the RCIADIC's *Final Report*, *VAJA1*, *Implementation Review*, *Victorian Government Response*, and *VAJA2* form the backbone of Victoria's criminal justice approaches to Aboriginal offenders. They also provide the base from which Aboriginal offenders and their offending behaviour have been problematized and governed over the past two decades. It is therefore necessary to explore the way Aboriginal offenders are positioned in these official documents, and ask: exactly who or what is being governed in the Victorian Department of Justice's approach to Aboriginal offenders? And, according to what authority and logics?

Governing Aboriginal Peoples in the Socio-political Sphere of Justice

What is governed by the Department of Justice's approach to Aboriginal offenders is not Aboriginal offenders as such, but rather the 'difference' between this population and the non-Aboriginal population. Moreover, this 'difference' is not presented in terms of offending behaviour – that is, Aboriginal offenders are not different to the non-Aboriginal population because they commit more crimes, or because they have a different history underling their offending behaviour. Rather, the 'difference' governed by the Department of Justice is the 'difference' experienced by *all* Aboriginal peoples in Victoria (and Australia), offenders and non-offenders alike. All Aboriginal peoples in Victoria are presented as 'different' because they are 'disadvantaged', 'over-represented' and plagued by a collection of 'underlying issues or factors'. As Table 3.1 shows, these three common features

---

5   The Victorian government is the only government in Australia (to date) to both undertake a review of the original Aboriginal Justice Agreement and renew a commitment to Aboriginal peoples with further objectives to be met through a second Agreement Phase.

6   In early 2011 the Victorian Department of Justice released a tender for the evaluation of VAJA2, with the aim of developing a third phase of the Victorian Aboriginal Justice Agreement in 2012.

of Aboriginal 'difference' are repeated throughout Victoria's framework for Aboriginal offender management.

**Table 3.1   The official documents' repeated discourse
of Aboriginal 'difference'**

	VAJA 1	VAJA 2	Implementation Review	Victorian Government Response
Disadvantage	27	28	128	18
Over-representation	30	50	108	7
Underlying Issues/factors	17	1	118	0
Number of pages in document	47	45	720	26

Note: This table illustrates the number of times the terms 'disadvantage', 'over-representation' or 'underlying issues/factors' appear in Victoria's official documents in relation to Aboriginal offenders.

This is not the first time Indigenous offenders have been located in terms of disadvantage or underlying issues. As Chapter 1 showed, several Australian and New Zealand researchers infiltrated the correctional literature in the past two decades. These researchers repeatedly argue Indigenous offenders are different to other offender populations because they experience a different history to these populations – a history marked by issues of disadvantage, over-representation and underlying issues such as colonization and dispossession of land (Cunneen 2006; Day 2003; Day, Howells and Casey 2003; Jackson 1988, 1995). However, Chapter 1 further showed how this discourse of difference was subsequently co-opted by the discourse of anti-social offenders and the infallible science of offending behaviour – the common features of Indigenous history became just another set of markers of anti-social behaviour and categorical risk. This experience is not common to the official documents or discourse in Victoria.

In Victoria, Aboriginal offenders are only presented in the official documents in reference to the problems facing all Aboriginal peoples. For example, the official documents state:

> We know that over-representation will not be reduced until the disproportionately high levels of disadvantage experienced by the Aboriginal community are tackled by all parts of government. (Department of Justice and Department of Human Services 2004: 5)

Or

Make no mistake, we have a small window before another generation of Indigenous hopes are lost to disadvantage and despair. (Department of Justice 2006: 3)

Thus, Aboriginal offenders are 'disadvantaged', 'over-represented' and plagued by 'underlying issues' because 'difference' – as understood in these specific terms – is the defining object in all Aboriginal peoples' lives. 'Difference' is both the subject and object position demarcated for Victoria's Aboriginal offenders. It is something that defines Aboriginal offenders' identity and something that is experienced by all Aboriginal peoples. Accordingly, it is 'difference' and not offending that must be governed by the Department of Justice.

This unusual manifestation of 'difference' in an offender population prompts the question, how has this come to pass in Victoria? That is, what has allowed Aboriginal 'difference' to supplant offending behaviour as the object of focus in the Department of Justice's approach to Aboriginal offenders?

The Collision of the Royal Commission into Aboriginal Deaths in Custody

There is a clear answer to this question: the Royal Commission into Aboriginal Deaths in Custody (RCIADIC). As illustrated at the beginning of this chapter, there is a fundamental connection between the RCIADIC and the chronology of the Department of Justice's official documents. These documents and agreements simply would not exist if the Royal Commission had not been conducted. However, the RCIADIC provided something more important than impetus. The RCIADIC, through its various products – the commission itself, the *Inquiries into Deaths in Custody*, and the *Final Report* – provided specific subject and object positions for Aboriginal peoples and Governments to occupy in all social and political spheres. These are the positions marked on Victoria's official documents. The discourse of Aboriginal 'difference' in the Department of Justice is a descendant of the RCIADIC and its demarcations.

The heritage of Victoria's official documents becomes apparent when looking at a sample of the individual reports of the inquiries into the deaths of Aboriginal people in custody. For example the *Report of the Inquiry into the Death of the Young Man who Died at Wujal Wujal on 29 March 1987* (Wyvill 1990a), explains:

The determination of the mechanics and circumstances of this death presents no problems but that is certainly not the end of the matter. By the Letters Patent issued in me, I am required to be concerned not only with how such a tragic death occurred, but also, and perhaps more importantly, why it occurred. While the answer to that perplexing question is of great importance for the grieving relatives, it is also of concern to the whole of our society if we are to understand the phenomenon that manifested itself at Wujal Wujal on the morning of Sunday 29 March 1987.

There is much about the death of this young man that can be understood in terms of the acute stresses suffered by Wujal Wujal Aboriginal people generally, young Aboriginal men specifically, and the deceased in particular. These have their origins in the impact of non-Aboriginal interaction on his people's lifestyle, values and their relationships to their land and each other.

Similarly, the *Report of the Inquiry into the Death of the Woman who Died at Ceduna on 18 February 1983* (Johnston 1990), states that:

This case serves to highlight the importance of health as a direct factor in the number of Aboriginal deaths in custody. I have made various references throughout this report to the poor health of the deceased. She died as a young woman. Although the deceased's state of health may have been exceptionally bad for the reasons discussed previously, it is clear that the Aboriginal people on the west coast of this State enjoy a much lower standard of health compared with the non-Aboriginal population and perhaps other Aboriginal people in this State.

Moreover the *Report of the Inquiry into the Death of the Young Man who died at Aurukun on 11 April 1987* (Wyvill 1990b) contends that:

Seventy-five years of the missionaries' management and control of virtually all aspects of the lives of Aurukun Aboriginals has denied people the full knowledge and experience of their own culture and its forms of social organization and left them dependent on white administrators making decisions and taking initiatives on their behalf. This combination of cultural denial and imposed dependency has left the Aboriginal people poorly equipped to deal with the social problems and decisions of their daily life and with the needs of administering the community as a whole in the present and in the future.

There are clear lines of descent between these Reports and the position of Aboriginal offenders in the Department of Justice. These Reports show how each death cannot be accounted for without looking at the broader issues surrounding Aboriginal peoples. The official documents state that Aboriginal peoples' presence in the criminal justice system will not change until the broader issues facing them are addressed (see in particular Department of Justice and Department of Human Services 2004: 5). These Reports claim that removal policies have denied Aboriginal peoples in custody and the community the knowledge and experience of their culture. The official documents state that past Government actions, such as removal, have had significant impacts on Aboriginal peoples and the disadvantage they experience (see in particular Department of Justice and Department of Human Services 2004: 21; Jackomos 2005: 25).

Yet, while the link between the discourse of the RCIADIC and Victorian official documents is clear, it is unclear what allowed the discourse of the RCIADIC to find a position of foundation and dominance in Victoria's criminal justice system.

The Impact of the RCIADIC Collision with Victoria's Criminal Justice System
There are two characteristics of the RCIADIC that lead to this position. First, the RCIADIC and its various products were not requested by the criminal justice system, not directed at an issue the criminal justice system actively wanted to address, nor regulated by the system's expertise. The RCIADIC was an external, independent audit of the criminal justice system's interactions with Aboriginal peoples, conducted in collaboration with Aboriginal peoples. Accordingly, the statements made by the RCIADIC did not simply juxtapose the discursive practice dominating the correctional sphere. Rather, they rendered the whole science of offending behaviour propagated by the correctional literature as being of no consequence to determining the 'truth' about Aboriginal peoples in criminal justice systems.

Second, the RCIADIC was excoriating and incendiary in nature. As the individual Reports demonstrate, the RCIADIC did more than just provide an account of Aboriginal offenders' different experiences; they repeatedly positioned the Australian Government as their *cause*. Thus, the RCIADIC did not collide with Australia's correctional history to be slotted in, ignored or transformed to contribute to the priorities of the correctional field (that is, the continued manufacture of anti-social offenders and their categorical risks to society). Rather, as the Attorney General stated in his Forward to the *VAJA2*, 'the Royal Commission into Aboriginal Deaths in Custody was such a moment – a profound wake up call that put the country's leaders on notice to stand up and take responsibility' (Department of Justice 2006: 3). The RCIADIC was something that demanded a response from Australia's criminal justice systems: to reconsider the subjectivity of all Aboriginal peoples and the role of all Government agencies in their formation.

These characteristics of the RCIADIC have influenced the Victorian Department of Justice in fascinating ways. They have provided the conditions from which this criminal justice system could become focused on the subject and object of Aboriginal 'difference' and not Aboriginal offending. They have also changed the conditions from which this criminal justice system engages with Aboriginal 'difference'. The Victorian Department of Justice is not positioned as a relay of power whose expertise in offending behaviour is needed to listen, judge and punish the figure of the offender. Instead, it is positioned as a deviant subject, whose problematic behaviour is revealed in the amount, state and life status of Aboriginal prisoners.

The RCIADIC's capacity to shift the role of the Department of Justice from governing authority to subject that requires better governance, implies something important about the broader mutual construction process explored by this book. The original rules of engagement outlined in Chapter 2 indicate that institutional bodies are marked by the history of their authority and their unquestioned capacity to listen and judge their subjects. In Victoria, the institutional body of the Department of Justice has had its authority questioned and its capacity to listen and judge Aboriginal subjects removed. More importantly, the institutional body of the Department of Justice has become the subject of scrutiny by a different authority – the RCIADIC. Thus, it is no longer sufficient to only ask in the Victorian context, who or what is governed and according to what logics? Rather, it is necessary to also ask, in the process of governing a population or a problem, what becomes *governable* about the institutional body in charge of this process? This is the question that is now answered in the Victorian context.

Negotiating Prescribed Roles in the Governance of Aboriginal Peoples

One of the most striking features of Victoria's official documents, is the clear association drawn between the Victorian Government's ability to 'recognize', 'acknowledge', 'understand', 'accept' or 'agree' with any of the ways of speaking about Aboriginal 'difference'.[7] This association is once again made apparent by the frequency with which these terms are used. As illustrated in Table 3.2 below, the words 'recognized' or 'recognition' appear in the context of discussing Aboriginal 'disadvantage', 'over-representation' and 'underlying issues', 230 times in the 720 pages of the *Implementation Review*.

Table 3.2   The official documents repeated discourse of 'recognition/recognized'

	VAJA 1	VAJA 2	Implementation Review	Victorian Government Response
Recognition	45	7	230	19
No. pages in document	47	45	720	26

Note: This table illustrates the number of times the words 'recognition' or 'recognized' appear in Victoria's official documents in relation to Aboriginal offenders.

Again, what is striking about the relationship between the Victorian Government's position of 'acknowledgement' and 'recognition' is not simply their repetition in official documents, but the different subject positions they provide for the Victorian Government to occupy.

First, the language of 'acknowledgment' and 'recognition' allows the current relationship between the Victorian Government and Aboriginal peoples to be positioned as different to earlier relationships. For example:

---

7   It is important to note that the Department of Justice uses the terms recognition, acknowledgement and understanding synonymously in the official documents.

> The Government understands that previous policies of separating Aboriginal children from their families continue to have a profound and lasting effect on economic, social and cultural outcomes of Aboriginal people in Victoria. (Department of Justice and Department of Human Services 2004: 21)

Or

> The Victorian Government accepts that past policies resulting in the removal of children have contributed significantly to the worse health and well-being of Koori families and communities. It is undertaking a number of initiatives to redress these disadvantages. (Jackomos 2005: 24)

Second, the language of 'acknowledgement' or 'agreement' specifies which issues affecting Aboriginal peoples are of priority for the Victorian Government and which, by implication, are not. For example:

> The Victorian Government acknowledges Aboriginal people as the rightful owners of their heritage and as having primary responsibility for its control and management. (Implementation Review Team 2004: 19)

Or

> The signatories [of the *Victorian Aboriginal Justice Agreement: Phase Two*] … agree that Koori communities are entitled to live in a safe, harmonious and nurturing environment free from racism and discrimination. (Department of Justice 2006: 20)

Finally, the language of 'recognition' acts to outline the new positions that Aboriginal communities can assume. These positions fall in line with both the acknowledgements of the current Victorian Government as well as the accepted 'facts' about Aboriginal peoples. For example:

> The Government recognizes that the Aboriginal community has the right to develop its own structures to service its needs, while maintaining the right to use mainstream services. (Department of Justice and Department of Human Services 2004: 11)

Or

> The signatories … recognize and respect the Koori connection to country and culture and the essential function that healthy and nurturing families have in improving justice outcomes. (Department of Justice 2006: 20)

Seeing the Department of Justice engage with Aboriginal 'difference' in these ways reveals something further about the RCIADIC's impact on Victoria's criminal justice system. The Victorian Government was not simply forced to accept the subject position demarcated for it by the RCIADIC, it *negotiated its subjectivity*. The Victorian Government reconstructed its position to make manifest the intelligibility of its perspectives and practices in relation to the RCIADIC. Accordingly, Aboriginal 'difference' is not only created by the Victorian Government (see the examples relating to the position of the current Government on the previous page of this chapter), but can also be maintained (see the examples of the accepted facts about the community on the previous page of this chapter) or even addressed by the Victorian Government (see the example of the new roles of the community in relationship to the Government on the previous page of this chapter).

The transformed position of the Department of Justice in its official documents reveals what has and has not been negotiable in this discursive practice. The Department of Justice has transformed its role from creator of Aboriginal 'difference' to include other elements (for example, maintainer and redresser). Yet, in doing so, it has reinforced the possibility that it is still a deviant subject. The official documents bear the markings of what Butler (1997) describes as 'excitable speech', whereby the Department of Justice must 'cling to' the terms of creating Aboriginal 'difference' in order to be recognized as having the potential to move away from that position. However, in clinging to these terms, the Department of Justice reinforces the possibility that it cannot change.

Furthermore, because these acts of speech are, in this sense, out of the Department of Justice's 'control' (Butler 1997: 15), the Department of Justice is incapable of reintroducing the object of offending behaviour. To do this, the Department of Justice would undo whatever ground it gained through acknowledging its role in creating Aboriginal 'difference'. It would become just another government body that cannot recognize or acknowledge the 'truth' about Aboriginal peoples: that the issue is 'difference' created by Governments, not offending behaviour of Aboriginal peoples.

Finally, because the Department of Justice has been denied the opportunity to reintroduce the object of offending behaviour, it has tried to negotiate a position of authority elsewhere. It has claimed capacity to manage Aboriginal 'difference'. Yet, the capacity of the Department of Justice to perform this task is unclear. Its capacity is still tied to the level and type of 'difference' marked on Aboriginal bodies, and these bodies' repeated appearance in the criminal justice system.

These fascinating features of Victoria's official documents imply something important about the way criminology should approach the mutual construction process. The focus when tracing mutual constructions of race and criminal justice should not be constrained to who or what is governed, or even how something becomes governable. Rather, it should also be turned to how those governing institutions or people of authority negotiate their role, and what logics and frameworks of knowledge restrict or support their governance.

Yet, the issue of governance is only one part of the broader construction process. As the Rule of Investment outlined in Chapter 2 explained, there are other important questions that need to be asked and answered, including: how does the machinery of power operate to facilitate these messy subject, object and authority positions in the practice of the institutional body towards Aboriginal offenders? And, what tactics and strategy of power have manifested through this machinery's operation?

Disciplining the Institutional Body

The emergence of both the RCIADIC discourse of governments *creating* Aboriginal 'difference', and the responding Victorian discourse of the Department of Justice's capacity to *maintain* or *redress* 'difference', has changed the Department of Justice's physical structure in the past decade. The institutional body has been transformed to include two new spaces where the problem of Aboriginal 'difference' is addressed: the Indigenous Issues Unit – renamed the Koori Justice Unit (KJU) in 2009 – and the Indigenous Policy and Services Unit (IPSU).

The appearance of these Units is interesting for three reasons. First, Aboriginal offender populations are the only population provided with dedicated Units in the Department of Justice. There are no separate, devoted spaces for women, Indo-Chinese or any other offender population that presents either disproportionately in Victoria's criminal justice system, or who have specific underlying issues associated with their offending behaviour. It is only the Aboriginal offender population that have become *recognizably* different in Victoria's criminal justice system. Moreover, it is only the specific issues of Aboriginal people that have been deemed as warranting the dedicated and separate attention of the Department of Justice.

Second, these Units act as parallel sites of justice. That is, after their opening, any approaches towards Aboriginal offenders appear inappropriate or at least questionable unless they are generated in these dedicated Units. Equally, any approaches towards mainstream offenders appear strange and out of place if they are generated by these separate, dedicated Units. Thus, these Units have become spaces where the different issues of Aboriginal offenders are not only recognizable but further *enclosed*.

Finally, these Units ensure that the subject and object of Aboriginal 'difference' takes a very specific shape in Victoria's criminal justice system. The KJU and IPSU have become *functional places* where the Government's position of maintaining and redressing Aboriginal difference is embodied in their operation. The functional nature of these Units is apparent in the objectives proposed for each.

The Enclosure of the 'Different' Problem of Aboriginal Peoples

The KJU was created as one of 18 Business Units within the Department of Justice. It was assigned four major objectives. First, the KJU is required to provide Department of Justice-wide policy in relation to Aboriginal peoples and communities. In performing this task, the KJU embodies the distinction drawn in the official documents between past and present Governments. The Unit exemplifies how the present Government is capable of providing policies that redress 'difference', whereas past Governments were only capable of providing detrimental policies that create 'difference'.

Second, the KJU is also responsible for providing Aboriginal programs and initiatives in relation to police, courts, community and corrections, and subsequently, monitoring and evaluating these programs. In performing these tasks, the KJU has taken on the additional function of clarifying what the current Victorian Government will acknowledge and recognize as the needs of Aboriginal peoples – the Unit has become yet another instrument of control and demarcation.

Finally, the KJU has been given the function of managing Koori career recruitment and development. This endowment allows the KJU to perform a very specific function; namely, the KJU acts to establish boundaries around the positions the Koori community can now occupy because the Victorian Government allowed them to share certain rights with the rest of the population (for example, the boundaries surrounding the rights of the Koori community to manage the heritage of its people but only in these specific spaces and objectives).

Thus, in every objective addressed by the KJU, this dedicated Unit also performs the function of embodying the Department of Justice's discourse of affecting Aboriginal 'difference'. The KJU is not alone in this performance. A similar process has taken shape in the IPSU.

The IPSU formed as one division within an existing Business Unit of the Department of Justice, Corrections Victoria. By occupying this different level of responsibility within the Department of Justice (that is, being only part of a Business Unit rather than being a Business Unit in itself), the IPSU is only assigned a single objective: the IPSU is responsible for developing, providing and delivering Aboriginal policy and services in both the Department of Justice's prisons and community corrections settings. Due to this singular responsibility, the IPSU forms the centre from which Victoria's correctional approach towards Aboriginal offenders emanates. Accordingly, the IPSU, like the KJU, has become a functional place; a place where the Department of Justice affects the levels of 'difference' Aboriginal offenders experience through the provision of programs and services.

This account of the KJU and the IPSU illustrates some of the core ways that the institutional body of the Department of Justice has transformed. The Department of Justice has not maintained its typical appearance as an unquestioned source of uniformity, bureaucracy and authority. Rather, it has re-emerged through the creation of these Units, as a curious subject whose questionable and problematic past is written on the surface for all to see. But, appearance isn't everything. If the surface is scratched on any one of these transformations to the institutional body, what is revealed is something that can only be described as messiness. The Koori recruitment strategy provides an excellent example of the messiness below the surface.

Scratching the surface of the Department of Justice's neat appearance
The Department of Justice recruits Aboriginal peoples because their presence allows the Department of Justice to better address its purpose of affecting Aboriginal 'difference'. As the following non-Aboriginal staff member explains:

> we would like to increase the number of Koori staff. I think that would be very relevant for having a more responsive system, not only for the individual offenders that they are dealing with, but for collegial relationships and how best to manage Koori staff. (non-Aboriginal staff member one)

However, as this staff member's statement further indicates, recruitment is not just about affecting Aboriginal 'difference'. It is also about managing Koori staff. The following two Aboriginal staff members' accounts shed light on the significance of this additional element of recruitment. They explain:

> When I came to Justice there were four Koori staff and now there are 60. The word gets around, so then Koori staff want to come and work in here. People working in the Units and the activities that are going on, they are real and meaningful, so it makes a difference. (Aboriginal staff member four)

And

> So we have a lot of Aboriginal people working in the justice system, I think there is over 60 now, but they are just about all the people who work in Aboriginal Units or Aboriginal positions. I can only think of two people I know across Corrections Victoria who are Aboriginal but work in a mainstream position … I think there are lots of reasons for that. The normal reason people will give from Corrections Victoria is that Aboriginal people don't like to lock up other Aboriginal people, and while there is some element of truth in that, I think it is more that despite how much we try there is still real discrimination when you are working in the prisons. Not so much in the employment procedures, I think they have done some really good things about trying to get people to work there, but just when you are in a prison everyday working with the officers, there is a lot of discrimination that goes on, so it would be a very hard place for an Aboriginal person to work. (Aboriginal staff member nine)

These statements provide insight into some of the complexity and tension attached to the Department of Justice's recruitment strategy and its role in affecting

Aboriginal 'difference'. The recruitment strategy is intended for all spaces and places of the Department of Justice (that is, not just the KJU and IPSU), but it does not have the same effect across the institutional body. Aboriginal people are not interested in working in places where they are still subjected to discrimination, but are interested in working in places where the work makes a difference to Aboriginal peoples and communities.

While the choices of Aboriginal people are not surprising, their effect on the institutional body is. The recruitment strategy is a mechanism for power's investment. It is a mechanism that targets the actions of the Department of Justice, allowing for actions like redressing difference to manifest. Moreover, it is a mechanism that only comes into effect when it aligns with other mechanisms in operation (that is, the opening of Aboriginal specific places to where Aboriginal peoples can be recruited). Finally, it is a mechanism which, through its alignment, sustains the effect of other mechanisms – spaces without discrimination, places with meaningful work and so on.

Yet, as the statements of Aboriginal staff members' illustrate, this mechanism is dependent on the actions, behaviour and judgements of Aboriginal peoples. It is only when the work is '*real and meaningful*' that Aboriginal people encourage other Aboriginal people to join. It is only when '*word gets around*' in the Aboriginal community that Aboriginal people want to work at the Department of Justice.

The tension between, and the complementary nature of, Government and Aboriginal peoples' actions in transforming the institutional body raises an interesting question about the tactics of power that have been invested in the Department of Justice.

What allows the Department of Justice to appear this way are the subtle investments of disciplinary power. To be clear, the appearance of disciplinary power in a criminal justice setting is not remarkable. Disciplinary power has been the stronghold of the prison for centuries; why wouldn't we therefore expect its markings on the body of an institution that oversees and directs the actions of the prison? What *is* remarkable about its appearance in this context is that in Victoria, the investments of disciplinary power do not filter through the Department of Justice to inscribe the offender's body; they stop at the institutional body. It is the institutional body that is subjected to the investments of enclosed spaces and functional places. It is the institutional body that is marked by the mechanism of the Koori recruitment strategy. It is the institutional body that is made docile. Thus, what must now be explored is: what does the institutional body's docility facilitate? That is, what is the overall strategy of these disciplinary investments?

Returning to an 'Ideal' Norm

There are two 'ideal' norms generated by these investments of power. These norms are apparent in the recruitment strategy previously discussed, but better illustrated through a further investment of power marked on the Department of Justice's institutional body: the examination.

The process of examination can be found in the operation of the Aboriginal Justice Forum (AJF). The Department of Justice holds an AJF four times a year. The AJF runs for approximately two days and is attended by key members of both signatory agencies within the Department of Justice and governmental and non-governmental Aboriginal bodies (such as the Victorian Aboriginal Legal Service). The purpose of the AJF is to report on the progress of initiatives outlined in the *Victorian Aboriginal Justice Agreement: Phase Two*, or in other words, to report on the Department of Justice's response and developments in relation to the RCIADIC.

Due to the collaborative nature of the AJF, the actions of the Department of Justice are no longer enclosed within the Aboriginal spaces and places created at Head Office. Rather, all actions, plans and progress made by the Department of Justice on the initiatives of the *Victorian Aboriginal Justice Agreement: Phase Two* are presented before representatives of Government and the Aboriginal community. Accordingly, every success and failure made in the Department of Justice's attempt to address Aboriginal difference is made visible for judgement. In this way, the AJF is a medium for examination.

Examining the actions of the institutional body
However, as the following Aboriginal staff member explains, it is not just the purpose of the AJF that facilitates examination, but also the promise of regular future occurrences:

> And we have an Aboriginal Justice Forum, there are four of those a year now
> instead of two, so our accountability, our obligations are really extreme, so you
> know you really need to be on top of what you are doing all the time and to not
> let anything slip. (Aboriginal staff member eight)

Thus, there is something that occurs through the AJF that is akin to what Foucault (1991a: 187) calls 'transforming the economy of visibility into the exercise of power'. The regular occurrence of the AJF makes staff of the Department of Justice feel as if their actions are under constant surveillance. They can '*not let anything slip*', even if they only have to present their work to an external audience once a quarter. This is the first technique of the AJF's process of examination.

The second technique involves allowing 'individuality to be introduced into the field of documentation' (Foucault 1991a: 189). As this Aboriginal staff member explains:

> There is also reporting that goes on. So we have an implementation report for
> VAJA2 and that has detailed in it every initiative, and everyone who has an
> initiative has to provide reports to us in particular formats which are then put
> into a traffic-light format. So if they are on target they will be green, if they
> are behind three months they will be amber and if there has been a significant
> delay they will be red. So we can go through them pretty quickly. Even though

we have 52 initiatives it can be tracked at every Forum where we are at, so it's not like people can't get a handle on what has happened to that. The same with our actions arising, we run a sheet on those, so that every action decided at the Forum has an action sheet and it doesn't come off until it is "action done". So every meeting, people can see all the actions arising. (Aboriginal staff member two)

While traffic-light breakdown of actionable items is a common bureaucratic mechanism, it still plays an important role in exposing the 'true' position of the Department of Justice in relation to Aboriginal peoples. Every action performed by the Department of Justice is documented, every step it does and does not take is revealed. The ability of the Department of Justice to reposition itself as capable of redressing Aboriginal 'difference' has become a calculable and analyzable object.

Something similar to this process of documentation appeared in Chapter 1. Chapter 1 showed how the register of meaning surrounding offending behaviour changed to one of 'operationality' (Lash 2002), whereby the need to know *why* something occurred was replaced by the capacity to understand *how* it operates. This change from 'why' to 'how' has occurred in the AJF through its process of examination. The focus in the AJF is *how* the Department of Justice has performed in relation to its targets, and *how* its performance can be documented in a traffic-light breakdown.

However, in the AJF's register of operationality, the target of operationalism has changed. It is *docility* that has been operationalized, not *deviance*. It is the ability of the Department of Justice to embody the subject position of affecting Aboriginal 'difference' that is coloured in green, amber and red. This is the first 'ideal' norm produced in and by the institutional body: a body whose non-aboriginal parts become docile in the development of Aboriginal 'difference', not active in redressing it.

A point of clarification is required at this time. It is doubtful that if this book focused on correctional approaches towards mainstream offenders these or any other investments of power would resonate in the institutional body for the purpose of disciplining *that* body. Foucault's *Discipline and Punish* serves as a perfect example of how the institution of the prison operates as a relay of power which, while marked with some investments of power (for example, spaces facilitating examination), is only marked to the extent that these investments facilitate change in the prisoner's body. So why, in Victoria, do we see the investments of disciplinary power directed at the institutional body?

Once again, the answer is derived from the totemic power of the RCIADIC. When the RCIADIC collided with Victoria's correctional history it did not simply force the Department of Justice to respond to its position as the creator of Aboriginal 'difference'. It also allowed for the emergence of Aboriginal peoples as the only authority in relation to other Aboriginal peoples. As this section of the chapter illuminates, the tentative position that the Department of Justice negotiated for itself in the official documents only operates *if* the Department of

Justice first relinquishes its authority of Aboriginal offender management (that is, through investments of disciplinary power like the recruitment strategy) and *then* relinquishes authority of its progress in becoming docile (that is, through investments like the AJF's examination). This is the other 'ideal' norm generated through the investments of the institutional body: the authority of Aboriginal people as the experts on governance.

Facilitating different actions for the institutional body

This second 'ideal' norm is more apparent in some of the other operations of the AJF. As the following two Aboriginal staff members explain:

> Obviously partnership is at the heart of it and the real information sharing, the openness, the transparency, the involvement in all critical decisions that affect people and the capacity building. By making sure we are supporting the community's ability to participate, recognizing straight away that there is a huge unequalness that sits in that relationship, so unless we are very careful to try and ensure that the community side is empowered and is supported, then it is meaningless to just put people around the table. (Aboriginal staff member two)

And

> The Justice Forum has got key representatives from everywhere as well as community people, and I think that is what gives us the strength; it's only been since this was launched that we have actually had any say in what was going on in Government. (Aboriginal staff member four)

Once again, these Aboriginal staff members' reveal the very contingent nature of the Department of Justice's transformation. The Department of Justice must ensure the Koori community is '*empowered*' and '*supported*' otherwise all of the Department of Justice's actions become '*meaningless*'. The Department of Justice must allow Aboriginal peoples to embody a position of authority otherwise the ability of the Department of Justice to affect Aboriginal 'difference' is disabled (or would operate to the wrong effect). Indeed, as the following Aboriginal staff members further explain, without community authorization, the actions of the Department of Justice – no matter how focused on the issue of redressing difference – will not take effect:

> It will not work unless they [the Aboriginal community] want it and are willing to work with it. There is no point in pushing something out the door and saying here is the money, or here is this program that worked over there and now we are going to put it over here, it just will not work. It will not work if you don't have community support and buy-in and that means participation from the development stages right through to the implementation and the evaluation of it afterwards. (Aboriginal staff member four)

And

> When working with the community you need to be very mindful not to build up
> any expectations. Certainly don't make promises that you can never keep … and
> if something can't be done, make sure that you go back and explain why it can't
> be done. (Aboriginal staff member eight)

This is the contingency of Victoria's response to the RCIADIC. The Department
of Justice can only become something more than the creator or contributor to
Aboriginal difference (that is, the first ideal norm), if it relinquishes its authority
and control over Aboriginal offender management to Aboriginal people (that is,
the second ideal norm).

The Emergence of Aboriginal Authority in Victoria

While the appearance of Aboriginal authority in the criminal justice system is a
new development for Victoria (and Australia), Aboriginal or minority voices and
experiences have found space in other correctional jurisdictions. Hayman (2006)
traces how Canadian Aboriginal women, included on the Task Force on Federally
Sentenced Women, were able to integrate Aboriginal experiences and language into
Creating Choices: The Report of the Task Force on Federally Sentenced Women
(Task Force on Federally Sentenced Women 1990). Considering how and why this
integration occurred, Hayman's work illuminates a key tension facing Aboriginal
participants in processes such as this. She shows how, on the one hand, Aboriginal
participants appear to 'capture' the authority and attention of non-Aboriginal
members of the Task Force (Hayman 2006: 79), however, on the other, Aboriginal
participants are subjected to the underlying presence of 'postcolonial guilt',
which neutralizes non-Aboriginal people and restrains them from questioning any
proposition made by Aboriginal people (Hayman 2006: 111).

Raising a similar issue, Phillips (2005, 2007; Phillips and Bowling 2003)
published a series of works on minority perspectives in the professional fields of
justice. These texts document the ways that black and Asian professionals in the
United Kingdom are recruited to address issues of discrimination. The texts show
how black and Asian people use this recruitment strategy to forge a collective
identity and position of authority in criminal justice systems.

However, Phillips' (2007) work also draws attention to the tension black and
Asian professionals experience when they need to criticize or raise concerns
about the institution that employs them. In particular, Phillips' work highlights
how black and Asian professionals may take less confrontational approaches, or
more subtle approaches when working with their employers, to address concerns
about discrimination. She proposes that this restraint is a result of the unequal
power relationship that is inherent in their employment. They are employed as
representatives of a group that has been discriminated against by institutions like
their employer.

These comparable studies raise some questions about the nature of Aboriginal authority in Victoria's criminal justice system and the mechanisms that sustain it. Certainly discussions with Aboriginal and non-Aboriginal staff indicate there is a level of mistrust between Aboriginal peoples and the Department of Justice. As the following Aboriginal staff member explains:

> ... when you are out in the region, people will go "who put this together?", and you have to say "no, no, this is our issue mate" and they go "oh yeah, well what can I do". (Aboriginal staff member three)

And, as the following non-Aboriginal staff member indicates:

> For me, being a non-Aboriginal person, I am heavily influenced really by what I am and am unable to do. There are just some areas where I won't go, where there is no point in me going there, where it won't be appreciated if I go there. This really restricts me more in what I do than would be the case in other non-Aboriginal Units ... I think this is because there is a large mistrust of non-Aboriginal people by Koories; and you can get over that, but you almost have to get over that with every individual person, like the word doesn't get around that you are alright. So it's very restrictive. (non-Aboriginal staff member five)

Yet, these statements illustrate something more than mistrust. They illustrate some of the complexity of Aboriginal authority in Victoria's criminal justice system. On one side, these statements indicate the concern from the community that actions and initiatives delivered through Aboriginal people may still come from non-Aboriginal mind-sets and have the potential to harm Aboriginal communities. They illuminate the potential for Aboriginal voices and experiences to be constrained in the ways that Phillips or Hayman describes. On the other side, however, these statements, along with some of the previous examples provided in this chapter (see for example pages 83 and 84 of this chapter), show how actions and initiatives that are not driven by Aboriginal authority in Government will be disqualified when they reach the community (for example, '*who put this together?*'). They demonstrate how Aboriginal voices can silence Government authority.

The 'new irony' of Aboriginal authority in the Department of Justice
There is something unique taking shape in Victoria's criminal justice system. Aboriginal people are not being asked to be representatives in an unchanged system, like the black and Asian people of Phillips' studies. Nor are they being asked to create and give language to a new system, from which they are subsequently restricted from examining, like the Aboriginal women in Hayman's study. Indeed, the issue in Victoria is not whether or not Aboriginal voices are to be heard or constrained, but rather, whether non-Aboriginal voices should be heard, and if so, what should they be allowed to say about Aboriginal issues. As one Aboriginal staff member explains:

> One of the things that I feel strongest about is that Government has tried for 200 years to have a corrections and justice system for all people including Aboriginal people, and it didn't work … whatever you say, that system did not work … if you are going to solve these problems, the solution has to come from within the Aboriginal community and you have to work with the Aboriginal community as equal partners to solve these solutions. And the Victorian Aboriginal Justice Agreement has just picked up on that … everything about the Victorian Aboriginal Justice Agreement is working towards letting us, the Aboriginal people, have our say in these issues that affect us. (Aboriginal staff member nine)

Thus, what appears to be taking place in the Department of Justice is something more closely aligned to what O'Malley (1998) described as the 'new irony' of liberal governance around Indigenous issues. O'Malley used this term to describe how Aboriginal people are appropriated by Government to play a variety of roles in order for Governments to then claim authority over the management of Aboriginal people's lives. O'Malley poses that the 'irony' of this process is that these appropriating Governments must accept Aboriginal structures and Aboriginal 'translations' of governance in order to operate. This is what is occurring in the Victorian Department of Justice. In order for the Department of Justice to claim any authority over the lives of Aboriginal peoples it must recruit Aboriginal peoples to govern its approaches. However, in hiring Aboriginal peoples, the Department of Justice must accept a different process of governance.

The 'irony' of Victoria's criminal justice system implies that mutual constructions of race and criminal justice are complex, unstructured and full of unexpected elements. It is not simply that notions of nationhood provide the conditions for specific legal and criminal justice practices to form. Nor is it simply that legal and criminal justice practices contribute to social constructions of race. Rather, the mutual construction process is determined by the way that each of these elements collides with a range of other location-specific factors and the resulting mess this collision creates.

In light of this, a further element of the mutual construction process has presented itself for exploration: resistances to power's investments in the mutual construction of race and criminal justice. This chapter shows how Victoria's mutual construction process is taking place within a complex mess of colliding elements. It also shows how it is the Department of Justice's Aboriginal staff who have been appropriated to manage this 'mess'. Thus, the question becomes, what exactly is taking place in the Aboriginal spaces and places of the Department of Justice? Are Aboriginal people simply accepting the discourse of 'difference' negotiated by the Department of Justice? What logics and frameworks of knowledge do they use to affect 'difference'?

Aboriginal Resistance in the Field of Governance

Aboriginal staff at the Department of Justice support a discourse of difference. However, they do not support the parameters for Aboriginal 'difference' set by the official documents. This is not to say that Aboriginal staff do not position Aboriginal peoples as disadvantaged, over-represented or plagued by underlying issues (as the official documents identified). Rather, Aboriginal staff simply refuse to confine the experiences of Aboriginal peoples to these three repeated terms. For example, as one Aboriginal staff member explains:

> People forget how recent this stuff is. So in 1962 work permits were established, and before that Aboriginal people had to get signed approval to apply for a job, and Aboriginal people were not welcome in schools. So when you are facing those things only occurring a generation ago, it's very hard to make that change now. (Aboriginal staff member nine)

The issue is therefore not whether or not the Department of Justice 'acknowledges' employment problems as an area of 'disadvantage'. Rather, it is that the Department of Justice and other members of society need to remember what they '*forgot*': the entire history that Aboriginal peoples experienced in relation to employment and the numerous disadvantages this presents.

Forgetting or ignoring parts of Aboriginal peoples' history was raised by a number of Aboriginal staff members. As the following Aboriginal staff members explain, there are a number of factors playing out in Aboriginal peoples' lives at any given time, which the Department of Justice and the non-aboriginal community do not take into account:

> People are lacking with knowing their identity, the stolen generation stuff. Obviously a prisoner does not have to be from the stolen generation to not know who they are, because their mother, father, grandmother, whatever, would have been affected by past Government policies. (Aboriginal staff member seven)

Or

> I remember a 30-year-old Aboriginal guy, very articulate, very smart, very switched on, and I remember saying "what makes you come back here?" and he said "I was made a ward of the state when I was young, adopted into a white family, made mistakes and have just been in and out of jail". All he knows is that while he is in there he has a routine. He knows what jobs he has to do for the day. He knows when he has his medication and knows all the rules about what he can and can't do. The minute he steps out that door, he has not got a clue about how to manage himself, and it just pushes him back into the same group and it's just the same cycle and no one will give them the chance. (Aboriginal staff member four)

Or

> If we go and do cultural awareness training at a prison it is common for people
> to go, "well, why don't Aboriginal kids go to school, they have the same access
> as anyone else and they should be going to school". And you are talking about 20
> years beforehand it was the stolen generation, where schools were a place where
> Aboriginal kids were taken from. Really commonly, families would send their
> kids off to school and they would never come back again. When do you get over
> that? (Aboriginal staff member eight)

For these Aboriginal staff members, talking about Aboriginal offenders or
populations does not just go hand-in-hand with explaining the expansive impacts
of past Government actions. Rather, it also goes hand in hand with showing the
current and future implications of past Government actions on the experiences,
behaviours and identities of Aboriginal peoples. Accordingly, regardless of
whether a person experiences removal from their families through past policies of
assimilation, removal from the community though their prison sentence, or only
observes members of their family and community experiencing these different
forms of removal, each person experiences the same 'disadvantage' and 'underlying
issues' of Aboriginal peoples, leading to Aboriginal peoples' 'over-representation'
in Victoria's criminal justice system. This is the complex relationship between the
past and present of Aboriginal peoples in Victoria.

The connection between the past and present of Aboriginal 'difference'
indicates a development in the discursive practice operating across the Department
of Justice. The history of Aboriginal 'difference' is constantly written and
rewritten. The RCIADIC wrote the history of Australian Government's creating
Aboriginal 'difference'. The Department of Justice rewrote this history in terms
of the present government redressing the past. Aboriginal staff members of the
Department of Justice are now writing the future of Aboriginal 'difference', as it
intersects with this past and present. Moreover, as these Aboriginal staff members'
words illuminate, it is not a process of writing one history over the top of another,
but of acknowledging the presence of the other when writing the next. Thus, there
exists in these accounts of Aboriginal 'difference' what Butler (1997: 28) once
called 'excessive historicity', where the history of 'difference' extends beyond the
individual staff member's experience of it.

Blurring the Boundaries between Offending and Non-offending Lifestyles

Aboriginal staff members are not, however, the only Aboriginal people rewriting
the future of Aboriginal difference. As a number of previous examples illustrate,
new developments for Aboriginal offenders will not take place unless they are
proposed by the Aboriginal community, or at least have community buy-in from the
beginning. It is here, in community proposed actions and authority, that something
unexpected has begun to form in the present and future history of Aboriginal and

criminal justice relations. The following two Aboriginal staff members' accounts illuminate this formation best:

> I think a strength and weakness of the Aboriginal Justice Agreement and our Unit is, whilst in the early stages of the implementation of the VAJA1 there may have been some hesitation and uncertainty of the Justice Agreement, I think that over the years we have proved ourselves to the community and we tend to get inquiries about everything, not just about Justice issues, "can you fix this", "we need that", you know, and so I think our reputation has probably grown and people have come to have confidence in us, or at least if we can't fix it we know where they can go with it. I see this as a good thing, but it is also a weakness of ours, because we actually get weighed down with a lot of stuff that is actually not our own. (Aboriginal staff member four)

And

> You find community workers will ring you and say "I have five kids who have already had 15 days each suspension at one school, all Aboriginal". The issue is that in half these blues [conflicts] they are claiming that it is racial abuse and that is the way that they have been taught to react to racial abuse ... so they will go to the principal and the principal will go "there is no proof in what you are saying about racial abuse, but you have admitted to smacking this other girl, so you have to be suspended". So the poor kid goes home with no closure, and I say to the worker, "but your responsibility is to go to the Equal Opportunity Commission and complain about it". We were lucky because we put that on the table and the Equal Opportunity Commission came down and ran a workshop down there with us ... you have to touch on those fuzzy areas. The worker, she was pulling her hair out, she didn't know what to do and that is our responsibility, finding solutions. (Aboriginal staff member three)

These statements reiterate a number of points previously made in this chapter. They reiterate the important role the community plays in shaping the actions of the Department of Justice, and the important role Aboriginal staff play in facilitating this process. However, these statements also illuminate two unexpected features that have become associated with these roles.

First, it is not simply that the Aboriginal community shapes the actions of the Department of Justice towards Aboriginal offenders. Rather, the Aboriginal community shapes the actions taken towards the community too. More importantly, the Aboriginal community asks for initiatives or actions that address the non-offending needs or concerns of the Aboriginal community.

Second, Aboriginal staff are not just responsible for facilitating the Aboriginal community's involvement in the Department of Justice. Aboriginal staff are also responsible for ensuring that the Department of Justice finds solutions for Aboriginal community problems.

In order to understand how this unexpected development in the Department of Justice has formed, it is necessary to consider *why* the Aboriginal community asks the Department of Justice (as opposed to other Government departments) to provide solutions for Aboriginal community problems. The following Aboriginal staff member's words shed some light on this occurrence:

> It doesn't make sense for us to be running housing or education policies or other sorts of things, but looking at the membership of the Forum and what we have the ability to influence, our authority is just strongest in the Justice area. (Aboriginal staff member two)

The reason why the Aboriginal community's non-offender-related issues have become the Department of Justice's responsibility is because it is in the Department of Justice, more than any other arm of Government, that the Aboriginal community have this opportunity for involvement.

Clarifying this point reveals more of the messiness, complexity and contingency at the heart of current and future Government and Aboriginal relations in Victoria. The Aboriginal community are appropriating whatever limited space is provided to Aboriginal people in the Department of Justice in order to address issues that may otherwise go ignored by Government. In doing so, the lines around the boundaries of criminal justice have started to extend. There is almost something akin to what Cohen (1985) highlighted when he spoke of the boundaries of punishment and control blurring when community-based orders emerged. However, the Aboriginal community are not being used by the Department of Justice to manage Aboriginal offending behaviour in new and different ways (as was the case in the communities of Cohen's work). Rather, the Aboriginal community use this opportunity to ask Victoria's criminal justice system to manage non-offending behaviour in their lives. It is non-offending lifestyles that are being brought into the gaze and responsibility of the criminal justice system, not offending lifestyles being made the responsibility of watchful citizens. This is the unfinished, complex, messy and unusual history of government and Aboriginal relations that is being written at the moment in Victoria's criminal justice arena.

In light of the unfinished nature of Victoria's criminal justice history, a final question arises: how do Aboriginal staff, sitting at the frontline of this history, negotiate these colliding and contradictory elements?

Blurring the Boundaries of Criminal Justice Experiences

What is overwhelming in discussions with Aboriginal staff is how often they explain their authority in terms of their common history with offenders. As the following four Aboriginal staff members explain, each staff member's knowledge of Aboriginal 'difference' is more intimate than what could be written in any official document:

Most of my colleagues, we've all had someone who has been incarcerated before, not all of us, but most of us and that kind of is that personal experience as well, which sort of helps you look at things a little bit differently. (Aboriginal staff member eight)

As Aboriginal people and I am one of them, things are just very close to home and going to prisons and talking to guys that are around the same age as my brother and my younger cousins, it can be very emotional, just seeing anybody in that situation, but when you are seeing the struggle of your own people it is very sensitive stuff. (Aboriginal staff member seven)

For me, and for everyone in our unit, we are all Aboriginal people. What you do at work, you see how it makes a difference. If we promise to run a program at a community corrections location and it does not happen, in two weeks I'll be out somewhere and one of the people who would have been coming to that program will be having goes about why the program didn't run. More importantly I know how important this stuff is, how what we do can change lives. What we do can make a difference to a person, which can make a difference to their family, which can make a difference to other families and to communities. (Aboriginal staff member nine)

And

When you have the level of involvement in the system as we do, it's just a part of each family's fight. Staff here, everyone has got someone who has been in, or who are somewhere in that process. So it is not like we are highly disconnected in that way, we have all that level of engagement and it is such a pervasive experience for most people. (Aboriginal staff member two)

Previous sections of this chapter show how the Koori recruitment strategy acts as a mechanism of power. The strategy allows Aboriginal staff to act as the authorities on Aboriginal difference and the experts on the Department of Justice's capacity to affect difference. The statements provided by staff above, demonstrate how recruited Aboriginal staff bring a new dimension to their role. Aboriginal staff contextualize their authority and expertise through their shared experiences of Aboriginal 'difference' and Government attempts to affect it. Aboriginal staff use a framework of *experience*, not just knowledge. Moreover, this framework of experience is not simply based on the experiences of Aboriginal 'difference' as they occur in the community. Rather, Aboriginal staffs' lives are shaped by the past and present history of Aboriginal offenders and their engagement in criminal justice systems.

The framework of experience of Aboriginal staff unveils a further element in the messy constellation of factors shaping the Department of Justice's approaches to Aboriginal offenders. Previously it was argued that Victoria's Aboriginal community appropriates the authority and presence of Aboriginal staff in the Department of Justice, bringing the gaze of the criminal justice system into their non-offending lives. The framework of experience indicates that even if this gaze was not requested by the community, the presence of Victoria's criminal justice system would still be felt in all Aboriginal peoples' lives. Thus, in Victoria, it is not only the roles and responsibilities of the criminal justice agency to the community that have been blurred; it is also the experiences of criminal justice in Aboriginal peoples' lives. The whole Aboriginal community is marked by the ongoing struggle of Aboriginal peoples in Victoria's criminal justice system.

Reversing Epistemic Violence

It seems then that something has emerged in Victoria's criminal justice system that is distinct from what Spivak envisaged with the concepts of 'worlding' and 'epistemic violence'. As explained in Chapter 2, these terms refer to the way the West engages with non-Western populations from the assumption they are encountering 'empty earth' on which they are entitled to write the inscriptions of the Western World. They also refer to the way the West further inscribes this earth with Western knowledge and epistemologies, which render non-Western populations as knowable, understandable and definable according to Western terms and concepts. The 'difference' of Aboriginal peoples that was wrought by Western epistemic violence through things like the *Proclamation of Governor Bourke* and the *Policy of Assimilation* is being reversed. The Department of Justice was forced through the unavoidable impact of the RCIADIC to remap the world of Aboriginal peoples in Victoria and re-inscribe it as a world marked by devastating differences – differences created by the actions of Western Governments. In doing so, the Department of Justice was requested to release its authority over the Aboriginal World; this was the only way that it could move to the position of affecting difference, not creating it. In gaining authority, Aboriginal staff have used their experiences to remap both the Aboriginal World and the Western World. They have mapped the Western World as capable of creating devastating differences in the lives of Aboriginal peoples and the world of Aboriginal peoples, as marked by these expansive and limitless devastating differences.

This unusual process of worlding illustrates something important about the investments of power in the Victorian Department of Justice. There are not just two ideal 'norms' facilitated in the Department of Justice: one where the Department of Justice is docile in redressing 'difference' and one where Aboriginal peoples are active authorities in this process. Rather, the 'Western' elements of the Department of Justice's body are made docile in order to render them *incapable of the authority* needed to relay any further investments of power to Aboriginal offenders. In contrast, the 'Aboriginal' elements of the Department of Justice's body have not only taken shape as an authority, but have allowed the institutional body to re-emerge as a relay of power *under their governance*. As this section illustrates, Aboriginal staff hired to occupy, manage and maintain the

'Aboriginal' elements or places of Department of Justice were not subject to the same investments of disciplinary power as other staff of the Department of Justice. Or more correctly, while they were subject to the same investments of disciplinary power (in the sense that these investments saw the creation of enclosed spaces within the Department of Justice that they needed to occupy), the strategy was different. These investments neither facilitated the docility of Aboriginal staff, nor presented Aboriginal staff as being simply a group of individual authorities on Aboriginal issues. Rather these investments allowed the shared experiences of these Aboriginal staff to emerge as a collective authority, and more importantly, as the only authority capable of listening to, judging and responding to the figure of the Aboriginal offender, the diverse demands of the Aboriginal community, and the actions of the Department of Justice in relation to Aboriginal peoples.

Some Final Implications and Conclusions

The changing authority of the Department of Justice allows this chapter to make some final implications about the mutual construction of race and criminal justice. This chapter has repeatedly illustrated the location-specific nature of Victoria's correctional approaches towards Aboriginal offenders. It traced how a constellation of location-specific factors – such as the specific history of Australia's colonization, the attempts of contemporary governments to respond to this history, and the deaths of 99 Aboriginal people in Australia's criminal justice system over the period of a decade – have forced open the criminal justice system to Aboriginal peoples. It has also shown how Aboriginal peoples use their authority to mark and transform the institutional body with Aboriginal knowledge and a framework of Aboriginal experience.

The findings of this chapter are reminiscent of those presented in the Introduction of this book by Bosworth (2004), Wacquant (2010a, 2010b) and Davis (2003). Both sets of findings show how constructions and regulations of racialized identities are intimately linked to the historical formations of criminal justice systems. Moreover, both illuminate how notions of nationhood and otherness are instrumental to both the development of criminal justice systems and the techniques that will see specific populations contained within them more often. However, this chapter reveals something more about the relationship between notions of nationhood, racialized identity and criminal justice practice. It reveals three fundamental structures supporting the mutual construction process.

First, fundamental to the mutual constructions of race and criminal justice are the *negotiations* of notions of nationhood, racialized identity and criminal justice practice. Thus, for example, the colonization of Australia, the demands of the RCIADIC, and the over-representation of Aboriginal peoples in criminal justice systems are common factors in each of Australia's States. Moreover, these common factors have seen each State form legal and criminal justice practices which are intimately linked to Australia's notions of nationhood and the regulation of Aboriginal peoples in Australia. However, the Victorian Department of Justice *negotiated* and *responded* to these common factors in its own way. The Victorian Department of Justice:

- developed multiple phases of the Aboriginal Justice Agreement;
- negotiated a role for itself in the governance of Aboriginal 'difference';
- transformed the spaces, places and functions of its body to enclose Aboriginal 'difference';
- provided space for Aboriginal authority to emerge; and
- subjected itself to a process of examination under Aboriginal expertise.

It is all of these location-specific negotiations which determine Victoria's criminal justice approaches towards Aboriginal offenders, not just the notions of nationhood circulating in Australia.

Second, the mutual construction process is *dynamic*; it is always subject to further negotiation. The demands from the Aboriginal community are constantly changing as trust with the Department of Justice develops. The responsibilities of the Department of Justice and its ability to remain docile in the management of Aboriginal peoples are under ever changing criteria in the examination process. The experiences of Aboriginal staff are constantly changing as more or less Aboriginal peoples enter Victoria's criminal justice system. Finally, as the experiences of Aboriginal staff change, so too does their understanding of Aboriginal offenders and the approaches necessary for their management. Thus, it is all of these *dynamic* factors that the Department of Justice negotiates in the mutual construction process.

Finally, the mutual construction process is *localized*. It has been numerous pages since this book even mentioned the science of offending behaviour. This science has been entirely silenced in discussions of the causes of Aboriginal offenders' over-representation in Victoria's criminal justice system, and the approaches taken by the Department of Justice to address it. This science is irrelevant to the multiple histories of 'difference' that are being mapped in the Western and Aboriginal Worlds, and these worlds' construction.

Thus, what this chapter reveals is not simply one of the first breaks in correctional history from the increasingly extending regulation of the discourse of science of offending behaviour, but more importantly:

- how location-specific and historical informed practices towards Aboriginal offenders emerged organically in Victoria's Department of Justice;
- how these practices position the 'Western' elements of the institution as capable of creating the differences experienced by all Aboriginal peoples, and the 'Aboriginal' elements of the institution capable of their redress;
- how this positioning is negotiated and performed by both parts of the Victorian Department of Justice through mediums like official documents, functional Units and frameworks of experience; and

- how it is this entire constellation of events and factors that inform the mutual constructions of race and criminal justice in Victoria.

But this is only one account of the mutual construction process at the local level; let us now consider another.

Chapter 4
Biculturalism:
Struggling to Maintain Dual Histories

The parameters surrounding the New Zealand Department of Corrections have seen its institutional body struggle to negotiate the mutual constructions of race and criminal justice. As a result, multiple figures of the Māori offender have been produced over the past 15 years.

The previous chapter provided the first of two case studies of the mutual constructions of race and criminal justice at the institutional level. It argued that mutual construction is a location-specific, negotiated and ongoing process. The present chapter provides the second of these two case studies. It explores how localized constructions of nationhood and racialized identity contribute to the formation, transformation and orientation of New Zealand's Department of Corrections.

New Zealand and its Department of Corrections were selected for this case study for the following four reasons:

1. *New Zealand's colonial history.* New Zealand has a different history of settler-colonization from Australia. New Zealand's history is hinged on the British Crown forming the Treaty of Waitangi in 1840 with some (but not all) Māori Chiefs. The Treaty of Waitangi provides the founding principles upon which any interaction between the New Zealand Government and Māori should be built. It dictates the shared and additional rights of Māori and Pākehā[1] in relation to the governance of New Zealand. Since its inception, New Zealand Governments have responded to the principles of the Treaty of Waitangi in a variety of ways. As a result, Māori have endured a range of experiences in New Zealand's society and criminal justice system.

2. *New Zealand's single Governmental approach.* The British Crown settled New Zealand as a single jurisdiction, not a federation. Accordingly, the Department of Corrections is responsible for the management of offender populations across New Zealand's North and South Island. This means that all correctional and community settings across New Zealand are governed by the same Department of Corrections' policies and practices.

3. *There is one Māori nation.* While the Māori nation comprises numerous *iwi* (tribes), all Māori share the same genealogy, world views, processes

---

1   Pākehā is a Māori word meaning person of predominantly European descent.

and culture. The unified nature of the Māori population has allowed Māori people across New Zealand's North and South Island to work together to protest against the New Zealand Government's treatment of Māori in all parts of society.

4. *New Zealand's approach to the tools, tactics and logics of global criminological literature.* The Department of Corrections practices a science of offending behaviour that focuses on targeting the anti-social attributes of offenders and managing the risk they pose to society. This science constitutes and regulates the position of Māori and Pākehā offenders. This science has, however, also been transformed to recognize and respond to the location-specific issues facing New Zealand and its populations.

A Change in Focus

In order to capture the proper dispersion of these location-specific elements in the formation and orientation of criminal justice in New Zealand, this chapter cannot share the previous chapter's focus. It cannot explore how the discourse of anti-social offenders and their categorical risks has been replaced by a discourse of location-specific 'difference', because this has not occurred in New Zealand. Instead, this chapter must address a different focus. It must present and analyse the tension between these global and local discursive practices, exploring how and why they emerge in New Zealand's correctional sphere, and what occurs at their many points of intersection and collision. To do this, this chapter asks: who or what is being governed in the New Zealand Department of Corrections' approach to Māori and Pākehā offenders? Who or what becomes governable through the Department of Corrections' approach? Using what authority, logics, and frameworks of knowledge? Supported by which tactics, tools and investments? To what end? And, what role do resistances play in these governing processes?

As with the previous chapter, this chapter draws on the official documents of the New Zealand Department of Corrections and interviews with Māori and Pākehā staff working in the area of Māori offending in order to answer these questions. The chapter uses this information across four sections. The first section provides a brief history of Government and Māori relations in New Zealand. It draws particular attention to the role of the Treaty of Waitangi in the formation of New Zealand's criminal justice system. The next three sections present and analyse the struggles the Department of Corrections has faced when trying to balance its responsibility to manage Māori and Pākehā offenders, with its obligations to Māori under the Treaty of Waitangi. These three sections focus on the way this ongoing struggle has changed the orientation of New Zealand's mutual constructions of race and criminal justice. These sections reveal the tools, tactics and investments of power, and bring attention to the corresponding performances of resistances.

A Brief Correctional History of Government and Māori Relations

New Zealand has a different history from Victoria and broader Australia. New Zealand was settled as a free society, and more specifically, as a society which was intended to mirror Britain. Accordingly, the priority in New Zealand's settlement was bringing Māori under British Crown control, not removing Māori rights to British land and law. In New Zealand, this priority was achieved when Māori and British relations were formalized into law with the development and signing of the Treaty of Waitangi in 1840.

The Treaty of Waitangi is an agreement between the British Crown and some Māori chiefs.[2] The agreement comprises three key principles. These principles outline the roles, responsibilities and relationships between the parties, stating that:

1. Māori cede sovereignty of New Zealand to Britain (however, in the Māori translation of the Treaty, only governance was ceded);
2. Māori retain full rights of ownership of their land, forests, fisheries and other possessions, but the Crown has an exclusive right to buy land from Māori if Māori wish to sell it; and
3. Māori are entitled to the same rights and privileges as British subjects.

A Contentious and Unstable Foundation for Government and Māori Relations

Successive New Zealand Governments have struggled to respect these principles and the roles, responsibilities and relationships they imply. For example, between 1844 and 1864 the British Crown 'bought' 91 per cent of New Zealand's South Island from the Ngäi Tahu. The Crown promised to leave adequate reserves for the Ngäi Tahu. It also indicated that Ngäi Tahu would continue to benefit from the settlement of their land. Neither of these outcomes occurred. The Crown left Ngäi Tahu with little to no space on the land and provided very little money in return for its sale.

The opportunity for Māori to address this or other breaches of the Treaty of Waitangi did not arise until 1975. In that year, the *Treaty of Waitangi Act* was passed, establishing with it the Waitangi Tribunal. The Waitangi Tribunal was established to hear and make recommendations on claims about potential breaches of the Treaty's principles. However, the Tribunal's powers were limited at the time of its inception. It was only empowered to hear claims of breaches occurring *after* the Tribunal's development (that is, post-1975).

It was not until 1985 that the Tribunal was granted powers to hear claims of breaches occurring *prior* to 1975 (see Bourassa and Strong 2002 for an account of

---

2   Not all Māori chiefs were present at the signing of the Treaty or agreed to its terms. It is not the purpose of this book to re-open or re-examine this issue further, for an examination of this kind see Orange (1987).

the development of the *Treaty of Waitangi Act 1975* and its impact on restitution of
Māori land). It was at this time, that the case of the Ngāi Tahu was brought before
the Tribunal – over a century after the original breach occurred. Yet, even though
a forum had been created to hear these grievances, the powers of the Tribunal
were restrained. The rulings of the Tribunal were – and are still – not enforceable
by law (Sorrenson 1995). Accordingly, when the Tribunal finally made a ruling
on the Ngāi Tahu case in 1991, its impact on Government and Māori relations
was limited. The Tribunal concluded that the Crown had acted unconscionably
and in repeated breach of the Treaty (Waitangi Tribunal 1991). The Tribunal
recommended that New Zealand's Government return some of the land to Māori
and make other concessions for Māori living on the land. But, the Tribunal could
not enforce any of its recommendations.

The Policy of Biculturalism

The fluctuating levels of recognition and priority afforded to the Treaty in New
Zealand have affected the position and experiences of Māori in New Zealand
society over time. This chapter shows the current, prominent place of Māori
in New Zealand's society and Government; a position where Māori culture and
practices are seen as a fundamental part of New Zealand's society, and where
Māori people are represented across Government and industry. Māori have only
recently occupied this position in New Zealand. Certainly when Māori protested
and formed activist groups and parties in the 1970s to demand recognition of their
rights, customs, land, language and culture (the catalyst for the development of the
Treaty of Waitangi Act 1975 and the Waitangi Tribunal), they did not occupy this
contemporary place (see Harris 2004 for an account of Māori protests over the past
40 years). In fact, it was not until the forth Labour Government of the late 1980s,
that the protests of Māori were formally addressed through the Government's
adoption of a Policy of Biculturalism (see Poata-Smith 1996, 1997 for further
detail).

Yet, the Policy of Biculturalism has received much criticism from Māori over
the past two decades. In particular, Māori have argued that the Policy has been used
as a means to 'indigenize' New Zealand's Government. That is, Māori processes
and knowledge are seen as being co-opted by New Zealand's Government in order
to legitimize the Government's Western practices towards Māori (see Tauri 1998,
1999; Tauri and Webb 2011 for further discussion of New Zealand's situation; see
Havemann 1988 for the broader discussion of 'indigenizing' the state).

This criticism of the Policy of Biculturalism was also raised in New Zealand's
first major report into Māori experiences in the criminal justice system: *The Māori
and the Criminal Justice System: He Whaipaanga Hou* (Jackson 1988).

The Māori and the Criminal Justice System
In the late 1980s, the then Department of Justice commissioned Moana Jackson,
a prominent Māori scholar, to produce a report on the relationship between Māori

and the criminal justice system. This Report was sought to develop a bicultural approach to justice and corrections in New Zealand that aligned with the Government's Policy of Biculturalism.

Jackson used this forum to raise several concerns about the Department of Justice and the broader New Zealand Government's approach to biculturalism. He claimed that:

> It is one of the weaknesses of current thinking on biculturalism that many institutions appear to believe that they can gain Māori perspectives or meet Māori needs without acknowledging the validity of Māori initiatives that may be contrary to their own. They also seem to feel biculturalism can be achieved without sharing the decision-making processes within a particular institution. These beliefs have resulted in instances of what may be called "cultural appropriation" which appear to satisfy the theory but certainly not the reality of biculturalism. (Jackson 1988: 206)

Thus, Jackson accused the Department of Justice of attempting to 'indigenize' its criminal justice practices. Jackson accused the Department of Justice of 'appropriating' Māori perspectives to suit the needs of the institution when working with Māori, but not using these perspectives to develop other initiatives by the Māori population.

The Department of Justice's response to Jackson's concerns was mixed. It rejected the claim of 'cultural appropriation'. However, it acknowledged the need to rethink its approach to biculturalism. It sought to incorporate Māori culture, processes and knowledge in better ways (see Patterson 1992).

At this point in New Zealand's history – a point where the mantra of biculturalism was strong but the practice was still under construction – the Department of Justice split into the Department of Corrections and the Ministry of Justice. One of the first requirements of the newly-formed Department of Corrections, was to determine how it, as a modern bicultural institution, would honour the obligations of the British Crown under the Treaty of Waitangi. One of the ways that the Department of Corrections approached this requirement was by recasting its obligations under the Treaty of Waitangi and reconstituting the relationship between Māori and Pākehā populations. The following excerpt from the *Framework for Reducing Māori Offending (FReMO)* illustrates this approach:

> Here in the Pacific, there are also many examples of cultural similarities co-existing alongside major cultural differences between any two groups. Māori and Pākehā share the modern values of "do-it-yourself Kiwi initiative", and "getting away to the beach for the weekend". But there are also huge differences between them, as in Tangihanga and funeral rituals. Many Māori, reflecting on a Pākehā funeral, will point to there being insufficient time for grief, and for support of the dead person's Whanau; while many Pākehā feel uncomfortable

with the outpouring of emotion and intimacy, and the days rather than hours spent at the deceased's side. (McFarlane-Nathan 1999: 8)

The Department of Corrections *negotiated* the demarcations of the Treaty of Waitangi with respect to its authority. The Treaty of Waitangi positioned the British Crown as responsible for providing Māori with the same rights and privileges as British subjects. The Department of Corrections simply presents Māori and Pākehā as sharing certain modern values. The Treaty of Waitangi positioned the British Crown as responsible for ensuring Māori are entitled to an additional set of rights that pertained to their particular ownership of a variety of possessions (that is, land and fisheries). The Department of Corrections simply presents Māori as entitled to their additional or particular values, ways of being or processes (such as the ones evoked during funeral rights).

The Department of Corrections' subtle renegotiations of the Treaty's demarcations caused a shift in responsibility. The emphasis changed from the sole *obligations* of the Department of Corrections to Māori and Pākehā populations, to the *capacity* of Māori and Pākehā populations to peacefully coexist and develop common values despite their differences. Māori and Pākehā are as responsible as the New Zealand Government for ensuring their ongoing welfare. Moreover, the responsibility of Māori within their relationship with Pākehā and the New Zealand Government has been set. Māori are entitled to some additional or particular values, ways of being and processes that do not preclude them from otherwise coexisting with, and sharing the same lifestyle of, Pākehā in New Zealand.

Over the past 15 years, the Department of Corrections has struggled to maintain this reading of its obligations under the Treaty of Waitangi. Specifically, it has struggled to find and maintain an acceptable balance between its responsibilities as an institution charged with the management of New Zealand's offender populations, and its reconstituted obligations to respect the shared and particular rights of Māori and Pākehā under the Treaty of Waitangi. It is this ongoing struggle that forms the lens through which this chapter can trace the mutual constructions of race and criminal justice in New Zealand. Using this lens, this chapter will now trace the various manifestations of this struggle in the Department of Corrections, and present the implications of this struggle for New Zealand's mutual construction process.

The First Struggle: Creating a Shared Science of Offending Behaviour

When the Department of Corrections formed in the mid 1990s, it conflated its responsibilities for managing offenders with its obligations under the Treaty of Waitangi. That is, the Department of Corrections created a science of offending behaviour that accounted for the shared and particular rights, values and processes of Māori and Pākehā in a framework of risk management.

The Department of Corrections did not explain *why* it took this approach to its responsibilities and obligations. Instead, it explained *how* the science of offending behaviour presented in the practical texts of the correctional literature was not suitable for use with Māori and Pākehā offenders. More importantly, it explained *how* and *why* this science of offending behaviour was not as transportable as the correctional literature claimed it to be. For example, *A Seein' 'I' to the Future: The Criminogenic Needs Inventory* (CNI), states:

> The LSI-R was developed using a Canadian offender population. Canadian offender may differ from their New Zealand counterparts in ways that reduce the accuracy of the LSI-R when used with the local offender population. (Coebergh et al. 2001: 3)

Furthermore, the *Risk of ReConviction: Statistical Models Predicting Four Types of Re-Offending (RoC)* explains:

> … investigators, particular in Canada, have introduced the concept of "risk/ need" scales … we believe that attempting to combine need and risk measures in a single scale in New Zealand would be premature. (Bakker, O'Malley and Riley 1999: 10)

Thus, the science of offending behaviour presented in the practical texts was a science of *Canadian* offenders' behaviour. It was not suitable for use with Māori and Pākehā offenders because its tools and techniques were not premised on these offenders' behaviour. Accordingly, what the Department of Corrections has produced instead is a location-specific science of offending behaviour that *can* account for the shared and particular rights, values and processes of Māori and Pākehā in New Zealand society within a framework of anti-social behaviour and categorical risk. This location-specific science of offending behaviour differs from its 'Canadian' or literature counterpart in four key ways.

1. A New Categorical and Predictive Factor: The Nature of Offences

There are separate risk and need scales in the Department of Corrections' science of offending behaviour. As a result, the register of operationality has changed. What has been operationalized in New Zealand's science of offending behaviour is the nature of the *offence*, not the anti-social behaviour of the *offender.*

Accordingly, the Department of Corrections must perform a different set of tasks before it can collect the information needed to identify, classify and divide its offender population into the appropriate categories of risk. The Department of Corrections must:

1. identify the *type* of offence committed by the offender; was it sexual or violent in nature? Was it drug related? Can it be classified as theft, property damage, or a driving offence?
2. identify the *timeline* of the offender's offence track-record; had it been six months, one year or five years since the last offence was committed?
3. classify the *seriousness* of the offence committed by the offender; did it warrant a custodial sentence?
4. divide the seriousness of the offence into distinct *categories*; was the offence serious enough to warrant a short, medium or long custodial sentence? (Bakker, O'Malley and Riley 1999)

Thus, according to this altered register of operationality, a high-risk offender is distinguished from a low-risk offender in New Zealand by the nature, trajectory and impact of their criminal career, not the number of anti-social attributes they possess.

2. A New Priority for Risk Management: Reducing the Threat of Serious Offences

Changing the nature of the factors associated with risk in New Zealand affects the priority for their management. The priority in the Department of Corrections' science of offending behaviour is to manage the *threat* of serious offences, not just the *risk* that offenders will offend again. As the *RoC* explains:

> Offenders with a probability of serious re-offending can be given priority in treatment or rehabilitative programmes. When treatment resources are limited and decisions must be made about who should receive them, this is best done on the basis of objective information about which offenders are most likely to commit serious crimes. (Bakker, O'Malley and Riley 1999: 28)

It is more efficient to reduce the probability that a high-risk offender will commit another *serious* offence, than it is to reduce the probability that they will commit any other *type* of offence. The issue is not how the offender is likely to behave in the future, but how their behaviour has measurable consequences for New Zealand society.

Thus, while the Risk Need Responsivity Model's (RNRM) claims of efficiency provided the impetus to relocate the figure of the offender from the scale of normality to a continuum of risk, the Department of Corrections' claims prompt a further shift. New Zealand offenders are to be located on a continuum of threat to society.

3. A New Scale of Need

Yet, while the threat of serious offences represents a different *problem* for the Department of Corrections to manage, the *solution* presented in the Department of Corrections' science of offending behaviour is largely the same as the one presented for Canadian offenders. As the *RoC* explains:

> Risk [as defined by the seriousness of the offence/threat of the offender] should be a guide as to who should have priority for rehabilitation; need [as determined by the attributes of the offender] should provide objective information about which aspects of individual functioning should be a priority for intervention. (Bakker, O'Malley and Riley 1999: 11)

To manage the threat of serious offences, the Department of Corrections must target the *attributes* of the most problematic offenders – those who threaten to commit the most serious crimes.

However, as New Zealand offenders do not, apparently, share much in common with Canadian offenders, the Department of Corrections has had to develop a new scale of 'need' in order to make these attributes operable. In order to target interventions to the appropriate attributes of the most problematic offenders, the Department of Corrections must perform yet another series of tasks. The Department of Corrections must:

1. Name and count the number of offender attributes present in the past six months; are they offence-related emotions and cognitions, an unbalanced lifestyle, or have they manifested as criminal associates and relationships (Coebergh et al. 2001).
2. Classify these attributes under two categories. Are they 'Offence Period' attributes; that is, attributes that are present in the period that 'starts the day before the offence and finishes at the completion of the offence'? Or, are they 'Pre-disposing Period' attributes; that is attributes that first appeared within the '6 months preceding the offence period'? (Coebergh et al. 2001: 5).
3. Determine the relationship between attributes that manifested in the 'Pre-disposing Period' and those that were present in the 'Offence Period'. Are they the same attributes throughout this time, if not, what has changed, and in what time period did change occur?
4. Determine the severity of the attributes that are directly related to the offence being committed. In general, attributes presented in the 'Pre-disposing Period' will not have any direct relationship on the offence unless they were also present in the 'Offence Period'.

It is only in completing these four tasks that the Department of Corrections can understand how much time, resource and effort they need to invest in order to manage their offender population and reduce the threat of serious offences in New Zealand society.

4. Accounting for Māori Culture-related Needs

As previously stated, the Department of Corrections has developed a location-specific science of offending behaviour that can account for the shared and particular rights, values and processes of Māori and Pākehā in New Zealand society. The three provisions described above allow the Department of Corrections to account for the *shared* rights, values and processes of Māori and Pākehā offenders. In the early 2000s, the Department of Corrections created a further assessment tool to identity and target the *particular* 'needs' of Māori offenders: the Māori Culture-Related Needs (MaCRN) tool.

According to the MaCRN tool, Māori offenders present with four particular 'culture-related' needs in addition to the general needs they share with Pākehā offenders (for example, offence-related emotions and cognitions, or criminal associates and relationships). The MaCRN tool proposes that Māori 'culture-related' needs can be identified, classified and targeted in a similar way to the general needs of offenders. As the *CNI* explains:

> MaCRN 1 – Cultural Identity, measures whether the offender has a **positive pro-social perception about being Māori or whether their perception about being Māori is negative and/or anti-social.** This is assessed on the basis of an offender's lack of pride and/or comfort about being Māori and/or whether pride and comfort are associated with anti-social behaviours, attitudes or beliefs. Once this is identified, the extent to which this perception precipitates thoughts and feelings that potentially predispose him/her to offending is examined. (Coebergh et al. 2001: 17, original emphasis)

> MaCRN 2 – Cultural Tension, measures the **nature and extent of the cultural tension** and the offender's capability of recognizing and pro-socially addressing this where it impacts on their personal, social and/or occupational functioning. (Coebergh et al. 2001: 18, original emphasis)

> MaCRN 3 – *Whanau* [family], is measured in two ways. The first category of assessment is lack of *whanau* contact and whether this has **negatively impacted** upon the functioning of the offender. The second category of assessment is the identification **of anti-social behaviours and attitudes within the offender's *whanau*** which may support and maintain offending behaviour. (Coebergh et al. 2001: 18, original emphasis)

> MaCRN 4 – *Whakawhanaunga* [extended family], examines whether the offender is **part of a group** (within the pre-disposing period) who they consider to be like a *whanau* to them. Once this has been identified, the importance of the group and/or the ways in which being part of this group has impacted upon their relationship with others is then assessed. (Coebergh et al. 2001: 18, original emphasis)

The definitions of the MaCRN and their place in New Zealand's science of offending behaviour illuminate how the Department of Corrections conflated its responsibilities for managing offenders with its obligations under the Treaty of Waitangi. What the Department of Corrections rationalized as being common amongst Māori and Pākehā offenders was not just their rights and privileges as British subjects. Rather, it was also their common right to have the Department of Corrections address their offending behaviour through its location-specific science of offending behaviour. What the Department of Corrections rationalized as being additional and particular to Māori was not just their ownership of certain possessions or processes. Instead, Māori offenders were rationalized as possessing an additional and particular problematic relationship with family and cultural processes, which influenced their engagement in offending behaviour. Thus, the obligations of the Department of Corrections under the Treaty of Waitangi were *operationalized* through the same register the Department of Corrections used to address its responsibility for managing offending behaviour.

Rejecting the Association between Māori Culture and the Behaviour of Māori Offenders

Using a single register to operationalize the Department of Corrections' obligations and responsibilities had serious ramifications for the construction of the Māori offender. It reintroduced the notion of criminal indigeneity.

Chapter 1 demonstrated how the ever-extending regulation of the practical texts and their science of offending behaviour ensured that the unique experiences of Aboriginal culture and history struggled to be heard as anything other than an additional and unique set of 'criminogenic needs'. A similar process occurred in New Zealand at this time. The unique history, rights and cultural processes of Māori people struggle to be accounted for in New Zealand's science of offending behaviour as anything other than 'culture-related' anti-social factors. Thus, it is the figure of the racially different Māori offender that is produced by the practice of the Department of Corrections at this time.

Not surprisingly, the MaCRN tool's association of Māori culture with Māori offender's anti-social behaviour was rejected by the broader Māori community. In 2002, Pirika Tame Hemopo, a Māori Department of Corrections staff member, brought a claim to the Waitangi Tribunal against the Department of Corrections.[3] Mr Hemopo claimed that the MaCRN tool disadvantaged Māori offenders. He raised concerns that the tool 'classified positive aspects of Māori culture and family as causing crime or as aggravating factors for sentencing' (Waitangi Tribunal 1995: 2).

---

3   The original claim also covered the RoC*RoI, but this part of the claim was largely removed when the Department of Corrections changed most of the contentious elements of this tool before the Tribunal hearing.

In response to Mr Hemopo's claim, the Waitangi Tribunal concluded that there were, 'certain shortcomings in the Department's management of the process by which MaCRNs were designed, implemented and evaluated', particularly in terms of 'having Māori culture used appropriately in the Department's dealings with offenders' (Waitangi Tribunal 1995: 16–17). The Waitangi Tribunal recommended that the Department of Corrections reconsider and determine if the MaCRN tool was in fact prejudiced against Māori. Shortly after this recommendation was released, the Department of Corrections discontinued the use of the MaCRN tool.

A common feature in the mutual construction process and its disparate effects
The findings of the Waitangi Tribunal and its impact on the Department of Corrections' actions are reminiscent of what occurred in the Victorian Department of Justice in relation to the Royal Commission into Aboriginal Deaths in Custody (RCIADIC). The conclusions and recommendations of the RCIADIC forced the Victorian Department of Justice (and other criminal justice systems operating in Australia) to stop their existing, prejudiced and detrimental approach to Aboriginal peoples, and devise new approaches. The finding and recommendations of the Waitangi Tribunal saw the MaCRN tool discarded by the Department of Corrections, and a new approach to Māori offenders developed.

However, there is a fundamental difference between these occurrences. The impact of the RCIADIC came from its irrefutable capacity to position Australian Governments as the creators of Aboriginal 'difference'. The Waitangi Tribunal did not share this capacity. Not only are the Tribunal's recommendations unenforceable by law, but the recommendations made in response to Mr Hemopo's claim only positioned the Department of Corrections as taking an *inappropriate* approach to using Māori culture in criminal justice practice, not as creating the underlying problem associated with their presence in criminal justice systems.

Accordingly, the changes that eventuated in New Zealand were not the same as those that took shape in Victoria. The findings and demands of the RCIADIC forced the Victorian Department of Justice to renegotiate and acquiesce much of its traditional capacity and authority to work with Aboriginal offenders. In contrast, as will be shown next, the findings and recommendations of the Waitangi Tribunal only required the Department of Justice to find a *better way* to use Māori culture in relation to its unquestioned science of offending behaviour.

The similarities and difference between Victoria and New Zealand's situation reiterates an important conclusion the previous chapter made about the method of engaging with the mutual construction process. It is no longer sufficient to only ask, who or what is governed and according to what logics? Rather, it necessary to also ask, in the process of governing a population or a problem, what also becomes *governable* about the institutional body in charge of this process? In the case of the Victorian Department of Justice, it was the *authority* of the institutional body that became governable. In the case of New Zealand's Department of Corrections, it is only the *products* of its unquestioned authority. Accordingly, while the first three provisions of the Department of Corrections location-specific science of offending behaviour are still used to regulate Māori and Pākehā 'risk' and 'need', the position of Māori culture has been negotiated for a second time.

The Second Struggle: Establishing the 'Māori World' and the 'Global World'

The Department of Corrections' second (and current) attempt to locate Māori culture in relation to Māori offenders focuses on the *differences* between Māori and Pākehā offender populations, not the commonalities *shared*. In doing so, the Department of Corrections has struck a new balance between its responsibilities for managing offending behaviour and its obligations under the Treaty of Waitangi. In this new construction of responsibilities and obligations, Māori culture, processes and values relate to the *subjectivity* of Māori offenders, not the *object* of offending behaviour. As a result, the criminal justice practices necessary to address Māori offenders and offending have undergone a corresponding change.

In the current approach of the Department of Corrections towards Māori offenders and offending, the MaCRN tool has been replaced with the Specialist Māori Cultural Assessment (SMCA) tool.[4] This tool is used by an independently contracted Māori assessor, not a correctional authority.[5] The assessment performed by the Māori assessor focuses on the cultural needs of Māori, based on their past and present connection to culture and their desire to change or enhance this connection. At the end of the assessment process, the Māori assessor produces a detailed report of the Māori offender's culture-related needs. The report recommends activities Māori offenders should undertake in order to change or enhance their relationship with culture. These recommendations are provided to both the Department of Corrections and Māori offenders (Policy Strategy and Research Group 2007).

The recommendations of the SMCA are then applied in places like Māori Focus Units (MFU). MFUs act as additional places within New Zealand prisons where the particular values, ways of being and problems of Māori are respected and addressed through Māori culture.[6] On a daily basis, Māori offenders in MFUs may undertake a variety of activities that align with the recommendations of the SMCA, including:

* undertaking courses on Māori culture;
* learning Māori language;

---

4   The SMCA was developed around the same time as the MaCRN and was being used in a few settings at the time that the MaCRN were brought before the Waitangi Tribunal. Since the recommendations of the Tribunal, the SMCA has been rolled out to other settings.

5   The Māori assessor does receive Department of Corrections' training as part of their employment.

6   At the time of writing this book, there are five Māori Focus Units operating in New Zealand's prisons.

- undertaking *whakapapa* (Māori genealogy) research; and
- working with a specialist Māori worker to foster relationships with the offender's *iwi* (tribe).

Thus, MFUs ensure that Māori offenders are immersed in the world of Māori culture and provide the tools, role models and functional spaces to re-engage Māori from a Māori World perspective.

Co-opting the Motivational Nature of Māori Culture

The Department of Corrections' current approach to Māori offenders does not conflate the responsibilities of the Department of Corrections to manage offending behaviour with its obligations under the Treaty of Waitangi. In fact, the current approach expressly states that Māori culture is a 'pro-social aspect' of Māori life and therefore, Māori offenders should receive separate practices that foster connection to it (Department of Corrections New Zealand 2008). Yet, even in the most separate of practices developed, Māori culture is co-opted by the extending reach and encompassing nature of New Zealand's science of offending behaviour.

Māori culture has become a key *motivational tool* the Department of Corrections can use to engage Māori offenders in its science of offending behaviour. For example, as the evaluation of the SMCA tool explains:

> By focusing on their (latent) cultural knowledge and experiences, participants are encouraged to see a culturally-enriched lifestyle as an accessible pathway out of offending. (Policy Strategy and Research Group 2007: 1)

Similarly, as the *Māori Strategic Plan 2008–13* explains:

> Evidence emerging from effectiveness evaluations show that the *Te Ao Māori* [the Māori World] approach strengthens the cultural identity of Māori offenders, improves their attitudes and behaviours and motivates them to participate in rehabilitation. (Department of Corrections New Zealand 2008: 12)

Moreover, as a recent evaluation of MFUs explains:

> *Whanau* [family] involvement, and adopting a positive and productive role within one's *whanau*, is an important message promoted by the MFU *kaupapa* [strategy or policy]. … It is a well-known principle of correctional research that offenders who establish themselves in a stable family situation are significantly less likely to re-offend. Consequently, evidence suggesting that the MFU experience motivates prisoners to re-establish and re-build relationships with their *whanau* is promising. (Policy Strategy and Research Group 2009: 28)

Māori culture has become a key *tactic* in New Zealand's science of offending behaviour. Māori culture has been made intelligible in terms of the Department of Corrections' logics (see in particular the evaluation of MFUs). It has been operationalized through the Department of Corrections' frameworks of knowledge (see in particular the *Māori Strategic Plan 2008–13*). And, as a result, Māori culture has been found to contain key motivational properties which can be used to encourage Māori offenders to enter the process that confirms the 'truth' of their threat to society and their undeniable risk of reoffending.

Māori culture has been co-opted in another way as well. By being identified as the only property or element that is *particular* to Māori offenders, Māori culture has, by default, confirmed what is *shared* amongst Māori and Pākehā offenders: their anti-social offending behaviour and its serious impacts on New Zealand's society. Māori culture has also become yet another *prop* in New Zealand's science of offending behaviour.

Thus, the struggle of the Department of Corrections to find an acceptable balance between its responsibilities and obligations has taken new form in the current phase of negotiation. More precisely, the specific actions of the Department of Corrections in developing the science of offending behaviour have been replaced by the capacity of this 'science' to become its own machinery. The science of offending behaviour is a science whose strength lies not only in its many tools for creation, but also in its practices' ability to both capture alternative discourses (for example, produce criminal indigeneity), and employ their alterity as another means for propagation (for example, co-opting pro-social Māori culture).

The Third Struggle: Māori Resistances in the Field of Governance

The strength of New Zealand's science of offending behaviour has been questioned by Māori staff at the Department of Corrections. More precisely, Māori staff do not use this science to rationalize Māori offending behaviour. Instead, they use a framework of experiences which shifts the association between Māori culture and Māori offending behaviour once more. As a result, another struggle has emerged in New Zealand's criminal justice system: the struggle between the official practice of the Department of Corrections' responsibilities and obligations, and the unofficial views of Māori staff infiltrating and transforming these practices' orientation.

The Logic of Choice

Māori staff agree with the Department of Corrections' recent positioning of Māori culture as a motivational tool for addressing Māori offending behaviour. Indeed, as the following Māori staff member explains, Māori culture plays a key role in allowing Māori to take responsibility for their offending behaviour:

For the majority of them, one of the things that might keep them out is reconnections with those traditional cultural values and making them relevant to contemporary society. We can't all go back and live on the land, we are living in towns and cities now, so it's about trying to make that whole idea of Māori culture something that is relevant today. (Māori staff member four)

Yet, while Māori staff support the official view on Māori culture, they do not necessarily share the belief that it is the anti-social nature of Māori offenders that needs to be addressed in 'motivated' Māori offenders. Rather, Māori staff locate Māori offending behaviour within a different set of parameters:

We still have to overcome the view from non-Māori communities that Māori culture is somehow connected to Māori over-representation in prisons. An example of that is the "Once Were Warriors" movie, which presented Māori as warlike tough-men who occasionally bash their wives … The theory is that a lot of young Māori men have lost touch with the reality of what it means to be Māori and instead they have picked up on the superficial warrior tough-guy stuff … What we have been trying to do is take that warrior concept and make it into a more positive thing, so it becomes about the warrior ethos of being centred on protecting and caring for your family. So that is the fundamental principle under the cultural approach to reducing re-offending, which is helping Māori to discover, or recover those traditional Māori values that held our society intact for so long prior to settlement and colonization. (Māori staff member three)

Thus the factors contributing to Māori offending behaviour cannot simply be identified by tracing the six months preceeding the offence period, or even in the day before – as the *RoC* instructs. Rather, Māori offending behaviour manifests because of three very broad factors that have taken shape over many years:

1. The Global World colliding with the Māori World in New Zealand's colonization and settlement;
2. Māori offenders' loss of connection to the Māori World; and
3. Māori offenders' incorrect reading of Māori culture.

This is not to say that Māori offending is caused by colonization and its ongoing effects, however. Rather, as the next two Māori staff members' discussions clarify, colonization and settlement only provide the conditions for a particular problem to manifest *in* Māori:

So we can't change history. … What we can do is help people to see that in a way that helps them to understand how they are reacting to it. So in a room full of 100 Māori, everyone will agree that colonization existed. But you will look across the whole range of the Māori sitting in that room and the effects of colonization for someone like me are far different than for someone who has grown up in a less privileged background ... Even your background you can't change. I can't help the way I was brought up, but what I can change is the way that I perceive it and the way that I react to it and the way that I move forward from here. I think it is always worthwhile to have that here and the reason is, it helps people understand that it might not necessarily be something wrong with them. But offending essentially comes down to an individual making a choice to do something. (Māori staff member three)

And

They can blame colonization all they like. Colonization was part of the problem, but we make choices as well. So in making our choices – and if offending was part of those choices – then we must be held responsible for that. If you look at people like myself, I was brought up in a colonized society, but I still have my language, I still have my traditional beliefs, I have succeeded like anybody else, so it comes down to choices and some people make some bad ones. (Māori staff member six)

Thus, colonization provides the conditions for some Māori to lose touch with their traditional Māori values or their language. Colonization allows some Māori to pick up on misrepresentations of the Māori image and engage in violent offending behaviour. However, colonization, the loss of Māori values and buying-in to some misrepresentations of Māori culture are not the *causes* of Māori offending behaviour, only the *parameters* within which offending behaviour exists.

What causes Māori offending behaviour is choice. The choice to '*blame*' colonization and not '*move forward*' from its effects. The choice to disengage with traditional beliefs, values and language and lose all that is additional and particular about Māori in New Zealand society. The choice to lose touch with the '*reality of what it means to be Māori*' and buy into some '*superficial*' image of Māori culture. These are the choices that Māori offenders are making, and these are the choices that define their offending behaviour. Thus, at the heart of Māori offending behaviour, are the discretional choices of individuals.

Locating the logic of choice in criminology
A logic of choice is not new to the correctional sphere. For the past two decades Correctional agencies have employed the methods and technologies of Cognitive Behavioural Therapy (CBT). As Chapter 1 explained, CBT teaches offenders that they have certain thinking errors that cause them to make incorrect choices in terms of their actions and behaviours. These teachings are based on a presumption that these individuals make incorrect choices like engaging in offending behaviour because of an innate abnormality or deficiency (a thinking *error*). Māori staff do not use this logic of choice. Rather Māori staff promote a logic of choice which is based on notions of free will and rational choice; where the individual may act or behave in a way that is disapproved by society, but they do so in sound mind.

Māori staff present Māori offending behaviour as stemming from Māori offenders' problematic relationships with culture and family that has developed because Māori offenders choose to disengage from culture. This choice is influenced by external factors, like colonization, and internal factors, such as the offender's perception of colonization's effects on Māori society. In this way, Māori staff's construction of Māori offenders greatly resembles the figure of the normalized offender propagated by the Good Lives Model (GLM) of offender rehabilitation's literature (presented in Chapter 1 of this book). The GLM figure of the normalized offender possesses certain common 'criminal' attributes, such as anti-social attitudes or associates, which have developed from a set of internal or external factors frustrating and influencing the type of choices they make when pursuing pro-social goals.

The return of the normalized offender in the Department of Corrections is significant. It represents the first break from the ever-extending grip of the science of offending behaviour in New Zealand. It also represents one of the first times that the figure of the normalized offender has gained traction in contemporary criminal justice practice. Thus the question becomes, why does this figure of normality not only appear in New Zealand, but also disqualify the utility of the science of offending behaviour in relation to Māori offenders?

The Authority of Experiences

The figure of the 'normalized' Māori offender takes hold in New Zealand's criminal justice practice because of Māori staff's experiences. Māori staff *know* that Māori offending is about choosing to '*blame*' colonization and its effects, because Māori staff shared the experience of colonization, but did not make this choice. As Māori staff member six explains (on page 115 in this chapter), '*I was brought up in a colonized society, but I still have my language, I still have my traditional beliefs, I have succeeded like anybody else*'. Māori staff *know* that Māori offending is about choosing to lose touch with the '*reality of what it means to be Māori*' and to buy into some '*superficial*' image of culture that leads to offending behaviour, because Māori staff share the experiences, pressures and problems facing Māori offenders, but do not make the same choices. As Māori Staff member three explains (also on page 115), '*I can't help the way I was brought up, but what I can change is the way that I perceive it, and the way that I react to it, and the way that I move forward from here*'. Thus, as was also the case in the Victorian context, a racialized framework of experience has emerged in an institutional body, displacing this body's Western framework of knowledge.

However, there are some crucial differences between Victoria and New Zealand's racialized framework of experience. As the previous chapter demonstrated, in Victoria, it was the *shared experiences* of Aboriginal staff, communities and offenders that provided staff of the Victorian Department of Justice with the authority to make decisions about Aboriginal offending behaviour. Aboriginal staff used this framework of experience to ensure that the Department of Justice approached Aboriginal offenders in terms of their past, present and future history of 'difference'.

In the case of the New Zealand Department of Corrections, the authority of Māori staff to position Māori offenders on a spectrum of normality and engage them with a logic of choice is based on the *diverse choices* Māori staff and Māori offenders make in relation to their common background and experiences. It is because Māori staff faced the same pressures as Māori offenders, but made choices leading to different experiences, that they can be sure that Māori offending is about choice, and as Māori staff member six explains (again, on page 115), '*some people make some bad ones*'.

Thus, the logic of choice and the accompanying framework of experience not only reposition Māori offenders away from the grip of the science of offending behaviour, but also determine their position in the broader Māori population. This logic and framework isolate and exclude Māori offenders from the realm of 'proper' Māori culture – Māori offenders are Māori who would mistakenly buy into some superficial notion of culture. Accordingly, Māori staff have not simply relocated Māori offenders from the Department of Corrections' continuum of threat to the Māori World's scale of normality. Rather, Māori staff have located Māori offenders at a particular *position* on the scale of normality – at the border of abnormality – and in doing so, Māori staff have recast the responsibilities of the Department of Corrections in terms of Māori offender management.

The consequences of unshared experiences

Relocating Māori offenders to the borders of 'proper' Māori culture raises an interesting point about the role that Māori staff play in the Department of Corrections' responsibilities and obligations. As indicated in the discussion of the SMCA and MFUs, Māori staff are recruited in order to both role-model positive associations with Māori culture, and to encourage Māori offenders to re-engage with culture. In other words, Māori staff are recruited to *fulfil* both the Department of Corrections' responsibility to manage Māori offenders' behaviour, and its obligations under the Treaty of Waitangi. Yet, the capacity of Māori staff to fulfil these roles is questionable. As the following Māori staff member explains, shared *choices* play a fundamental role in motivating Māori offenders to engage with Māori culture, not shared *backgrounds*:

> we have been using a group called "Mahi-Tahi" who are comprised of former gang members, criminals and prisoners, people who are known to prisoners inside, who have adopted the Māori cultural way of living and who then go and present that to people who they probably used to be in gangs with. They are very credible these guys, because they have been there, whereas if I turned up they would just look at me and probably, just by the way I talked, they would know that I had never shared their experiences in life. As far as they would be concerned I have had a privileged upbringing. The way they put it is, "you talk like one of them, how could we trust you". Whereas guys that have tattoos all

over the face and are known to be former gang members are very credible and they get talking to these guys and they start turning them around as well. (Māori staff member three)

What is '*credible*' to Māori offenders is the Māori ex-offender who shares their experience of losing connection with culture and who has chosen to re-engage with Māori culture. It is not the Māori staff member whose connection to culture has never changed.

Drawing a distinction between these two ways of being a 'culturally endowed' Māori highlights an important distinction between Victorian and New Zealand racialized correctional histories. In the case of Victoria, there is only one story inscribed on the bodies of Victoria's Aboriginal population: '*the struggle of our people*'. This single struggle means that Aboriginal offenders, Aboriginal staff members in Government and Aboriginal communities share the same history of Aboriginal 'difference' in Australia, regardless of any specific experiences in that history. This is not the case in New Zealand. Māori offenders, Māori staff and the broader Māori community share New Zealand's history of colonization, however, their subjectivity is marked by the different choices they made in interpreting and balancing the Māori World after it collided with Global World.

Herein lies the nature of the final struggle facing Māori staff and the broader Department of Corrections. The Department of Corrections employs Māori staff to fulfil its obligations and responsibilities to Māori offenders. Māori staff use this role to renegotiate how the Department of Corrections demarcates its responsibilities and obligations. In doing so, Māori staff introduce a logic of choice and a framework of Māori experience to replace the Department of Corrections' science of offending behaviour. Yet the framework of Māori experience excludes Māori staff from performing the roles necessary to address Māori offending behaviour and the problematic choices of Māori offenders. Māori staff cannot act as role-models for Māori offenders because Māori staff do not share the choices Māori offenders have made in terms of culture, and therefore, have not shared the experiences that result. Accordingly, any Māori staff member attempting to act as a role-model for Māori offenders will be met with mistrust – '*you talk like one of them, how could we trust you?*'

The struggle facing Māori staff as they renegotiate the Department of Corrections' responsibilities and obligations to Māori implies something important about the role of resistances in the mutual construction process. The original rules of engagement outlined in Chapter 2 indicated that there are resistances to power's investments. It was argued that resistances take form through negotiated performances of identity, whereby each person's actions are individually determined by the way they position and understand their identity in their immediate situation, in upcoming situations, and in broader society.

In New Zealand, the actions of the Department of Corrections' *institutional body* are marked by investments and resistances to power, not just the bodies of the individuals that this institution governs. The actions of the Department of Corrections have been marked by the way its Māori staff position and understand their identity in relation to a number of factors, including:

- their responsibilities and roles in the Department of Corrections' institutional body,
- their shared and diverse experiences with Māori offenders; and
- the broader position of Māori culture in the Māori World and the Global World.

As a result, the actions of Māori staff within the institutional body have repositioned the obligations and responsibilities of the Department of Corrections to Māori offenders. Māori staff have presented the Department of Corrections as responsible for addressing the *choices* Māori offenders make across their lifespan.

Māori staff's actions therefore reveal another dimension to Foucault's (1998: 96) claim that 'just as the network of power relations ends by forming a dense web that passes through apparatuses and institutions, without being exactly localized in them, so too the swarm of points of resistance traverses social stratifications and individual unities'. Māori staff's actions reveal how points of resistance *also* pass through 'apparatuses' and 'institutions', affecting how certain 'social stratifications' and 'individual unities' become possible. That is, Māori staff negotiate the undesired division of Māori subjectivity that took shape through the tools and tactics of colonization in broader society by developing a logic of choice. This logic of choice presents the subjectivity of all Māori as being determined by the choices they make, not the dividing actions of Government. This logic of choice has, through the actions of Māori staff, been presented as the guiding logic for governing the past, present and future lives of Māori offenders.

Thus, it is no longer sufficient to only ask, what role do resistances play in the mutual constructions of race and criminal justice? Rather, it is necessary to also ask, in what ways are institutional bodies marked by their own process of resistance? Whose performances of identity are marked on the institutional body? What elements of identity are negotiated in their performance? What effects do these elements have on both the subjects that are governed by an institution and the subjectivity of the institution that has become governable? And how do all these elements of power and resistance's investments in institutional and individual bodies affect how certain 'social stratifications' and 'individual unities' become possible?

This chapter has already answered many of these questions in the New Zealand context. However, there is something more that can be said about how the elements of power and resistance's investments in the Department of Corrections' institutional body affect the way that certain 'social stratifications' and 'individual unities' become possible in New Zealand.

Being marked by another history

Māori staff's bodies are not just marked by their own performances of identity. They are also marked by both the Department of Corrections' and the broader New Zealand Government's struggle to negotiate the obligations outlined under the Treaty of Waitangi. Māori staff are expected to both *fulfil* the responsibilities and obligations of the Department of Corrections under the Treaty of Waitangi, and *legitimize* the way the Department of Corrections negotiates them. As the following three Māori staff members explain:

> One of the difficulties we have goes back to past injustices, about not trusting a government department, not just the Department of Corrections. That is partly what our role is, to be in the middle of it, to negotiate and gain trust and get a good relationship going. (Māori staff member six)

> There is not anywhere that is as hard to work as here as Māori. By that I mean that the issues are difficult, the public support is not as strong as if we were selling health or education, not many people want correctional services except when something goes wrong, but everyone thinks that health is naturally a good thing, so most Māori organizations and tribes are all focused on that building model. (Māori staff member three)

And

> For some people in the community we are still an extension of colonization, so for many of them it is still about, "let's lock up all the Māori who won't behave the way we want them to". (Māori staff member four)

Thus, Māori staff are located right '*in the middle*' of both the Department of Corrections' and the broader New Zealand Government's struggle to negotiate the obligations outlined under the Treaty of Waitangi. And, as a consequence, Māori staff have been made *responsible* by both the Department of Corrections and the Māori community for the actions of New Zealand Governments. Māori staff have been made responsible for both resolving and contributing to the effects that the New Zealand Government has had on the lives of Māori across time.

Accordingly, in the case of New Zealand, it is not just the institutional body of the Department of Corrections that has been marked by notions of nationhood and location-specific negotiations of racialized identity. Rather, it is also that in the process of race and criminal justice's mutual construction, the racialized identity of the Department of Corrections' Māori staff has been marked by the 'excessive historicity' of New Zealand's institutions and their dense web of power relations.

Some Final Implications and Conclusions

This chapter explored the location-specific negotiation of notions of nationhood and racialized identity that lie at the heart of the Department of Corrections' formation. It showed how New Zealand's unique settler-colonial history provided the conditions for the Department of Corrections to emerge as a 'bicultural' institution in the early 1990s. It further demonstrated how this emergence required the Department of Corrections to negotiate the shared and separate rights of Māori and Pākehā. It illuminated how this negotiation brought the Department of Corrections' focus to the dual presence of Māori and Global Worlds, and the location of Māori offenders within and between. And, it illustrated how the Department of Corrections has repeatedly struggled to maintain the borders between the two Worlds, having to repeatedly renegotiate the shared and separate rights of Māori and Pākehā. In light of the nature of the Department of Corrections' struggles, it is now possible to present another facet of the mutual construction process: the parameters within which mutual construction is negotiated.

The parameters of negotiations are the *parameters of the two Worlds* within which the Department of Corrections, the New Zealand Government and Māori have been situated. Accordingly, New Zealand's mutual constructions of race and criminal justice are fundamentally tied to the Department of Corrections':

- *need* to recognize the presence of two Worlds – a need prompted by the New Zealand Government's Policy of Biculturalism and its heritage in the principles of the Treaty of Waitangi;
- struggle to create clear *boundaries* between the Worlds – a struggle created by the way that the Department of Corrections negotiated the policy of biculturalism in correctional settings (that is, using a single register of operationality to determine both the Department of Corrections' responsibilities for the management of Māori and Pākehā offenders, and its obligations to Māori offenders under the Treaty of Waitangi);
- inability to *maintain* the boundaries between Worlds in practice – an inability resulting from the Department of Corrections' decision to develop a location-specific science of offending behaviour which had the capacity to co-opt the presence of Māori culture; and
- capacity to make Māori staff responsible for the *ongoing negotiation* of the two Worlds, the changing boundaries between them, and the obligations of the Department of Corrections and the Māori community within them – a capacity that is possible because Māori staff's bodies are marked by the presence of two Worlds, the changing boundaries between them, and the obligations of the Department of Corrections and the Māori community within them.

Yet, while the parameters within which mutual construction occurs have only become apparent in New Zealand's process of construction, they are not unique to this jurisdiction. In retrospect, the Victorian Department of Justice's process of mutual construction is also guided by certain parameters within Australia.

When the first settlers of Australia declared Australia as belonging to no one, they erased the presence of the Aboriginal World. Accordingly, what became negotiable 200 years later was not how to account for the Aboriginal World or, what borders lie between the Global World and the Aboriginal World. Rather, what became negotiable was how to account for Aboriginal peoples and any remnants of the Aboriginal World *within* the Global World. As such, it is not just that the Victorian Department of Justice has had to negotiate factors like the colonization of Australia, the demands of the RCIADIC, and the over-representation of Aboriginal peoples in criminal justice systems. Rather, it has had to negotiate these factors within these specific *parameters*. As a result, the Department of Justice has created a separate part *within* its Western institution where the problem of Aboriginal 'difference' can be enclosed alongside the Aboriginal peoples whose knowledge and experience can address this problem.

Thus, the parameters within which mutual construction becomes negotiable are those that are created from the collision of two Worlds and the resulting *recognition* and *positioning* of those Worlds. Accordingly, what this chapter reveals is not simply how negotiated, location-specific and historically informed practices towards Māori and Aboriginal offenders have emerged organically in New Zealand's Department of Corrections and Victoria's Department of Justice. Rather it has also shown how these practices were unlikely to emerge in any other way within these jurisdictions' parameters.

Chapter 5

Diverse History, Common Practice

The mutual constructions of race and criminal justice are about our past, present and future. The previous two chapters have demonstrated how localized constructions of racialized identity contribute to the formation, transformation and operation of criminal justice systems. They show how location-specific, historical and contemporary constructs of Aboriginal and Māori offenders entered Victoria and New Zealand's criminal justice systems, transforming their spaces, functions and operations. The present chapter changes the orientation of this book and explores the way that penal logics and technologies contribute to the construction of racialized identity.

This chapter explores how the principle of responsivity – a principle for effective classification and treatment that emerged from the literature documented in Chapter 1 – has been approached by the Victorian Department of Justice and the New Zealand Department of Corrections in relation to Aboriginal and Māori offenders. The focus is on the technologies and tools used in the practice of responsivity, and the subject positions Aboriginal and Māori offenders are expected to occupy in relation to this practice.

To perform this exploration, the chapter has been split into three sections. Section one provides a brief history of responsivity. It reflects on some of the tensions surrounding this principles' development and the implications this holds for correctional practice. Sections two and three illustrate the respective ways that Victoria and New Zealand apply the principle of responsivity in practice. These sections illuminate the common and diverse elements of Victoria and New Zealand's practice and discuss the implications these have for the mutual construction process going forward.

A Brief History of the Risk Need Model's Principle of Responsivity

As indicated in Chapter 1, the principle of responsivity emerged from the Risk Need Responsivity Model (RNRM) as a core component for effective offender classification and treatment (alongside the risk and need principles). The responsivity principle dictates that effective treatment occurs when correctional agencies identify possible variances in their offender population's personality and cognitive-behavioural characteristics. Such variances may result from internal factors, such as an offender's level of intellectual functioning, or external factors, such as inappropriately designed or delivered treatment programs (Ogloff and Davis 2004).

Yet, it is unclear from this description of responsivity what correctional agencies should do once they identify that there are variances in their offender population. Should agencies provide their offender populations with the same treatment techniques and programs notwithstanding any variances? Should agencies provide their offender populations with the same techniques and programs, but change the form of delivery to address variances? Or, should agencies develop and provide separate and specific forms of treatment and delivery for offender populations depending on the variances they present with? Based on the limited guidance the RNRM texts provide, correctional agencies could choose any one of these options to increase the effectiveness of their practice, yet each represents a wholly different approach towards the treatment of offenders.

Given the clear gap in direction provided by the RNRM texts, one might expect that the principle of responsivity would have received further discussion and development elsewhere, for example, by practitioners grappling to provide responsive practice. This is not the case. The principle of responsivity has generated very little discussion in the correctional literature since its emergence. To illustrate, when using common databases for scholarly publications, the term 'offender rehabilitation' returns over 5,600 publications, the terms 'risk' and 'offender rehabilitation' return over 2,700 publications, and the terms 'responsivity' and 'offender rehabilitation' only return 67.[1]

The lack of literature on responsivity is not the only factor limiting its implementation. The principle has also lacked development within this small collection. Much of the literature that has been produced about responsivity simply re-states the original, unfinished account provided by the RNRM texts, without any propositions for elucidation. For example, Bonta and Cormier (1999: 240), in their review of corrections research in Canada, simply state that the responsivity principle 'calls for the matching of modes and styles of treatment to offender characteristics', without indicating how this match is achieved, or how these modes, styles and characteristics are comprised. Similarly, Gendreau (1996b) accepts and employs an unchanged version of the risk, need and responsivity principles in his proposal for effective intervention with offenders.

Even when researchers acknowledge the limitations surrounding the responsivity principle, they provide few solutions. For example, both Kennedy (1999) and Looman, Dickie and Abracen (2005) outline the literature's neglect of the principle and discuss the implications for effective practice. Yet neither suggests a remedy for this problem. Kennedy (1999) proposes that correctional agencies could resolve this issue by considering both internal and external factors that may hinder an offender's learning – a proposition that only slightly deviates from the original directions of the RNRM. Similarly, Looman, Dickie and Abracen (2005) provide recommendations about *which* internal and external factors should

---

1   Search conducted using Web of Science (ISI), Australian Public Affairs – Full Text (Informit), Expanded Academic ASAP (Gale) and JSTOR databases on 6 April 2012.

be acknowledged by correctional agencies, but fail to indicate *how* correctional agencies could address these factors in practice.

An Alternative Reading of Responsivity

Discussions of responsive service delivery have not been entirely omitted from the literature. Rather, a very small body of texts was published in the last decade providing correctional agencies with directions for delivering such services. The problem with these texts however, is that they are based in the Good Lives Model (GLM) of offender rehabilitation, which, as Chapter 1 showed, has gathered little traction in correctional practice.

To be clear, the GLM does not present a 'principle of responsivity' or any other 'principle'. The GLM does, however, provide a comparable instruction for correctional agencies in terms of addressing offender variances. The GLM indicates that correctional agencies must individualize their program delivery so that they can better address and enhance the pro-social characteristics and attributes of offenders (Ward 2002a, 2002b; Ward and Stewart 2003b). The GLM calls this process 'offender enhancement'. It encourages correctional agencies to enhance the characteristics and attributes that allow offenders to be 'responsive' to life's challenges when released, not just those which allow offenders to be 'responsive' in correctional settings.

Day, Howells and colleagues produced several publications in the past decade which build on the GLM's foundations. These scholars propose that the principle of responsivity is embedded in the GLM process of addressing 'offender readiness', not just reflected in the broad GLM premise of offender enhancement (Day, Tucker and Howells 2004; Howells and Day 2003; Howells, Day and Davey 2005; Williamson et al. 2004).

Correctional agencies address offender readiness when they recognize and work with factors affecting an offender's willingness to change their behaviour. To do this, correctional agencies must focus on two groups of factors:

1. internal factors of the offender – including the offender's cognitive, affective, behavioural, volitional and personal identity factors; and
2. external factors surrounding the offender – including their location, opportunity, resources, support, program/timing and target (Ward et al. 2004).

When correctional agencies recognize and work with these offender factors, offenders are more likely to be 'ready' to receive treatment and be responsive to its effects (Howells, Day and Davey 2005).

Birgden (2004) proposes a similar development of the principle of responsivity. Birgden argues that the GLM's concept of offender enhancement only encapsulates internal responsivity factors; that is, factors that are concerned with the treatment of offenders and the relationship of the offender and clinician in the treatment process. Birgden proposes that correctional agencies must also consider external responsivity factors. External responsivity factors include the overall culture of the correctional organization. Birgden contends that through a therapeutic jurisprudence approach (where the law and its agents have a therapeutic effect), the culture of the correctional agency can support the offender rehabilitation process, ensuring that offenders are more likely to be responsive to treatment.

Addressing offender readiness and fostering therapeutic jurisprudence provide correctional agencies with two avenues to operationalize the principle of responsivity at both an individual and institutional level. Yet, neither of these proposed avenues has gained much attention in correctional practice.[2] This is because both are misaligned in the correctional field's discursive practice.

Regulating the Orientation of Responsivity in Criminal Justice

Offender readiness and therapeutic jurisprudence are based in the GLM's construction of normalized offending behaviour. While providing correctional agencies with more guidance about how to operationalize the responsivity principle, these propositions also recommend sustaining a figure of the offender the correctional sphere has rejected. Specifically, they ask correctional agencies to engage in the so-called 'dangerous' process of looking beyond the management of specified risk factors and locate offenders' behaviour in those factors that frustrate good decision making (Ogloff 2002: 249).

In contrast, the RNRM's unfinished explanation of responsivity finds foundation in correctional literature and practice because of the dominance of the RNRM's science of offending behaviour in these spheres. The seemingly incomplete instruction of acknowledging and identifying possible variances in offender's personality and cognitive-behavioural characteristics is unproblematic because correctional agencies are also instructed to acknowledge, identify, record and target the innate deficiencies of their offender population – their anti-social attributes. Variance is just another facet of deficiency.

Given both the limited instruction provided by the principle of responsivity and the principle's location in the correctional literature's discursive practice, the question becomes, how do Victoria and New Zealand approach this principle in relation to Aboriginal and Māori offenders? How do these correctional

---

2   The propositions about therapeutic jurisprudence have gained some foundation in Victoria's criminal justice sphere. These propositions appear in the Reducing Reoffending Framework: Setting the Scene document of the Department of Justice, which was co-developed by Birgden. As the title suggests, this document was created in 2004 to 'set the scene' for further developments to Victoria's correctional practice based on a mixture of RNRM, GLM and Therapeutic Jurisprudence approaches. However, shortly after its publication, both developers of the Framework left their roles at the Department of Justice and as a result, there have been no further developments in Victoria based on a therapeutic jurisprudence approach.

jurisdictions, whose criminal justice agencies have been transformed by location-specific notions of nationhood, negotiate this universal principle for effective treatment? How do they negotiate this principle's potential to construct criminal indigeneity in their society?

Responsivity in the Victorian Department of Justice

Responsivity is provided with two definitions within the Victorian Department of Justice: an official documents definition and an Aboriginal staff definition. The appearance of two definitions in Victoria is not surprising. Chapter 3 illustrated that there have been numerous times in the Department of Justice's history when the history of Government and Aboriginal relations was written by Government, only to be rewritten by Aboriginal peoples. What is notable about the two definitions of responsivity, however, is that they are a *product* of the writing and rewriting process, not another *example* of it.

The official documents of the Department of Justice define responsivity as follows:

> [The Victorian Department of Justice will] make mainstream and positive justice-related services more responsive and inclusive of the needs of the Koori community. This will be measured by the:
>
> - proportion of people accessing positive criminal justice system-related services who are Koori; and the
> - number of Koories employed in criminal justice system-related agencies. (Department of Justice 2006: 20)

This definition of responsivity is interesting for a number of reasons. First, the 'features' of responsivity closely align with those of 'culturally appropriate' practice. Culturally appropriate practice took shape in the criminological literature in the early 1990s, but has foundations in psychology's much longer history of cross-cultural therapy (see for example Carter and Qureshi 1995; Choney, Berryhill-Paapke and Robbins 1995; Lee and Armstrong 1995; Pedersen 1995). While the phrase 'culturally appropriate' is used to describe any attempts by institutions to take into account the cultural knowledge and practices of a specific population, this phrase has taken on particular meaning in relation to Indigenous offenders. In this context, culturally appropriate practice refers to correctional agencies recognizing that mainstream practices are *inappropriate* for Indigenous offender populations. It also refers to correctional agencies providing steps to address this problem (see for example Jones, Masters, Griffiths and Moulday 2002; Jones, Loredo, Johnson and McFarlane-Nathan 1999; Hylton 1995; Zellerer 2003). The two most common steps recommended for correctional agencies are:

1. recruit Indigenous staff to perform a variety of roles – including redeveloping practices, delivering programs and engaging the community; and
2. develop programs that are appropriate for Indigenous offenders – for example, programs with cultural content.

There are few differences between these steps towards 'culturally appropriate' practice and the Department of Justice's account of responsivity. Responsivity is about Koori employment and Koori offenders accessing appropriate programs.

Where there is difference is in the emphasis placed on measuring these features. The Department of Justice does not simply become 'responsive' when it creates 'positive criminal justice system-related services', or when it develops positions for Aboriginal peoples within them. Rather, responsivity comes into effect when the 'proportion' of Aboriginal peoples accessing services and the 'number' of Aboriginal employees increases or reaches some undefined threshold. Likewise, it is only when there is an increase in the occurrence of these things (Aboriginal peoples accessing services and being employed) that the Department of Justice becomes 'more responsive and inclusive of the needs of the Koori community'. In other words, responsivity has been rationalized through the logic and discourse of human resources. It has been operationalized in terms of outcome measures for performance.

The Aboriginal and non-Aboriginal staff members of the Victorian Department of Justice, however, provide a different definition for responsivity. As the following three staff members explain:

> They [Koori offenders] are not responsive to mainstream programs; that is why we are setting up all these Koori specific ones. (non-Aboriginal staff member five)

> I think responsive would be the fact that you can actually get them to participate in the programs, because it means that you've got something right, in that you are giving them something that they are interested in and that they want to participate in. (Aboriginal staff member eight)

And

> I think it's about getting people to do the programs. (Aboriginal staff member seven)

On the surface these staff members' statements simply qualify the previous definition of responsivity. They suggest that in order for the Department of Justice's performance measures of responsivity to come into effect, it must undertake a series of tasks. The Department of Justice must:

- recognize that Aboriginal offenders are not being responsive to mainstream programs;
- establish Aboriginal specific programs;
- make sure Aboriginal specific programs give Aboriginal offenders '*something that they are interested in and that they want to participate in*'; and
- facilitate the process by which Aboriginal offenders will '*do the programs*'.

There are, however, two crucial differences. First, the subject position in relation to responsivity has changed in staff members' accounts. Aboriginal offenders are also set a role in relation to responsivity, not just the Department of Justice. Second, the discourse of measurement is missing from staff members' accounts. Aboriginal offenders and the Department of Justice simply become responsive if Aboriginal offenders access and participate in programs set up for them.

The different discourses regulating these accounts indicate something important about the position responsivity has taken in the Victorian context. Both Victorian accounts present responsivity as a subject position; as something that both the Department of Justice and Aboriginal offenders become. In contrast, the RNRM positions responsivity as an object; as a collection of variances that need to be identified alongside the other factors of innate offending behaviour. This observation leads to a second.

The only commonality of Victoria's accounts of responsivity is that neither contributes to the RNRM's science of offending behaviour. The official documents and Aboriginal staff provide distinct accounts of responsivity. In one account responsivity is a fluid structure; in the other it is static. In one account responsivity is demarcated as a subject position for the Department of Justice; in the other it is a subject position for both the Department of Justice and Aboriginal offenders. In one account responsivity is a problem; in the other it is an outcome. Noting the differences between these accounts, it would be easy to assume these points of divergence are just another example of writing and rewriting Aboriginal history in the Victorian context. This assumption would be premature and incorrect. Both accounts of responsivity illustrate what it means to be responsive in the Victorian Department of Justice.

Demonstrating this important distinction are the two key programs identified by both the official documents and Aboriginal staff as exemplars of responsivity: the Marumali Program and the Koori Cognitive Skills Program.

Marumali: The Worlding of Aboriginal Offenders

The Marumali program took shape within the Department of Justice in the mid 2000s. The program was implemented in order to contribute to the broad initiative of reducing Aboriginal offenders' re-offending rates (Department of Justice 2006: 38). In particular, the program was meant to aid the strategy of 'addressing characteristics that put offenders at high risk of re-offending' (Department of Justice 2006: 38). Yet, the Marumali program was neither developed by the Department of Justice, nor geared for delivery to offender populations. The program was developed to support survivors of the Stolen Generations,[3] as the website for the program explains:

> The Marumali model of healing is unique, original and unparalleled. While based on the healing of one individual, it offers an effective framework, structure and process which supports the healing of all survivors, whether removed to institutional care, foster care or adoptive families. The pathway to recovery involves mind, body and spirit, addresses the issue of identity and is seen as an ongoing journey or process. It is able to take account of state/territory variations in how removal policies were implemented, and illuminates the trans-generational effects on survivors, their families and the communities they were removed from. It does this in a way which contains and effectively manages the distress and risk that such realizations might otherwise invoke in Aboriginal participants. (Marumali 2007)

While the Department of Justice uses the Marumali program to contribute to its goal of reducing re-offending, it is not the purpose of the program. The Marumali program is run by Aboriginal people, for Aboriginal people. It provides them with the tools to locate their identity in past Government policies, such as removal. The Marumali program is about *Aboriginal 'difference'* and its construction by Government.

This is not the first time that the object of Aboriginal 'difference' has replaced the object of offending behaviour when discussing Aboriginal offenders. Chapter 3 demonstrated how the Department of Justice has repeatedly proposed through its official documents, staff and operations, that Aboriginal offenders are defined by their differences. Thus, while the purpose of the Marumali program – supporting members of the stolen generation – appears divorced from the Department of Justice's goal of reducing re-offending, it is consistent with the Department of Justice's broader discursive practice in relation to Aboriginal offenders.

An unusual ritual of confession
The Marumali program allows Aboriginal offenders to enter the discursive practice of Aboriginal 'difference'. As the following Aboriginal staff member's description

---

3   The Stolen Generations refers to the generations of Aboriginal children who were forcibly removed from their families and communities through a range of Australian Government policies and practices. For example, in the 1940s all Australian states adopted policies to assimilate Aboriginal peoples of mixed descent. In the 1950s and 1960s this policy evolved to removing Aboriginal children, placing them with white Australian families and not allowing them to practice Aboriginal language or culture.

of the program illustrates, the Marumali program makes a vital contribution to this discursive practice:

> The common issues [facing Aboriginal offenders] and it's one of the reasons why we have Marumali ... are the dispossession and the fact that the restriction to education, the discrimination, all those factors come into the reason why they are there.

> But after undergoing a program, for example like Marumali, the comments, the general comment back and feedback from them is that if they had have know all this about themselves all these years ago they wouldn't be in the position they are in now.

> So you know that that program is actually working. So if they take nothing else back out with them, they are going to take the stuff that they have learnt about themselves and about the reason why some of their family members are the way they are: it's because of what's happened. So it also gives them a bit more understanding of how they fit into their family and hopefully gives them a bit of an idea about where they can go to from there when they get out. (Aboriginal staff member eight)

This Aboriginal staff member's description of the Marumali program illuminates three fascinating points about the contributions of the program to the discursive practice of Aboriginal 'difference'. First, the Marumali program engages Aboriginal offenders in a discursive ritual of Aboriginal 'difference'. But, unlike the other ritual of discourse presented in this book (see page 26 in Chapter 1), this ritual is reversed. Aboriginal offenders are not expected to divulge prescribed words that are met by scripted judgements from correctional authorities like the anti-social offender in Chapter 1. Rather, the correctional authority teaches Aboriginal offenders the words they should speak. Through the Marumali program Aboriginal offenders are expected to '*learn about themselves*'. How? By first listening to accounts about how they and their family '*are the way they are ... because of what's happened*' and then trying to understand '*how they fit*'. Aboriginal offenders are expected to first listen and then tell their own story of how they and their family have been subject to '*dispossession*', '*restrictions to education*' and '*discrimination*'. Aboriginal offenders are expected to first listen and then tell their own story about how these '*differences*' have led them to being '*in the position that they are in now*', as one of many over-represented Aboriginal peoples in the criminal justice system. Accordingly, the confessions that Aboriginal offenders either make within the confines of the program, or take away with them to tell another time, is a learnt confession. It is a confession that is taught by the correctional authority that knows the 'truth' behind why they are there, even if the offenders are not yet aware of it.

Second, the Marumali program acts as a constitutive technology in the construction of Aboriginal 'difference'. The Marumali program requires Aboriginal offenders to understand where they fit in relation to their family, health, education and so on. In doing so, it introduces the discourse of Aboriginal 'difference' within which Aboriginal offenders locate and constitute themselves. Thus, by helping Aboriginal offenders '*learn about themselves*' and learn about the '*common issues*' that they and other Aboriginal peoples face, issues that contribute to '*the reasons why they are there*', the Marumali program further allows for Aboriginal offenders to constitute themselves as being different to other populations because they are 'disadvantaged', 'over-represented' and subject to numerous 'underlying issues'.

The constitutive nature of this process draws attention to a final interesting feature of the Marumali program: the 'authorities' that teach the confession and then listen and judge its repetition. The authorities are Aboriginal peoples. The confession that Aboriginal offenders learn to retell in their own words is the story of Aboriginal 'difference' that Aboriginal staff have been telling since they came to the Department of Justice in the mid 1990s.

Perhaps this is a new dimension to what Butler (1990) meant when she spoke of performed identities as being a 'copy of copy'. Aboriginal offenders are being asked to locate themselves in the story of Aboriginal 'difference' that has been written, erased, revised and transformed numerous times by both the Australian Government and Aboriginal peoples. Yet, Aboriginal offenders are not being asked to repeat and locate themselves in the Australian Government's account of Aboriginal 'difference'. Rather, they are being asked to repeat an *Aboriginal* account of 'difference'. They are being asked to locate themselves in the world of Aboriginal experience, and in doing so, continue and expand the boundaries of Aboriginal 'difference'.

The Koori Cognitive Skills Program: A Change in Conversation

The Koori Cognitive Skills Program appears to be like any other cognitive behavioural therapy (CBT) program for offenders. Thus, like the CBT programs discussed in Chapter 2, it aims to address the lack of problem-solving skills that lead to offending lifestyles.

What makes this program a '*Koori*' Cognitive Skills Program however, is the means by which it has been developed and delivered. The Koori Cognitive Skills Program, while based on James McGuire's Offence-Focused Problem Solving Program, has been adapted by a Koori registered psychologist, in consultation with the Koori community and their elders.

While numerous adaptations have been made, the five most illustrative include:

1. 'A Talking Stick, which was introduced as a tool to assist communication, connection and participation of all group members in discussions and debriefing' (Atkinson and Jones 2005: 21);

2. 'A traditional, gender-based culturally relevant activity, which was integrated into the program. Such as inscribing a shield for the men, and basket-weaving for the women. It was intended for traditional activities to occur during sessions when appropriate, and between sessions too, if desired' (Atkinson and Jones 2005: 21);

3. 'Three boxes were provided in the Aboriginal colours of red, black and yellow. Group members were encouraged to write down and "post" details of offences into the red box, worries into the black box and feedback into the yellow box, for use in subsequent group activities' (Atkinson and Jones 2005: 21);[4]

4. The content of role-playing scenarios was changed to reflect issues and concerns more likely to arise in the Aboriginal community (Atkinson and Jones 2005); and

5. 'It was intended that the final session of the program incorporate some elements of a 'rite of passage', including a ceremonial burning of the contents of the boxes, and the formal presentation of certificates for graduation' (Atkinson and Jones 2005: 21).

The Koori Cognitive Program appears largely symbolic in practice, especially in comparison to the Marumali program. The Marumali program provides Aboriginal offenders with a forum to trace their history and locate their identity, the Koori Cognitive Skills Program provides Aboriginal offenders with a talking stick and other symbols that they can use when discussing their erroneous thought processes. However, this judgement prematurely assumes the Koori Cognitive Skills Program and the Marumali program were developed in order to facilitate the same affect in the actions and cognitions of Aboriginal offenders. This is not the case. The Marumali program allows offenders to enter and locate themselves in the history of Aboriginal 'difference'. The Koori Cognitive Skills Program positions the offender in relation to their offending behaviour, and asks them to respond. How the Koori Cognitive Skills Program does this is fascinating.

Disciplinary tactics for an unusual responsibilization strategy
Aboriginal offenders undergoing the Koori Cognitive Skills Program are subject to a progressive set of disciplinary tactics, which ultimately makes Aboriginal offenders responsible for their past, present and future behaviour. The process begins with the components surrounding Aboriginal offenders' behaviour being broken down. The components are classified in terms of thinking errors, problematic associations, appropriate and inappropriate behaviours and so on.

---

4   The colours of the boxes represent the three colours of the Aboriginal flag. The flag has a yellow circle centred on the background of black and red blocks of colour. The yellow circle represents the sun, which in Aboriginal culture is the giver of life and protector. The block of red colour represents Australia's red earth to which Aboriginal people have a spiritual relationship. The block of black represents the Aboriginal people of Australia.

Once their thoughts have been reclassified, Aboriginal offenders are engaged in a process that sees them taught how to recognize when their thoughts are erroneous, and how to think in more appropriate and rational ways about the situation they are in. Once they have been taught this information, Aboriginal offenders enter a final judgement which examines their capacity to move through the CBT process on their own. This examination either sees them classified as having successfully lowered their risk to a manageable level, or as being problematic, dangerous and risky.

Responsibilizing offenders for their past and future actions is not an unusual feature of contemporary penal practice. Nor is the appearance of a responsibilization strategy in a penal program modified to better match the 'variances' of its participants, unique to the Koori Cognitive Skills Program. Both Hannah-Moffat (2000, 2001, 2004b, 2006, 2011; Hannah-Moffat and Yule 2011) and Pollack (2005, 2007, 2009) explore the different ways that 'gender-responsive' and women-focused practices in Canada deploy responsibilization strategies. Both scholars show how these strategies not only produce better neo-liberal citizens, but also construct the subjectivity of prudent women within neo-liberal society.

Hannah-Moffat (2000, 2001, 2004b, 2006, 2011; Hannah-Moffat and Yule 2011) contends that feminist scholars and practitioners have infiltrated the Correctional Service of Canada with a notion of women's empowerment. This notion recognizes and responds to women offenders' common history of abuse, trauma, and disempowerment. However, Hannah-Moffat further illustrates how this notion of empowerment is regularly co-opted in practice, changing the orientation of women-focused programs. Hannah-Moffat's work on the 'Creating Choices' framework in Canada (2000, 2001, 2004a), for example, shows how the notion of empowerment deployed in this framework, does little more than empower prisons while responsibilizing women. Women-focused practices developed under this framework 'empower' women to make a predetermined and value-laden set of choices about how to conduct their lives, which, if they fail to make, justify the punitive responses of the penal system.

Similarly, Pollack (2005, 2007, 2009) argues that 'gender-responsive' practices are restrained and affected by the prison setting and its traditional logics and techniques. Pollack illuminates how socio-economic experiences of women – such as abuse, trauma and disempowerment – are quickly recast in prison settings in terms of the maladaptive coping skills or 'risk factors' they produce. Women are encouraged and 'empowered' to talk about their drug and alcohol abuse, relationship problems, or even complete psychological disturbances, such as personality disorders, that are associated with their experiences, but *not* the abuse or trauma that lead to them. Moreover, Pollack demonstrates how women are taught to internalize problematic associations (such as drug and alcohol abuse) and risk factors (such as personality disorder) as *their story*. In doing so, women become responsible for the management of these factors post-release. In fact, if women choose to discuss how these factors might relate to their past abuse, their discussions are re-presented to them by psycho-correctional authorities as examples of how they have failed to make progress and take responsibility for their choices.

A point of difference in Victoria's responsibilization strategy

There are parallels between Canada's gender-responsive programs and practices and Victoria's Aboriginal responsive programs and practices. However, there is also a point of difference. The cultural elements included in the Koori Cognitive Skills Program are not cultural 'factors' like abuse or trauma. They are props, methods and rituals of culture. When Aboriginal offenders are asked to discuss their offending behaviour, they are assisted by a talking stick. When Aboriginal offenders are asked to listen to other offenders talk about their offending behaviour, and locate their cognitions in a spectrum of errors, they do so while engaging in a culturally relevant activity. When Aboriginal offenders are asked to identify and separate the details of their offence from their emotions, they do so while considering the meaning of the different colours of the Aboriginal flag. In other words, the cultural props, methods and rituals used in the Koori Cognitive Skills Program are not the focus of this responsibilization process. Aboriginal offenders are not responsibilized to be better Aboriginal people. Their engagements with these props, methods and rituals are unbound and unconfined to any particular strategy.

Thus, the Koori Cognitive Skills Program facilitates a very different development in Aboriginal offenders than the Marumali program. The Marumali program allows Aboriginal offenders to understand how the world of Aboriginal 'difference' was created for them by Australian Government actions. It allows Aboriginal offenders to tell *their story* of forced separation from culture by Australian Governments, and how this separation facilitates their appearance before the correctional agency at this time. The Koori Cognitive Skills Program does not share this focus on Government actions. Rather, the Koori Cognitive Skills Program allows Aboriginal offenders to understand that it is only *their* actions – which are supported by their engagement with indigeneity and culture – that will move Aboriginal peoples beyond this point of 'difference'. It is through engagement with indigeneity and culture that the world of Aboriginal peoples can take new form within Western society. This is the 'rite of passage' that Aboriginal offenders undertake within the confines and constructs of the Koori Cognitive Skills Program.

Aboriginal Staff: The Crucial Dimension

While each of these 'responsive' programs facilitates different actions in Aboriginal offenders, they are not the catalyst for Aboriginal offenders choosing to participate in them. Rather, Aboriginal offenders participate in these programs because of Aboriginal staff. As the following non-Aboriginal staff member explains:

We know that the key is Aboriginal people working in those areas. One of the big flagships for that is our Koori Cognitive Skills Programs, where a mainstream Cognitive Skills Program run in prisons and Community Corrections Services for years and very few Aboriginal prisoners attend, all of a sudden we have a Koori Cognitive Skills Program and while the model and the program manual is different, the prisoners don't know that before they walk in the door, all they see is that the program now, instead of being delivered by a Corrections Psychologist, is co-facilitated by an Aboriginal person.

We ran it in four prisons this year and just because of that one factor of having an Aboriginal person involved, at three of those prisons we had to turn prisoners away because we had too many people wanting to be in the group. So it's just this amazing turn around, just by involving Aboriginal people in these programs. (non-Aboriginal staff member nine)

The fundamental role Aboriginal peoples play in the Koori Cognitive Skills Program's delivery indicates the fragile nature of the constructive and transformative practices taking place in the name of responsivity. Before Aboriginal offenders will enter the rituals of discourse provided through the Marumali and Koori Cognitive Skills Programs, they must first choose to accept the *authority* that delivers these rituals, and judges their progress in them. It is the appeal and trust in the authority of Aboriginal people that is the catalyst for Aboriginal offenders entering the Marumali and Koori Cognitive Skills Programs.

Aboriginal staff are fundamental to Victoria's Department of Justice and all its interactions with Aboriginal offenders. Chapter 3 demonstrated how the Koori recruitment strategy could not operate unless Aboriginal peoples saw other Aboriginal people in the Department of Justice doing meaningful work for Aboriginal communities. As explained, it is only when '*word gets around*' in the Aboriginal community that Aboriginal people want to work there. Additionally, Chapter 3 further shows how, once recruited, Aboriginal staff became the only authorities capable of listening to, judging and providing approaches for both Aboriginal offenders and the Aboriginal community. They became the only means by which the Department of Justice could reach the Aboriginal community and get the response of '*oh yeah, well what can I do*' about a Department of Justice related issue, instead of just the defensive question of '*who put this together?*'

The operations of the Marumali and Koori Cognitive Skills Program indicate that Aboriginal staff allow the Department of Justice to perform yet another function in relation to Aboriginal 'difference'. Aboriginal staff provide the means for the institutional body of the Department of Justice to reach Aboriginal offenders and get a positive response of engagement. As the non-Aboriginal staff member explains above, Aboriginal offenders do not know the content or processes of an Aboriginal specific program before they start. They do not know if these programs will have the same mainstream practices as all the other programs, or if they will incorporate the cultural and historic elements that they do. Rather, what makes

Aboriginal offenders choose to engage in these programs is the sight or knowledge of an Aboriginal person being involved in its delivery.

In light of this additional role for Aboriginal staff, it is now possible to explain how the distinct discourses of responsivity circulating in the Department of Justice relate to one another, how these complementing discourses came to take the shape that they do, and what this implies for the mutual construction process.

The Relationship between the Two Versions of Responsivity in Victoria

As previously stated, there are two versions of responsivity in the Victorian Department of Justice. There is one that the Department of Justice becomes, maintains and increases when a proportion of Aboriginal peoples access positive criminal justice system-related services and a number of Aboriginal peoples are employed in criminal justice system-related agencies. There is also one that Aboriginal offenders become when they access and participate in programs specifically set up for them by the Department of Justice. Having mapped these programs and services, the contingent nature of these accounts of responsivity are apparent. One way of being responsive cannot come into effect without the other. Aboriginal offenders cannot become responsive until the Department of Justice sets up the programs that they can access and participate in, and the Department of Justice cannot be measured on its responsivity until Aboriginal offenders access these programs. Aboriginal offenders will not access the programs or want to participate in them until the Department of Justice allows an Aboriginal person to deliver the programs. The Department of Justice cannot be measured on their responsivity until they hire more Aboriginal peoples to deliver the programs. Thus, responsivity only comes into being when both the Department of Justice and Aboriginal offenders perform certain actions that make them 'responsive'. Responsivity is a circular process that requires both the Department of Justice and Aboriginal offenders to *continuously* perform their demarcated roles. This account does not, however, explain why it is these two elements in particular that have been associated with Aboriginal offender responsivity in Victoria.

It is these elements in particular because these are the elements that align with the broader discursive practice operating in Victoria's criminal justice system in relation to Aboriginal peoples. In the same way that Chapter 3 shows how the position of the Department of Justice in relation to Aboriginal peoples' 'difference' was in flux (that is, difference was something that the Department of Justice could create, maintain, redress and so on), so too is the Department of Justice's position in responsive practice in flux. Responsive practice is not a binary state; it is something which the Department of Justice must continuously strive to facilitate. Responsivity is something the Department of Justice must maintain, increase and so on as the number of Aboriginal peoples employed and the proportion of Aboriginal peoples accessing criminal justice services change.

Moreover, Chapter 3 documents how the Department of Justice attempted to shift its role in relation to Aboriginal 'difference' by authorizing Aboriginal peoples to manage Aboriginal offenders in the ways that they see fit. Aboriginal authority and management has also become a measure of responsivity in the Department of Justice. In order to be responsive, the Department of Justice must hire more Aboriginal peoples to provide and deliver specially designed services and programs for Aboriginal offenders in the ways that they see fit.

Finally, when Aboriginal offenders engage in programs such as Marumali and become 'responsive', they enter into the same process of 'worlding' traced in Chapter 3. Aboriginal offenders enter the process of mapping the world of difference that Aboriginal peoples experience. They further contribute to this process through locating their story within myriad other accounts of Aboriginal 'difference'. Similarly, when Aboriginal offenders engage in the Koori Cognitive Skills Program and become 'responsive', they are provided with the tools and mechanisms that enable them to create a new world of indigeneity. When Aboriginal offenders become 'responsive' they not only enter a process of being managed by Aboriginal peoples in ways that these people see fit, but also enter a process of managing their future in ways that are fit for an Aboriginal person.

These 'responsive' practices illuminate an important development in the discursive practice of Aboriginal 'difference' circulating in the Victorian Department of Justice. The Department of Justice embodies responsivity when it releases control of Aboriginal offenders to Aboriginal peoples. However, its capacity to be 'responsive' is not measured until Aboriginal offenders attend and participate in programs. Moreover, Aboriginal offenders' responsivity is contingent on the Department of Justice creating programs in which they are keen to attend and participate. However, what ultimately makes Aboriginal offenders 'responsive' is their capacity to take control of their construction of difference and begin to construct a new position beyond its current confines. Thus, Victoria's approach to the responsivity principle is both a continuation of the discursive practice of difference and a final process of examination. The capacity of the Department of Justice to redress Aboriginal 'difference' is ultimately reliant on the judgements and actions of Aboriginal peoples.

Victoria's approach to Aboriginal offender responsivity illustrates the final piece in Victoria's account of the mutual constructions of race and criminal justice. Chapter 3 shows how Victoria's location-specific and negotiated notions of nationhood and racialized identity transformed the operation of the Department of Justice. It shows how the Department of Justice became an institutional body marked by the history of Aboriginal 'difference'. Another facet of the construction process is now apparent. This marked institutional body has negotiated penal tools and logics, changing their orientation when used with Aboriginal offenders. The Department of Justice has transformed and employed tools and logics of responsivity which construct the past, present and future of Aboriginal offenders. In doing so, these tools and logics establish the 'truth' of Aboriginal 'difference' in Victoria. They make the whole process of a negotiating and transforming institutional body *necessary* in the Victorian context.

Responsivity in the New Zealand Department of Corrections

Like Victoria, the New Zealand Department of Corrections provides two accounts of responsivity. First, there is an official documents account, which states:

> To the Department of Corrections, being responsive means having an organization and staff capable of developing and delivering services that are effective and appropriate for Māori. This includes:
>
> - providing appropriate training and development for staff to be able to deliver services in a manner that respects Māori values and supports Māori processes;
> - increasing the involvement of Māori staff at all levels of the Department, to support Māori-to-Māori service delivery, and influence change at a management level to improve overall services for Māori; and
> - incorporating Māori values in the Department's organizational policies, practices, processes and culture. (Department of Corrections New Zealand 2003: 9)

There are obvious parallels between this account of responsivity and the one presented in Victoria's official documents. Both accounts reflect elements of culturally appropriate practice (for example, changes to staff composition and training), and both measure responsivity in terms of departmental actions. There is also a clear point of difference. Victoria's official documents present offender access and participation as a key component of responsive programs and services. New Zealand's documents present respectful services that incorporate Māori processes as their key component. Consequently, while Victoria's account lends itself to developing culturally *specific* programs for Aboriginal offenders, New Zealand's account only lends itself to culturally *respective* programs that incorporate Māori values alongside their Pākehā counterparts.

The difference between Victoria and New Zealand's accounts of responsivity reflects a broader difference in these jurisdictions' penal practice. As Chapter 3 demonstrates, the social and penal history of Victoria provided the conditions for Aboriginal people to:

- enter into a separate and different part of the Victorian Department of Justice;
- develop programs about the separate and different experiences of Aboriginal peoples; and

- deliver these programs in separate or different ways to Aboriginal offenders (for example, Marumali and the Koori Cognitive Skills Program).

In contrast, the social and penal history of New Zealand provided the condition for the Department of Corrections to emerge from a social policy of biculturalism, focused on recognizing and respecting the values and process of the Māori World in the Global World, only to subsequently have the Department of Corrections:

- struggle to position the Māori World alongside the Global World; and
- have its Māori staff construct the balance between these worlds in a slightly different way than the official documents.

In light of these histories, it is not surprising that Māori staff provide a slightly different account of responsivity than the Department of Corrections' official documents. Māori staff propose:

> Responsiveness is about how we work with people to achieve meaningful results. Responsiveness is about the quality of our relationships and the methodology of people engagement we provide both in our written and spoken form. (Māori staff member two)

> When talking about responsiveness, the programs that we have developed are important, but there are a whole lot of other things that surround that ... it's everything, the policies we develop, the staff, even our own Māori staff, they might be Māori but even the way they relate to other Māori might need a tune up. (Māori staff member three)

And

> Responsivity is not about dealing with a minority population, but dealing with a very discrete group of people who share a common set of cultural values and norms, who are very unique in terms of those cultural norms, who occupy a fairly important part of New Zealand society and who are a major group in our corrections system. (Māori staff member four)

For Māori staff, responsivity is not just about respecting the presence of the Māori World in the Global World. Rather, it is about ensuring the relationship between the two Worlds and populations is correctly balanced. For Māori staff, responsivity is about:

- recognizing the specific position of Māori in society and the correctional setting;
- acknowledging the role Māori play in shaping these environments; and

• ensuring the method of engagement in these environments allows for quality relationships to develop between all parties – Māori and Māori, and Māori and Pākehā.

The differences between the official documents and Māori staff accounts of responsivity are familiar. Chapter 4 shows how the official documents of the Department of Corrections and Māori staff propose different methods and mechanisms for getting Māori offenders to disengage from offending behaviour and re-engage with Māori culture. When Māori offenders are approached from the Global World, their innate offending behaviour is targeted, while the pro-social features of their culture are respected. When Māori offenders are approached from the Māori World, the choices of Māori offenders to disengage from culture and engage in offending behaviour are challenged and baselines for connecting with culture in the Global World and Māori World are presented. A similar pattern is followed in terms of responsivity. The official documents propose that existing services which target innate deficiency should be revised to incorporate and respect the pro-social features of Māori culture. Māori staff emphasize working with Māori offenders in meaningful ways, in order to recognize the unique position and culture of Māori in society. The question therefore becomes, how is responsivity practiced in the Department of Corrections? To answer this question it is necessary to explore the operation of a multi-faceted 'responsive' practice identified by both the official document and Māori staff: The Te Piriti Special Treatment Program.

The Ritualistic Cultural Assessment of Māori offenders

The Te Piriti Special Treatment Program is a bicultural treatment program that is delivered at a 60-bed facility for child sex offenders. The program is delivered to Māori, Pacific Islander and Pākehā offenders and is grounded in a Cultural Perspective Policy comprising four goals:

1. To create a 'culturally supportive' environment for staff (Larsen et al. 1998: 391). Support in this context refers to actions such as providing Māori staff with 'the opportunity to attend network *hui* (meetings)' (Larsen et al. 1998: 391).
2. To provide bicultural training for staff. Training focuses on staff learning to follow the principles of the Treaty of Waitangi, and includes staff participating in a cultural and Treaty awareness program (Larsen et al. 1998: 392).
3. To manage the 'action phase' of the cultural and Treaty awareness program. This phase includes building and maintaining relationships with local *iwi* (tribe) for consultative processes.
4. To revise 'policies and processes to improve service delivery to Māori' (Larsen et al. 1998: 393). This goal primarily relates to two actions:

    a. securing funding for a cultural consultant who informs the cultural policies of the unit and assesses Māori offenders; and

    b. adapting the treatment process so as to incorporate bicultural content.

Māori staff identify the cultural assessment process that occurs when the Māori offender first enters this program, and the bicultural therapy process they receive post-assessment, as exemplars of Māori offender responsivity in practice.

Another unusual ritual of confession

The cultural assessment process is provided by a cultural consultant, who is also referred to as a Māori assessor. The assessment is focused on a number of variables including: cultural identity, knowledge of *whakapapa* (genealogy), the potential presence of *Mate Māori* (a 'sickness' related to a person's actions) or *Makutu* (being cursed by an external source), knowledge of Māori traditional values and beliefs, knowledge and experience of *Marae* (sacred open meeting place) protocol, status of *Te Reo* (language and culture), level of cultural skills (including crafts), motivation to develop *tikanga Māori* and relationship with *whanau* (nuclear and extended family).

    The following two Māori staff members' discussion presents the fundamental features of this 'responsive' process:

> What is interesting, are these cultural assessments that we operate, which is really a conversation with an offender about his 'Māoriness' rather than his "offendingness". (Māori staff member 3)

> And it's having a huge effect on Māori offenders. The whole process works on the idea that if you can motivate an offender, then that offender will get some sort of treatment. But a lot of our offenders are not motivated, or will take some time to get motivated … [so] they will go into this two hour assessment, this one-to-one with the Māori assessor. By the end of it they are asking for a rehabilitation program. (Māori staff member 4)

> And they are not being directed that way, they are just being engaged from a totally different perspective and at the end of it they go "whoa, actually when I think about it, I need to get my shit together". (Māori staff member 3)

Thus, the cultural assessment process serves as a ritual of discourse. When Māori offenders enter the cultural assessment process they are not simply engaged by a Māori assessor who talks to them about '*Māoriness*'. Rather, they are required and expected to provide statements about the current state of their '*Māoriness*'. They are expected to account for their knowledge, skills, experience and involvement in Māori culture, language, world views, craft, family and society. When Māori offenders speak these statements about '*Māoriness*', their speech unfolds in a power relationship. The Māori assessor (a person of cultural authority and stature) not only hears and records what is said, but also draws out how they came to be located in this current state of '*Māoriness*'. When Māori offenders provide their prescribed confession to a person who not only presents as an authority on '*Māoriness*', but also represents '*Māoriness*' in its proper formation, Māori offenders are able to reflect on what they have said and make the un'*directed*' judgement that, '*whoa, actually when I think about it, I need to get my shit together*'.

Both the ritualistic nature of this 'responsive' cultural assessment process, and the effect that it has on Māori offenders, enhance our understanding of the Department of Corrections' approach towards Māori offender responsivity. Responsivity is entirely dependent on the position of Māori offenders and the capacity of the Department of Corrections to facilitate movement within and away from this position. The question is, however, what exactly is the position that Māori offenders are being moved away from, and where are they being moved towards?

Locating Māori offenders in the discourse of discretional choice
The cultural assessment process clearly positions Māori offenders as having a problematic relationship with their culture. Yet, it is unclear if this relationship manifested because Māori offenders *chose* this lifestyle (Māori staff's discourse of discretional choice), or because of their *innate deficiencies* (the official document's science of offending behaviour). The following Māori staff members' discussion about the purpose and effect of cultural engagements such as those contained in the cultural assessment process clarifies this issue:

> One of the things I've seen in the time that I have been here is, with most Māori offenders, Māori culture, if presented to them in the right way, and by that I mean in an honest, challenging way, can have a profound effect on the way that they see themselves, and then can give some baseline from which they can measure their behaviour.

> When they are in prison, because there are not a lot of other distractions, there is that opportunity to start working through that with them. So, "who are you" and "what do you think that means" and "how does that fit into what you do and how you behave towards your family?"

> Which is more than just about lecturing them, it is actually about presenting them with a really clear understanding of what it means to be Māori and then inviting them to say, "how does that fit with your actual behaviour?" "What do you want to do about it?" and "here are some practical things you can do to get there". (Māori staff member three)

When the Māori assessor engages Māori offenders, they are engaging Māori offenders who have *chosen* this problematic lifestyle and *chosen* to disengage from culture. Hence the necessity to ask Māori offenders who they think they are and how they got that way, and to present them with an '*honest*' and '*challenging*' understanding of what it means to be Māori, in order to provide a baseline from which to compare.

The reappearance of the discourse of discretional choice is not surprising in the context of the cultural assessment process. As Chapter 4 shows, this discourse is founded in the experiences of Māori staff; the cultural assessment process is developed and delivered by a Māori person whose experiences of discretional choice act as a baseline for judging Māori offenders' behaviour. However, the above Māori staff member's account illustrates more than just the presence of the discourse of choice. It presents three further features of the ritualistic and 'responsive' engagements of the Department of Corrections with Māori offenders.

First, it is not simply that Māori offenders are required or expected to provide statements about their '*Māoriness*'. Rather, it is the Māori assessor that teaches them both the statements they must speak and how to position themselves as the subjects of those statements. Thus, in these 'responsive' approaches, the Māori offender is expected to consider '*who are you*' and '*what do you think that means ...?*' by first listening to '*honest*' and '*challenging*' accounts about what it means to be Māori and the choices that lead away from that position, and then trying to understand '*how does that fit into what you do and how you behave towards your family?*'.

Second, these 'responsive' engagements are constitutive in nature, not just ritualistic. Māori offenders are not only provided with the conditions to construct their offending behaviour in terms of the choices they made. Rather, they are also allowed to construct their 'true' position in society through this process. They are provided with a '*baseline*' of the Māori assessor from which they can compare their past, current and future behaviours and choices and recognize their 'true' position as being a cultural Māori subject.

Finally, this process does more than just allow Māori offenders to reflect on their behaviour and ask for a rehabilitation program. It allows Māori offenders to reflect on: the choices they have made, where those choices have led them, and where that position is in comparison to Māori who choose to remain in contact with their culture. It '*invites*' them, but does not '*lecture*' them, to decide what they are going to do about these choices.

Taking responsibility for Māori choices
A similar ritual was observed in the Victorian Department of Justice's approach to Aboriginal offender responsivity. Victoria's 'responsive' programs, such as the Marumali program, allow Aboriginal peoples to present Aboriginal offenders with an understanding of what it means to be an Aboriginal person in Australia. Victoria's responsive programs teach Aboriginal offenders how to locate themselves in

their understanding of Aboriginal 'difference', and invite Aboriginal offenders to consider how they can move beyond that position.

However, as has consistently been the case, while the mechanisms, props and tactics operating in the Victorian Department of Justice and the New Zealand Department of Corrections are the same, distinct, localized outcomes arise. In Victoria, this ritual allows for Aboriginal offenders to locate themselves in the history of disadvantage, over-representation and underlying issues. It allows Aboriginal offenders to be regulated by the discursive practice of Aboriginal 'difference'. In New Zealand, this ritual allows for Māori offenders to locate themselves in terms of the current state of their *'Māoriness'*. It allows them to be regulated by the discursive practice of discretional choice. The New Zealand ritual:

- constructs Māori offenders as capable of making rational choices;
- constitutes Māori offenders as having made choices that divide and exclude them from their proper place in both the Māori and Global World; and
- presents Māori offenders as capable of taking *responsibility* for their return to the rightful place of Māori within and between these Worlds through their choices.

The appearance of this responsibilization strategy in the cultural assessment process is interesting. Unlike the responsibilization strategy presented in Victoria's Koori Cognitive Skills Program, this strategy does not leave culture as an unbound property. Rather, culture and Māori offenders' past, present and future connections to it are located at the very heart of the strategy. However, this is not to say that culture is co-opted like women's 'empowerment' was in the gender-responsive responsibilization strategies illuminated by Hannah-Moffat and Pollack. Rather, this responsibilization strategy allows Māori offenders to take responsibility for being good Māori, cultural citizens, who have a connection to culture that is meaningful, real and a 'true' expression of the Māori World, not neo-liberal Māori subjects who perform culture in prudent ways.

But, even with these enhancements to our account of Māori offender responsivity, something remains unclear: what happens next? What happens when Māori offenders ask to participate in a rehabilitation program, or ask to be provided with the *'practical things'* that get them back to the baseline of Māori culture?

The Bicultural Therapy Process and the Re-emergence of Innate Deficiency

Once Māori offenders complete the cultural assessment process they begin the bicultural therapy process. It is here that they receive the rehabilitation program that they have asked for and the *'practical things'* that they need to do to move towards their proper position in the Māori and Global World.

According to the official documents of the Department of Corrections, the bicultural treatment process has two key features. First, offenders receive a series of mainstream cognitive behavioural therapy/social learning theory-based modules. These modules combine the developments from the 'best practice' literature (presented in this book as the 'practical texts' of the correctional literature), with the successful operations of other specialist units in the Department of Corrections, such as Kia Mārama[5] (Nathan, Wilson and Hillman 2003: 12). The modules are focused on areas such as: 'group norm building, offending patterns, sexual reconditioning, victim empathy, relationship skills and sexuality education, mood management and relapse prevention' (Nathan, Wilson and Hillman 2003: 12).

The second key feature of the bicultural therapy process is *tikanga Māori* (Māori customs and traditions). Primarily, *tikanga Māori* are incorporated into the therapeutic environment surrounding the delivery of the modules. Thus, when offenders work on areas such as group norm building or relapse prevention in the therapy rooms, they are also exposed to *tikanga Māori* such as '*awhi* [to embrace], *tautoko* [to support], *aroha* [all encompassing love], *wairu* [spirit], *whanaungatanga* [active family support], *whakapapa* [genealogy], *whakapiripiri* [introduction], and *hākari* [feast]' (Nathan, Wilson and Hillman 2003: 14).

How these diverse features interact within the bicultural therapy process is explained by the following Pākehā staff member:

> What we ended up doing was installing a cultural milieu where a whole lot of Māori practices, prayer and all that sort of stuff was embedded in the very practice of running the unit. It was integral to it rather than added on to it. So we had the cultural milieu and then within that we had a standard CBT program, which had nothing to do with the culture, but somehow it seemed that by putting it in that environment, it made it a lot more attractive to Māori, Māori are much more prepared to go there and the reporting of experiences have been a lot more positive. (Pākehā staff member one)

This account of the bicultural therapy process illuminates the disciplinary mechanisms and tools embedded within the Department of Corrections' 'responsive' practice. One of the first things to occur in the bicultural therapy process is Māori offenders, together with a corrections psychologist and a Māori healer, break down aspects of their offending behaviour (such as offending patterns, sexual deviations or poor relationship skills) so that these problematic behaviours can be identified and targeted. The therapy process then teaches Māori offenders the actions they need in order to replace these problematic behaviours and achieve the better result of a pro-social lifestyle (such as enhancing victim empathy or developing relationship skills). Then, through modules such as group norm building or sexual reconditioning, an optimal sequence is established for offenders' new, pro-social actions to operate. Finally, through modules such as mood management and relapse prevention, this optimal sequence is fixed in place

---

5   Kia Mārama was the first specialist prison treatment program for child sex offenders established in New Zealand.

and the offender is taught how to become the manager of their own pro-social life. The Māori offender is taught how to recognize when they are at risk of slipping up and what they can do to their cognitions and behaviours to address this problem.

Another unusual responsibilization strategy
The mechanisms of New Zealand's bicultural therapy process are almost identical to those used in Victoria's Koori Cognitive Skills Program. Moreover, both 'responsive' programs deploy a responsibilization strategy that sees offenders become the managers of their new pro-social lives. However, this is where the similarities between Victoria and New Zealand's criminal justice practice end. The cultural props, methods and rituals of the Koori Cognitive Skills Program are not the subject of this program's responsibilization process. Rather, they *facilitate* the responsibilization of Aboriginal offenders, allowing these offenders to engage in a CBT process that they might otherwise ignore. In contrast, the bicultural therapy process not only draws on cultural elements to *facilitate* a responsibilization strategy, but further *co-opts* these elements' presence in order to *deliver* the strategy.

At the end of the cultural assessment process, Māori offenders are moved to a point where they will *ask* for the tools and practical steps that allow them to become responsible for their cultural lives. The bicultural therapy process, drawing on Māori offenders' willingness and motivation to engage in programs that incorporate Māori customs and traditions, delivers a *different* responsibilization strategy than requested. The responsibilization strategy embedded in the bicultural therapy process teaches Māori offenders how to become the manager of their pro-social, *neo-liberal life*, not good cultural citizens in the Māori World. The bicultural therapy process co-opts Māori culture, and the desires of Māori offenders to engage in it. Thus, if Māori offenders become disillusioned and question the '*practical things*' the bicultural therapy program teaches them, the bicultural therapy process responds by reinstating their desire for culture. Māori offenders who struggle in the bicultural therapy process are encouraged to meet with the cultural consultant. The cultural consultant is expected to once more discuss the offender's desire for a cultural life and the associated *need* to stay within the bicultural program which provides them with opportunities to engage in *tikanga Māori* (Larsen et al. 1998; Roberston et al. 1999).

Relaying the same struggles to Māori offenders
The appearance of this second responsibilization strategy (the strategy for responsibilizing neo-liberal citizens) is not surprising in New Zealand's context. The New Zealand Department of Corrections has repeatedly struggled to maintain a balance and separation between the Māori and Global Worlds. The Department of Corrections has used frameworks, discourses, mechanisms and strategies of the Global World that co-opt elements of the Māori World. Yet, what is surprising here, is that the tension between these Worlds and the struggle of the Department

of Corrections to negotiate it is being *relayed* to the Māori offender through these 'responsive' practices.

When offenders are engaged from the Māori World (for example, through the cultural assessment process), they are engaged from a world where offending behaviour is a side effect of a choice to disengage from Māori culture. Accordingly, Māori offenders are provided with a strategy that will see them become cultural Māori subjects, who happen to also be acceptable neo-liberal subjects in the Global World. When Māori offenders are engaged from the Global World (for example, through the bicultural therapy process), they are engaged from a world where offending behaviour is a result of their innate deficiencies. Accordingly, Māori offenders are provided with a strategy that will see them become better neo-liberal subjects, who happen to also have some acceptable cultural customs and traditions from the Māori World.

This observation illuminates a final element of New Zealand's approach to Māori offender responsivity. Unlike the Victorian Department of Justice, the New Zealand Department of Corrections does not approach Māori offender responsivity as an extension of its discursive practices. Nor does the New Zealand Department of Corrections' approach to responsivity represent just as an extension of the institutional body's role within its discursive practice. Rather, the Department of Corrections' approach *extends* the messiness of New Zealand's correctional history to the lives of Māori offenders. The Department of Corrections provides Māori offenders with the tools and strategies to locate themselves neither within nor between the Māori or Global Worlds as they currently stand.

Victoria and New Zealand's 'Responsivity' and the Mutual Construction Process

In light of Victoria and New Zealand's 'responsive' approaches, it is now possible to provide two final implications about the mutual constructions of race and criminal justice. First, in the mutual construction process, the tools for construction can be 'emptied'. I do not use the term emptied here to suggest that the actions associated with responsivity in Victoria and New Zealand have no meaning, or are empty gestures. Rather, I use this term to indicate how neither of these jurisdictions' practices of responsivity adheres to the prescriptive guidelines of the criminological literature. Neither jurisdiction propagates responsivity as a tool for identifying racial deficiencies.

Moreover, I use the term empty to indicate how penal tools and logics, such as those used under the banner of responsivity, have become vessels or shells within which various local descriptive practices are stored. The Department of Justice's 'responsive' practice embodies and extends Victoria's practice of Aboriginal 'difference'. The Department of Corrections' 'responsive' practice extends New Zealand's struggle to negotiate its discursive practice in a single, consistent manner. Thus, what is produced through the vessel of 'responsivity' are all the subject and object positions required to make location-specific discursive practices *necessary*.

Second, the mutual constructions of race and criminal justice encompass the past, present and future of jurisdictions and populations in a complex process. What this and the past two chapters have revealed are:

- Notions of nationhood are tied to the history of a jurisdiction's *formation*. In Victoria, it was notions of Aboriginal peoples' uncivilized ways that allowed the British Crown to claim Australia as empty land. In New Zealand, it was the notion that Māori had potential for civilized agreement that lead to the signing of the Treaty of Waitangi.
- Notions of nationhood are negotiated by contemporary criminal justice systems, and result in transformed criminal justice *practices*. In Victoria, these notions lead to the enclosure of Aboriginal 'difference' within the institutional body of the Department of Justice. In New Zealand, it was the struggle to locate and find balance between the Māori and Global World that transformed the Department of Corrections.
- Transformed criminal justice systems provide the foundations from which contemporary *penal tools and logics* are negotiated, 'emptied' and refilled. In Victoria, responsivity encapsulates Aboriginal 'difference', in New Zealand, it was the struggle of two worlds.
- Negotiated penal tools and logics are capable of *constructing the future* of racialized peoples, such that their future both responds to its constructed past, and allows for racialized populations to extend the boundaries of its comprehension. The 'responsive' Aboriginal offender becomes capable of *creating* the future of Aboriginal 'difference' according to Aboriginal knowledge and experience. The 'responsive' Māori offender is made into a better neo-liberal subject while asking to be made a good, cultural Māori citizen.

A final conclusion can now be drawn about the mutual construction of race and criminal justice. The mutual construction process is negotiated and ongoing. It is negotiated by both the criminal justice system and the offender with whom the process ultimately resides. It is ongoing because individual and institutional bodies continue to subjectively perform their negotiated roles in the history of mutual construction. Thus, it is not just that the mutual construction of race and criminal justice is about the past, present and future. Rather, it is also that the process of construction will continue to expand the boundaries of our comprehension of racial identity and criminal justice practice.

Conclusion

The starting premise of this book was that race and criminal justice are mutually constructed. That is, racialized notions of nationhood are fundamental to the formation and orientation of criminal justice; and criminal justice tools, technologies and logics propagate specific racialized identities in society. The core argument of this book is that while criminology plays a small role in the mutual constructions of race and criminal justice, its impact on the mutual construction process is disproportionately large.

Criminology rarely produces accounts of the mutual construction process. Instead, it largely fixates on racialized peoples' over-representation in criminal justice systems, and propagates the same two limited and contrasting explanations for their disproportionate presence. The absence of criminological accounts of the mutual construction process and the inability of criminology to move beyond limited explanations for racialized peoples' over-representation are related. They both occur because of the ways criminological literature has changed in the past two decades: the literature has become a medium for practice and has subsequently acted as a repository for propagated 'truths'.

A Medium for Practice

The emergence of the Risk Need Responsivity Model of offender classification and treatment in correctional literature allowed the literature to become the key source of texts that have provided correctional agencies with the principles, techniques and approaches they now use in the development of practice (see for example Andrews, Bonta and Hoge 1990). This medium for practice has produced an 'infallible science' of offending behaviour that distorts the distribution of race and criminal justice in theory and practice. This 'science':

- *disqualifies* the lived experiences of racialized peoples – claiming that race is not a major factor in offending behaviour;
- *conflates* the socio-economic markers associated with racialized peoples' experiences of colonization, disadvantage and marginalization, with those of 'risk'; and
- *criminalizes* the experiences of racialized people – processing them through the same register of operationality as used for anti-social offending behaviour.

For these reasons, criminologists have largely struggled to move beyond claims that racialized people are a particular problem in criminal justice systems, or that racialized peoples' problems in criminal justice systems occur because of inappropriate Western tools and logics. Racialized people have become ensnared in a system that supports and sustains their repeated presence in custody, and consequently, criminologists have been denied the material needed to develop an account of anything else.

A Repository for Propagated 'Truths'

The function of the correctional literature has changed again in the past decade, taking with it the capacity for criminologists to produce accounts of mutual construction. The recent literature has become a repository for texts that serve *only* to confirm the success of the infallible science of offending behaviour in practice. This altered function has allowed for the science of offending behaviour to appear as the *only* science of offending behaviour.

In the decade following the emergence of the science of offending behaviour in criminological literature and practice, it has become *easier* for criminologists to continue to produce texts about the science of offending behaviour, *harder* for criminologists to produce texts about anything other than this science, and *necessary* to abide by this science's rules.

The science of offending behaviour is self-propagating. It comes complete with logics, tools, and rituals to produce both the figure of the anti-social offender, and the need of correctional agents to manage this figure's risk. Accordingly, there is no obvious reason for criminologists to depart from the science in order to produce texts about anything else – this science's 'truths' are self-evident and their practice is largely unquestionable. As a result, criminologists now have a variety of jurisdictional practices that can be explored either individually or comparatively. Furthermore, the science is couched in claims of 'best practice' and 'what works'. It is therefore necessary for criminologists to work in some way with the logics, tools and technologies of this science, even if they want to change it, or risk the implication that their alternate proposition is 'poor practice' and an example of 'what doesn't work'.

It is this insidious nature of the science of offending behaviour in practice that affects the capacity of criminologists to produce accounts of mutual construction. Or more precisely, it has forced criminologists to transform the criminological literature into a repository for the science's 'truths' (and only those 'truths') and as a result, criminological accounts of the mutual construction process are absent.

Ironically the very forum once used by criminologists to foster movement in correctional practice from 'nothing works' to 'what works' now serves to reinforce and stifle digression from this new prevailing dogma. As Foucault (1980d: 83) would phrase it, the correctional literature has become the repository for a 'unitary body of theory which [acts to] filter, hierarchize and order ... [various local and alternative claims to attention] in the name of some true knowledge and some arbitrary idea of what constitutes a science and its objects'. Thankfully, there is no reason why criminology theory or practice must remain this way.

Charting a New Path for Criminology

Criminology now has a unique connection to correctional practice. By allowing correctional literature to become a source of advice for practitioners, criminology has become the key informant and confidante for criminal justice. Criminologists can and should use this connection to practice to change the relationship between criminology and criminal justice once more. Specifically, I propose that criminologists become *local* confidantes and *global* informants.

By these terms I mean criminologists should:

- listen to their local criminal justice practitioners and consumers, focusing on who speaks about what;
- trace the markings on local institutional and individuals bodies, focusing on the localized investments of power and resistance that have produced them; and
- contribute to a global narrative about trends in practice, focusing on the performance of identity at the local level and how local performances are shaped by the excessive local history of the individual and the excessive historicity of their circumstances in global society.

This is the process that was employed throughout the second section of this book as it applied the Rules of Engagement to the mutual constructions of race and criminal justice in the Victorian Department of Justice and the New Zealand Department of Corrections.

Many other scholars already perform these roles in their work and encourage others to follow suit (see for example, the majority of the scholars referred to in the Introduction of this book – Hannah-Moffat, Hudson, Liebling, Phillips and so on). However, what I invite criminologists to do is also change the way they operate within these roles. I propose that criminologists use the insights gained from acting as local confidantes and global informants to support the *organic development* of criminal justice practice at the local level. That is, criminologists should use these insights to further act as a local confidante to criminal justice practitioners – supporting their efforts to maintain promising location-specific practices – and also become a global informant to local criminal justice, recommending to practitioners suitable alternative practices from other jurisdictions when change is required.

Thus, I contend criminology can combat the problematic mutual constructions of race and criminal justice by *facilitating movement* within it. To provide some momentum for criminology, I offer the following five insights as a local confidante and global informant on the mutual constructions of race and criminal justice.

1. Race and Criminal Justice are Dispersed in Location-specific Ways

The mutual construction process is influenced by constellations of location-specific factors. As this book illuminates, location-specific factors:

- influence the development of correctional systems – for example, the development of New Zealand's 'bicultural' Department of Corrections;
- transform the orientation of criminal justice – for example, the transformed objectives of the Victorian Department of Justice (from managing offenders to addressing Aboriginal 'difference');
- struggle to remain in focus when they collide with other factors – for example, the Department of Corrections' struggle to reconcile its responsibility to manage offending behaviour with its obligations under the Treaty of Waitangi; and
- nullify the influence of other factors circulating within the correctional system – for example, the Victorian Department of Justice's approaches to Aboriginal offending, which primarily continue to address Aboriginal 'difference' in Australia, rather than the innate deficiencies of anti-social offenders.

Accordingly, it is not that there is *a* proper dispersion of race and criminal justice that criminology has ignored or distorted. Rather, race and criminal justice is inherently tied to place: they are dispersed in location-specific ways and the relationship between them is influenced by location-specific factors. It is the role of criminologists to document how the constellation of location-specific factors is comprized in their jurisdiction, and to inform the broader criminological field about the effect this constellation has on the ways race and criminal justice are dispersed.

2. The Parameters Surrounding the Mutual Construction Process Produce Predictable Effects on Race and Criminal Justice's Dispersions

Despite the diversity inherent in the mutual construction process, there are some parameters within which location-specific factors emerge. These parameters relate to the position of the Western World in society, and affect the mutual construction process in three consistent ways:

- Western superiority, racial deficiency – when Western perspectives and processes are largely unquestioned by a society, the location-specific factors that emerge position racial differences in terms of either deficiency or deviance from society's norm. Australia's Policy of Assimilation, and the resulting stolen generation, exemplifies this relationship between parameters and factors. The process of assimilation was founded on the belief that Aboriginal language and culture were deficient in comparison to those of white Australians. Aboriginal parents were also presented as incapable of caring for their children to the same standard as white Australian parents. As a result, Aboriginal children were removed from their families, placed with white Australian families, and not allowed to practice Aboriginal language or culture – some of the key 'differences' experienced by Aboriginal offenders and communities.

- Questionable Western practice – when Western perspectives and processes are present, but their superiority is in question, the constellation of location-specific factors that emerge change. These constellations include constructions of racial differences that appear in reference to the questionable nature of the Western World. For example, when the incendiary and excoriating findings of the Royal Commission into Aboriginal Deaths in Custody (RCIADIC) emerged in Australia, the capacity of Australia's Government to manage Aboriginal peoples was questioned. Within these parameters, Victoria's location-specific constellation began to include factors such as the Department of Justice creating separate and dedicated Units that would redress the 'difference' Australian Governments created for Aboriginal peoples.

- Coexisting ways of being – when a society positions the Western World as capable of coexisting alongside another world, both worlds' frameworks of knowledge are positioned in kind. Within these parameters, the issue of acceptable similarities and differences between worlds become the focus of location-specific factors, and the identity of racialized and non-racialized populations is constituted accordingly. This is why New Zealand's location-specific constellation of factors includes the attempts of the Department of Corrections to account for Māori culture first as an additional feature of Māori offenders' innate offending behaviour, and then as a core element of Māori subjects, who happen to also exhibit innate offending behaviour.

Thus, what this book reveals is not simply how the position of the Western World determines the parameters within which race and criminal justice are dispersed. Rather, it further shows how the position of the Western World can change over time within one society, can manifest in different ways between societies, and how at each point in time when change occurs, the mutual constructions of race and criminal justice respond and adapt.

I propose that criminologists use these parameters to guide how they support the organic development of criminal justice practice at the local level. In particular, criminologists should use parameters to guide what constitutes a *relevant* practice for their jurisdiction – a practice that has been successful in jurisdictions that operate in similar parameters, not just with similar populations or problems – and when practitioners are more likely to accept this information, when the parameters are in flux.

3. The Mutual Construction Process is Negotiated by Criminal Justice Systems

The parameters within which constellations of location-specific factors emerge do not determine what will be marked on institutional bodies. Rather, the mutual construction process is *negotiated* by institutional bodies.

A key example of this negotiation was provided in the book's account of the two enclosed Aboriginal Units in the Victorian Department of Justice. These Units were dedicated to addressing Aboriginal 'difference'. They emerged because the Victorian Department of Justice reconstructed its position to make manifest the intelligibility of its perspectives and practices in relation to the RCIADIC. In doing so, the Victorian Department of Justice not only negotiated the location-specific factors surrounding its practice, but also shifted the parameters within which these factors could emerge. That is, the Department of Justice's actions legitimized the RCIADIC suggestion that Western frameworks of knowledge were mistaken in their understanding of Aboriginal peoples up until that point.

This account is not used to suggest that intuitional bodies have the capacity to *control* the constellation of location-specific factors they negotiate. The ongoing struggle of the New Zealand Department of Corrections to locate Māori culture illustrates that this is not always the case. This struggle was marked by multiple efforts of the Department of Corrections to negotiate its responsibilities as an institution charged with the management of New Zealand's offender populations, and its reconstituted obligations to respect the shared and particular rights of Māori and Pākehä under the Treaty of Waitangi.

Accordingly, what occurs at the local level of the mutual construction process is not merely the remnants of local histories which have marked all bodies within a jurisdiction. Rather, what this book reveals is how the mutual construction process is influenced by the way that correctional institutions *choose* to conduct themselves within their history, and the struggles they face in their conduct. Thus, I propose that it is in *conversation* with institutional bodies that criminology is likely to have the greatest impact in facilitating and supporting the organic development of criminal justice practice.

In the past decade, a debate has been sparked about the potential for conversations like this to occur under the banner of 'public criminologies'. While I encourage criminologists to negotiate this debate in their own terms (see in particular the special issues of *Criminology and Public Policy* (2010), and *Theoretical Criminology* (2007) for the range of positions that have been taken by criminologists), I also want to provide one piece of advice about how criminologists' conversations with institutional bodies should occur in the context of racialized populations and racialized criminal justice issues. This advice is contained in the next insight provided by this book.

4. Racialized Staff Negotiate Location-specific Dispersions of Race and Criminal Justice and are made Responsible for their Dispersion

There are negotiations taking place within the institutional body other than those presented above. This book provides one of the first accounts of the complex and messy roles racialized people have been asked to perform within criminal justice systems of settler-colonial societies. This account illuminates three key roles.

First, racialized peoples are not simply recruited by criminal justice institutions to act as authorities on racialized offenders' behaviour. Rather, racialized staff are expected to provide the type of authority that aligns with the way criminal justice institutions have chosen to conduct themselves. For example, while both Aboriginal people and Māori were hired by their jurisdiction's criminal justice system to act as authorities for their people, the authority they are expected to provide is different in practice. Aboriginal staff of the Victorian Department of Justice are expected to provide authority on the management of Aboriginal 'difference', whereas Māori staff of the New Zealand Department of Corrections are expected to provide particular authority over the management of Māori offenders' culture, but not necessarily their offending behaviour.

Second, the authority racialized staff choose to provide in practice is actually determined by their *experiences* of living within their jurisdiction's constellation of location-specific factors. For example, Aboriginal staff used their authority to implement the Marumali Program in the Department of Justice – a program about the ongoing effects of Australia's assimilation policies on all Aboriginal peoples. Aboriginal staff implemented this program because they knew from their experiences of these policies, that this was the '*struggle of our people*'. In contrast, Māori staff attempted to create programs that would challenge Māori offenders about the choices they made in their lives. These choice-focused programs were important to Māori staff because they knew from the experiences they did and did not share with Māori offenders, that choice is the central issue in Māori offending behaviour. Thus, the negotiations of racialized staff do not take shape in the same way as their broader institutional body's negotiation. It is not about *choosing* to do something within certain parameters. Rather, it is about *performing identity*.

Finally, because racialized authority has taken on a performative function in criminal justice, the lines between racialized peoples and institutional bodies' experiences of location-specific factors have blurred. This book provides examples of how the lines have blurred between:

- the experiences of offenders and non-offenders – where Aboriginal staff, communities and offenders share the same experiences of disadvantage, over-representation and underlying issues;
- the responsibilities of criminal justice agencies to offenders and those to non-offenders – where Aboriginal communities request the Department of Justice's involvement in their non-offending lives because the Department

of Justice plays such a pivotal role in Aboriginal offenders' lives through its Aboriginal staff;

- the responsibilities of communities to offenders' and to the institutions that hold them – where the Department of Corrections utilizes Māori staff to encourage Māori *iwi* to become involved in Māori offenders' lives in the ways that the Department of Corrections sees fit.

In authorizing racialized staff, racialized staff have been positioned as the only constant within the blurred arena of race and criminal justice. As a result, racialized staff both play a core role in negotiating the mutual construction process in a location, and have been made the frontline staff for its success and failure.

I previously proposed that it was in conversation with institutional bodies that criminology is likely to have the greatest impact. In light of the roles that racialized staff play in the mutual construction process, I am not advocating for criminology to hold this conversation with institutions. Rather, I contend it is the role of criminologists to ensure conversations about racialized populations and racialized criminal justice issues occur within criminal justice institutions, and, more importantly, that these conversations are held with racialized peoples, so their experiences are incorporated and they can have a voice in their own responsibilization.

5. The Mutual Construction of Race and Criminal Justice is Ongoing and Cyclical

The programs and practices created by correctional institutions to address racialized offenders' offending behaviour make racialized offenders responsible for their future in location-specific ways, and according to the negotiated frameworks of knowledge and experience of correctional agencies and their racialized staff. This book reveals the ongoing and cyclical nature of the mutual construction process. It shows how:

- correctional agencies negotiate the histories of racialized peoples as these histories relate to the obligations of the institution;
- racialized staff renegotiate the obligations of the institution as they relate to their experiences of living this history;
- racialized offenders are asked to locate themselves within and amongst both of these negotiated histories;
- racialized offenders are also made responsible for how they negotiate these histories in their future;
- racialized offenders' performance of their identity in their future affects the location-specific factors associated with racialized peoples; and
- correctional agencies negotiate the new addition to the constellation of factors.

Thus, to conclude, at the heart of mutual construction is an ongoing process of negotiation and performance which is capable of transforming the practice of institutions. The current mutual construction process is slow moving and requires significant investment and negotiation before transformation can take effect, as the following Aboriginal staff member explains:

> These systems, they are a bit like a huge boat, you just can't turn them around in two seconds, it is going to take awhile. (Aboriginal staff member four)

But, if criminologists act as local confidantes and global informants, they can provide the critical momentum to release this mutual construction process from the problematic and over-simplistic bifurcated discourse of over-represented racialized peoples that has stifled organic development in criminal justice practice for far too long.

References

Allan, A. and Dawson, D. 2004. 'Assessment of the risk of reoffending by indigenous male violent sexual offenders', *Trends and Issues in Crime and Criminal Justice*, 280, 1–6.

Andrews, D. 1999. 'Principles of effective correctional programs', in *Compendium 2000 on Effective Correctional Programming*, Volume 1, edited by M. Serin. Ottawa: Correction Services Canada.

Andrews, D. and Bonta, J. 1995. *The Level of Service Inventory – Revised*. Toronto: Multi-Health Systems.

Andrews, D. and Bonta, J. 2001. *Level of Service Inventory – Revised Profile Report*. North Tonawanda: Multi-Health Systems.

Andrews, D. and Bonta, J. 2010. *The Psychology of Criminal Conduct*. Fifth Edition. Cincinnati: Anderson Publications.

Andrews, D., Bonta, J. and Hoge, R. 1990. 'Classification for effective Rehabilitation: Rediscovering Psychology', *Criminal Justice and Behaviour*, 17(1), 19–52.

Andrews, D., Bonta, J. and Wormith, J. 2006. 'The recent past and near future of risk and/or need assessment', *Crime and Delinquency*, 52(1), 7–27.

Andrews, D., Zinger, I., Hoge, R., et al. 1990. 'Does correctional treatment work? A clinically relevant and psychologically informed meta-analysis', *Criminology*, 28(3), 369–404.

Andrews, D., Zinger, I., Hoge, R., et al. 1990c. 'A human science approach or more punishment and pessimism: A rejoinder to Lab and Whitehead', *Criminology*, 28(3), 419–29.

Armitage, A. 1995. *Comparing the Policy of Aboriginal Assimilation: Australia, Canada and New Zealand*. Vancouver: University of British Columbia Press.

Ashcroft, B. 2001. *On Post-Colonial Futures: Transformations of Colonial Culture*. London: Continuum.

Atkinson, G. and Jones, R. 2005. *An Evaluation of the Koori Cognitive Skills Program Pilots for Corrections Victoria: Final Report*. Melbourne: Victorian Department of Justice.

Aveling, N. 2004. 'Critical whiteness studies and the challenges of learning to be a "white ally"', *borderlands e-journal* [online] 3(2). Available at: http://www.borderlands.net.au/vol3no2_2004/aveling_critical.htm [accessed 23 December 2009].

Bakker, L., O'Malley, J. and Riley, D. 1999. *Risk of Reconviction: Statistical Models Predicting Four Types of Re-Offending*. Wellington: New Zealand Department of Corrections.

Beccaria, C. 1775. *An Essay on Crime and Punishment.* London: F. Newbery.

Beck, U. 1992. *Risk Society: Towards a New Modernity.* London: SAGE.

Beck, U. 1998. 'Politics of risk society', in *The Politics of Risk Society*, edited by J. Franklin. Cambridge: Polity Press, 9–22.

Beck, U. 2000. *World Risk Society.* Cambridge: Polity Press.

Beck, U., Giddens, A. and Lanash, S. 1994. *Reflexive Modernization: Politics, Tradition and Aesthetics in the Modern Social Order.* Cambridge: Polity Press.

Bentham, J. 1780. 'An introduction to the principles of morals and legislation', in *An Introduction to the Principles of Morals and Legislation: Jeremy Bentham*, edited by J. Burns and H. Hart. London: Methuen.

Berger, M. 1999. *White Lies: Race and the Myths of Whiteness.* New York: Farrar Straus Giroux.

Bernstein, R. 1994. 'Foucault: Critique as a philosophic ethos', in *Critique and Power: Recasting the Foucault/Habermas Debate*, edited by M. Kelly. Massachusetts: Massachusetts Institute of Technology, 211–42.

Bhabha, H. 1994. *The Location of Culture.* London: Routledge.

Birgden, A. 2004. 'Therapeutic jurisprudence and responsivity: Finding the will and the way in offender rehabilitation', *Psychology, Crime and Law*, 10(3), 283–95.

Birgden, A. and McLachlan, C. 2004. *Reducing Re-offending Framework: Setting the Scene Part No. 1.* Melbourne: Victorian Department of Justice.

Bonta, J. 1996. 'Risk-needs assessment and treatment', in *Choosing Correctional Options that Work: Defining the Demand and Evaluating the Supply*, edited by A. Harland. London: SAGE, 18–32.

Bonta, J. 1997. *Offender Rehabilitation: From Research to Practice* (Research Report no. 1997–01), Ottawa: Solicitor General.

Bonta, J. 2002. 'Offender risk assessment: Guidelines for selection and use', *Criminal Justice and Behavior*, 39(4), 355–79.

Bonta, J. and Cormier, R. 1999. 'Corrections research in Canada: Impressive progress and promising prospects', *Canadian Journal of Criminology*, 41(2), 235–47.

Bonta, J., LaPrairie, C., and Wallace-Capretta, S. 1997. 'Risk prediction and re-offending: Aboriginal and non-aboriginal offenders', *Canadian Journal of Criminology*, 39(2), 127–44.

Bosworth, M. 1996. 'Resistance and compliance in women's prisons: Towards a critique of legitimacy', *Critical Criminology*, 7(2), 5–19.

Bosworth, M. 1999. *Engendering Resistance: Agency and Power in Women's Prisons.* Aldershot: Ashgate.

Bosworth, M. 2004. 'Theorizing race and imprisonment: Towards a new penality', *Critical Criminology*, 12(2), 221–42.

Bosworth, M. and Carrabine, E. 2001. 'Reassessing resistance: Race, gender and sexuality in prison', *Punishment and Society*, 3(4), 501–15.

Bourassa, S. and Strong, A. 2002. 'Restitution of land to New Zealand Maori: The role of social structure', *Pacific Affairs*, 75(2), 227–60.

British Society of Criminology. 2011. British Society of Criminology Conference Programme 3–6 July 2011, Northumbria University.

Broadhurst, R. 1997. 'Aborigines and crime in Australia', *Crime and Justice: A Review of Research*, 21, 407–68.

Brown, M. 2000. 'Calculations of risk in contemporary penal practice', in *Dangerous Offenders: Punishment and Social Order*, edited by M. Brown and J. Pratt. London: Routledge, 93–108.

Buchan, B. and Heath, M. 2006. 'Savagery and civilization: From *terra nullius* to the "tide of history"', *Ethnicities*, 6(1), 5–26.

Butler, J. 1990. *Gender Trouble: Feminism and the Subversion of Identity*. London: Routledge.

Butler, J. 1997. *Excitable Speech: A Politics of the Performative*. London: Routledge.

Carach, C., Grant, A., and Conroy, R. 1999. 'Australian corrections: The imprisonment of indigenous people', *Trends and Issues in Crime and Criminal Justice*, 137, 1–6.

Carrabine, E. 2004. *Power, Discourse and Resistance: A Genealogy of the Strangeways Prison Riot*. Aldershot: Ashgate.

Carter, R. and Qureshi, A. 1995. 'A typology of philosophical assumptions in multicultural counselling and training', in *Handbook of Multicultural Counselling*, edited by J. Ponterotto, J. Casas, L. Suzuki and C. Alexander. Thousand Oaks: SAGE, 239–62.

Cheliotis, L. and Liebling, A. 2006. 'Race matters in British prisons: Towards a research agenda', *British Journal of Criminology*, 46(2), 286–317.

Choney, S., Berryhill-Paapke, E. and Robbins, R. 1995. 'The acculturation of American Indians: Developing frameworks for research and practice', in *Handbook of Multicultural Counselling*, edited by J. Ponterotto, J. Casas, L. Suzuki and C. Alexander. Thousand Oaks: SAGE, 73–92.

Coebergh, B., Bakker, L., Anstiss, B., et al. 2001. *A Seein' "I" to the Future: The Criminogenic Needs Inventory (CNI)*. Wellington: Psychological Services, New Zealand Department of Corrections.

Cohen, S. 1985. *Visions of Social Control*. Cambridge: Polity Press.

Cunneen, C. 2001. *The Impact of Crime Prevention on Aboriginal Communities*, Sydney: New South Wales Crime Prevention Division and Aboriginal Justice Advisory Council.

Cunneen, C. 2006. 'Racism, discrimination and the over-representation of Indigenous people in the criminal justice system: Some conceptual and explanatory issues', *Current Issues in Criminal Justice*, 17(3), 329–47.

Cunneen, C. 2011. 'Indigeneity, sovereignty and the law: Challenging the process of criminalisation', *University of New South Wales Faculty of Law Research Series*, paper 11, New South Wales: University of New South Wales.

Cunneen, C. and McDonald, D. 1997. *Keeping Aboriginal and Torres Strait Islander People Out of Custody: An Evaluation of the Implementation of the Recommendations of the Royal Commission in Aboriginal Deaths in Custody*.

Canberra: Office of Public Affairs, Aboriginal and Torres Strait Islander Commission.

Davis, A. 2003. *Are Prisons Obsolete?* New York: Seven Stories Press.

Davis, B. 1999. *The Inappropriateness of the Criminal Justice System – Indigenous Australian Criminological Perspective.* Paper to the 3rd National Outlook Symposium on Crime in Australia, Mapping the Boundaries of Australia's Criminal Justice System, 23 March 1999, Canberra, Australia.

Day, A. 2003. 'Reducing the risk of re-offending in Australian indigenous offenders: What works for whom?', *Journal of Offender Rehabilitation*, 37(2), 1–16.

Day, A., Giles, G., Marshall, B. and Sanderson, V. 2004. 'The recruitment and retention of indigenous criminal justice agency staff in an Australian state', *International Journal of Offender Therapy and Comparative Criminology*, 48(3), 347–59.

Day, A., Howells, K. and Casey, S. 2003. 'The rehabilitation of indigenous prisoners: An Australian perspective', *Journal of Ethnicity in Criminal Justice*, 11(1), 115–33.

Deakin University Australia and Australian and New Zealand Society of Criminology. 2011. ANZSOC Conference Programme: The 24th Annual ANZSOC Criminology Conference: Crime and the Regions from the local to regional, national and international, 28–30 September 2011. Geelong: Deakin University.

Department of Corrections New Zealand. 2008. *Māori Strategic Plan: 2008–2013.* Wellington: New Zealand Department of Corrections.

Department of Justice. 2006. *Victorian Aboriginal Justice Agreement: Phase Two.* Melbourne: Indigenous Issues Unit, Victorian Department of Justice.

Department of Justice and Department of Human Services. 2004. *Victorian Aboriginal Justice Agreement: Phase One.* Melbourne: Victorian Department of Justice.

Department of Justice, Department for Community Development, Department of Indigenous Affairs, Western Australia Police Service, the Aboriginal and Torres Strait Islander Commission, the Aboriginal and Torres Strait Islander Services and Aboriginal Legal Service of Western Australia. 2004. *Western Australian Aboriginal Justice Agreement.* Perth, Western Australian Department of Justice.

Durie, M. 1996. *Māori Culture Identity and its Implications for Mental Health Services.* Palmerston North: Department of Māori Studies, Massey University.

Durie, M. 1998a. *Whaiora: Māori Health Development.* Aukland: Oxford University Press.

Durie, M. 1998b. *Te mana, Te kawanatanga: The Politics of Māori Self-determination.* Auckland: Oxford University Press.

Durie, M. 2001. *Māori Ora: The Dynamics of Māori Health.* Auckland: Oxford University Press.

Durie, M. 2003. *Nga Kahui Pou: Launching Māori Future.* Wellington: Huia.

Durie, M. 2005 *Nga Tai Matatu: Tides of Māori Endurance.* South Melbourne: Oxford University Press.

During, S. 1995. 'Postmodernism or post-colonialism today', in *The Post-Colonial Studies Reader*, edited by B. Ashcroft, G. Griffiths and H. Tiffin. London: Routledge.

Duster, T. 2001. 'The "morphing" properties of whiteness', in *The Making and Unmaking of Whiteness*, edited by B. Rasmussen, E. Klinenberg, I. Nexica, and M. Wray. Durham: Duke University Press, 113–37.

Elder, C., Ellis, C. and Pratt, A. 2004. 'Whiteness in constructions of Australian nationhood: Indigenes, immigrants and governmentality', in *Whitening Race: Essays in Social and Cultural Criticism*, edited by A. Moreton-Robinson. Canberra: Aboriginal Studies Press, 208–21.

Fee, M. 1995. 'Who can write as other?', in *The Post-Colonial Studies Reader*, edited by B. Ashcroft, G. Griffiths and H. Tiffin. London: Routledge.

Feeley, M. and Simon, J. 1992. 'The new penology: Notes on the emerging strategy of corrections and its implications', *Criminology*, 30(4), 449–74.

Findlay, M., Odgers, S. and Yeo, S. 2005. *Australian Criminal Justice.* Third Edition. Victoria: Oxford University Press.

Finnane, M. and McGuire, J. 2001. 'The use of punishment and exile: Aborigines in colonial Australia', *Punishment and Society*, 3(2), 279–98.

Finnane, M. and Richards, J. 2010. 'Aboriginal violence and state response: Histories, policies and legacies in Queensland 1860–1940', *The Australian and New Zealand Journal of Criminology*, 43(2), 238–62.

Foucault, M. 1967. *Madness and Civilization: A History of Insanity in the Age of Reason.* London: Tavistock.

Foucault, M. 1969. *The Archaeology of Knowledge.* London: Routledge.

Foucault, M. 1980a. 'The eye of power', in *Power/Knowledge: Selected Interviews and Other Writings 1972–1977*, edited by C. Gordon. New York: Pantheon Books, 146–65.

Foucault, M. 1980b. *Power/Knowledge: Selected Interviews and Other Writings 1972–1977.* New York: Pantheon Books.

Foucault, M. 1980c. 'Truth and power', in *Power/Knowledge: Selected Interviews and Other Writings 1972–1977*, edited by C. Gordon. New York: Pantheon Books, 109–33.

Foucault, M. 1980d. 'Two lectures', in *Power/Knowledge: Selected Interviews and Other Writings 1972–1977*, edited by C. Gordon. New York: Pantheon Books, 78–108.

Foucault, M. 1981. 'The order of discourse', in *Untying the Text: A Post-structuralist Reader*, edited by R. Young. London: Routledge and Kegan Paul, 48–78.

Foucault, M. 1985. *The Use of Pleasure: Volume Two of The History of Sexuality.* New York: Pantheon Books.

Foucault, M. 1990. *Politics Philosophy Culture: Interviews and Other Writings 1977–1984.* London: Routledge.

Foucault, M. 1991a. *Discipline and Punish: The Birth of the Prison.* London: Penguin Books.

Foucault, M. 1991b. 'Politics and the study of discourse', in *The Foucault Effect: Studies in Governmentality*, edited by G. Burchell, C. Gordon and P. Miller. London: Harvester Wheatsheaf, 53–72.

Foucault, M. 1991c. 'Questions of method', in *The Foucault Effect: Studies in Governmentality*, edited by G. Burchell, C. Gordon and P. Miller. London: Harvester Wheatsheaf, 73–86.

Foucault, M. 1991d. *Remarks on Marx: Conversations with Duccio Trombadori.* Translation R. Goldstein and J. Cascaito. New York: Semiotext(e).

Foucault, M. 1998. *The History of Sexuality One: The Will to Knowledge.* Ringwood: Penguin Books.

Foucault, M. 2000a. 'Nietzsche, genealogy, history', in *Aesthetics, Method, and Epistemology: Essential Works of Foucault 1954–1984*, Volume 2, edited by J. Faubion. Middlesex: Penguin Books, 369–92.

Foucault, M. 2000b. *Power: Essential Works of Foucault 1954–1984*, Volume 3. Ringwood: Penguin Books.

Foucault, M. 2002. 'The subject and power', *Power: Essential Work of Foucault 1954–1984*, Volume 3, edited by J. Faubion. London: Penguin Books, 326–48.

Foucault, M. 2007. *Security, Territory, Population: Lectures at the College de France 1977–1978.* Basingstoke: Palgrave Macmillan.

Foucault, M. 2008. *The Birth of Biopolitics: Lectures at the College de France, 1978–1979.* New York: Palgrave Macmillan.

Frankenberg, R. 2001. 'The mirage of an unmarked whiteness', in *The Making and Unmaking of Whiteness*, edited by B. Rasmussen, E. Klinenberg, I. Nexica, and M. Wray. Durham: Duke University Press, 72–96.

Garland, D. 1995. 'Penal modernism and postmodernism', in *Punishment and Social Control*, edited by T. Blomberg and S. Cohen. Hawthorne: Aldine de Gruyter.

Garland, D. 2001a. *The Culture of Control: Crime and Social Order in Contemporary Society.* Oxford: University of Chicago Press.

Garland, D. 2001b. *Mass Imprisonment: Social Causes and Consequences.* London: SAGE.

Gendreau, P. 1996a. 'Offender rehabilitation: What we know and what needs to be done', *Criminal Justice and Behavior*, 23(1), 144–61.

Gendreau, P. 1996b. 'The principles of effective intervention with offenders', in *Choosing Correctional Options That Work: Defining the Demand and Evaluating the Supply*, edited by A. Harland. London: SAGE.

Gendreau, P. and Andrews, D. 1990. 'Tertiary prevention: What the meta-analysis of the offender treatment literature tells us about "what works"', *Canadian Journal of Criminology*, 32, 173–84.

Giddens, A. 1990. *The Consequences of Modernity.* London: Polity Press.

Giddens, A. 1994. *Beyond Left and Right.* Cambridge: Polity Press.

Giddens, A. 1998. *The Third Way.* Cambridge: Polity Press.

Giroux, H. 1999. 'Rewriting the discourse of racial identity: Toward a pedagogy and politics of whiteness', in *Becoming and Unbecoming White: Owning and Disowning a Racial Identity*, edited by C. Clark and J. O'Donnell. London: Bergin and Garvey.

Goldie, T. 1995. 'The representation of the indigene', in *The Post-Colonial Studies Reader*, edited by B. Ashcroft, G. Griffiths, and H. Tiffin. London: Routledge.

Gomez, L. 2010. 'Understanding law and race as mutually constitutive: An invitation to explore an emerging field', *Annual Review of Law and Social Sciences*, 6, 487–505.

Greenfeld, L. and Smith, S. 1999. *American Indians and Crime*. Washington DC: Bureau of Statistics.

Hale, C., Hayward, K., Wahidin, A. and Wincup, E. 2009. *Criminology*. Second Edition. Oxford: Oxford University Press.

Hall, D., Green, M., Chambers, G., and Lea, R. 2006. *Tracking the Evolutionary History of the Warrior Gene in the South Pacific*. Paper to the 11th International Human Genetics meeting, Brisbane, 6–10 August.

Hannah-Moffat, K. 2000. 'Prisons that empower: Neo-liberal governance in Canadian women's prisons', *British Journal of Criminology*, 20, 510–31.

Hannah-Moffat, K. 2001. *Punishment in Disguise: Penal Governance and Federal Imprisonment of Women in Canada*. Toronto: University of Toronto Press.

Hannah-Moffat, K. 2004a. 'Gendered risk at what costs: Negotiations of gendered risk in Canadian women's prisons', *Feminism and Psychology*, 14(2), 234–49.

Hannah-Moffat, K. 2004b. 'Losing ground: Gendered knowledges, parole risk, and responsibility', *Social Politics*, 11(3), 363–85.

Hannah-Moffat, K. 2005. 'Criminogenic needs and the transformative risk subject: Hybridizations of risk/need in penality', *Punishment and Society*, 7(1), 29–51.

Hannah-Moffat, K. 2006. 'Pandora's box: Risk/need and gender-responsive corrections', *Criminology and Public Policy*, 5(1), 1301–11.

Hannah-Moffat, K. 2011. 'Sacrosanct or flawed: Risk, accountability and gender-responsive penal politics', *Current Issues in Criminal Justice*, 22(2), 193–215.

Hannah-Moffat, K. and Maurutto, P. 2010. 'Re-contextualizing pre-sentence reports: Risk and race', *Punishment and Society*, 12(3), 262–86.

Hannah-Moffat, K. and Yule, C. 2011. 'Gaining insight, changing attitudes and managing "risk": Parole release decisions for women convicted of violent crimes', *Punishment and Society*, 13(2), 149–75.

Harris, A. 2004. *Hikoi: Forty Years of Māori Protest*. Wellington: Huia Publishers.

Havemann, P. 1988. 'The indigenization of social control in Canada', in *Indigenous Law and the State*, edited by B. Morse and G. Woodman. Dordrecht: Foris Publications, 71–100.

Hayman, S. 2006. *Imprisoning Our Sisters: The New Federal Women's Prisons in Canada*. Montreal: McGill-Queen's University Press.

Hogg, R. and Carrington, K. 2001. 'Governing rural Australia: Land, space and race', in *Rethinking Law, Society and Governance: Foucault's Bequest*, edited by G. Wickham and G. Pavlich. Oxford: Hart Publishing, 43–60.

Holdaway, S. 1996. *The Racialisation of British Policing*. London: Macmillan.

Home Office. 2006. *A Guide to Anti-Social Behaviour Orders*. London: Home Office.

Howells, K. and Day, A. 1999. 'The rehabilitation of offenders: International perspectives applied to Australian correctional systems', *Trends and Issues in Crime and Criminal Justice*, 112.

Howells, K. and Day, A. 2003. 'Readiness for anger management: Clinical and theoretical issues', *Clinical Psychology Review*, 23(2), 319–37.

Howells, K., Day, A. and Davey, L. 2005. 'The future of offender rehabilitation', in *Issues in Australian Crime and Criminal Justice*, edited by D. Chappell and P. Wilson. Chatswood: LexisNexis Butterworths.

Hucklesby, A. and Wahidin, A. 2009. *Criminal Justice*. First Edition. Oxford: Oxford University Press.

Hudson, B. and Bramhall, G. 2005. 'Assessing the "other": Constructions of "Asianness" in risk assessment by probation officers', *British Journal of Criminology*, 45(5), 721–40.

Hylton, J. 1995. 'Social policy and Canada's aboriginal people: The need for fundamental reforms', in *Popular Justice and Community Regeneration: Pathways of Indigenous Reform*, edited by K. Hazlehurst. Westport: Praeger, 3–20.

Implementation Review Team. 2004. *Victorian Implementation Review of the Recommendations from the Royal Commission into Aboriginal Deaths in Custody: Discussion Paper*. Melbourne: Victorian Department of Justice.

Jackomos, A. 2005. *Victorian Government Response to the Implementation Review of the Recommendations from the Royal Commission into Aboriginal Deaths in Custody*. Melbourne: Indigenous Issues Unit, Victorian Department of Justice.

Jackson, M. 1988. *The Māori and the Criminal Justice System He Whaipaanga Hou – A New Perspective: Part 2*. Wellington: New Zealand Department of Justice.

Jackson, M. 1995. 'Justice and political power: Reasserting Māori legal processes', in *Legal Pluralism and the Colonial Legacy: Indigenous Experiences of Justice in Canada, Australia, and New Zealand*, edited by K. Hazlehurst. Avebury: Aldershot, 243–63.

Johnston, E. 1990. *Report of the Inquiry into the Death of the Woman who Died at Ceduna on 18 February 1983*. Canberra: Australian Government Publishing Service.

Jones, R., Loredo, C., Johnson, S. and McFarlane-Nathan, G. 1999. 'A paradigm for culturally relevant sexual abuser treatment: An international perspective', in *Cultural Diversity in Sexual Abuser Treatment: Issues and Approaches*, edited by A. Lewis. Brandon: Safer Society Press.

Jones, R., Masters, M., Griffiths, A. and Moulday, N. 2002. 'Culturally relevant assessment of Indigenous offenders: A literature review', *Australian Psychologist*, 37(3), 187–97.

Joudo, J. 2008. 'Responding to substance abuse and offending in Indigenous communities: Review of diversion programs', *Research and Public Policy Series*, no. 88. Canberra: Australian Institute of Criminology.

Kennedy, S. 1999. 'Responsivity: The other classification principle', *Corrections Today*, 61, 48–51.

La Prairie, C. 2002. 'Aboriginal over-representation in the criminal justice system: A tale of nine cities', *Canadian Journal of Criminology*, 44(2), 181–208.

Larsen, J., Robertson, P., Hillman, D. and Hudson, S. 1998. 'Te Piriti: A bicultural model for treating child molesters in Aotearoa/New Zealand', in *Sourcebook of Treatment Programs for Sexual Offenders*, edited by W. Marshall, Y. Fernandez, S. Hudson and T. Ward. New York: Plenum Press, 385–98.

Lash, S. 2002. *Critique of Information*. London: SAGE.

Latimer, J. and Foss, L. 2005. 'The sentencing of aboriginal and non-aboriginal youth under the young offenders act: A multivariate analysis', *Canadian Journal of Criminology and Criminal Justice*, 47(3), 481–500.

Lea, R. and Chambers, G. 2007. 'Monoamine oxidase, addiction, and the "warrior" gene hypothesis', *New Zealand Medical Journal*, 120(1250), 5–10.

Lee, C. and Armstrong, K. 1995. 'Indigenous models of mental health intervention: Lessons from traditional healers', in *Handbook of Multicultural Counselling*, edited by J. Ponterotto, J. Casas, L. Suzuki and C. Alexander. London: SAGE.

Lombardo, P. 2011. *A Century of Eugenics in America: From the Indiana Experiment to the Human Genome Era*. Bloomington: Indiana University Press.

Lombroso, C. 1876. *L'Uomo Delinquente*. Milan: Hoepli.

Lombroso, C. 1898. 'Why homicide has increased in the United States – II', *North American Review*, CLXVI(494), 1–11.

Looman, J., Dickie, I. and Abracen, J. 2005. 'Responsivity issues in the treatment of sexual offenders', *Trauma, Violence and Abuse*, 6(4), 330–53.

Lum, D. 2011. *Cultural Competent Practice: A Framework for understanding diverse groups and justice issues*. Fourth Edition. Belmont: Cengage Learning.

Martinson, R. 1974. 'What works? Questions and answers about prison reform', *The Public Interest*, 35, 22–54.

Maurutto, P. and Hannah-Moffat, K. 2007. 'Understanding risk in the context of the youth criminal justice act', *Canadian Journal of Criminology and Criminal Justice*, 49(4), 465–91.

McFarlane-Nathan, G. 1999. *FReMO Framework for Reducing Māori Offending: How to Achieve Quality in Policy and Services to Reduce Māori Offending and Enhance Māori Aspirations*. Wellington: Psychological Service, New Zealand Department of Corrections.

McGuire, J. 2000. 'Can the criminal law ever be therapeutic?', *Behavioural Sciences and the Law*, 18, 413–26.

McGuire, J. 2002a. *Offender Rehabilitation and Treatment: Effective Programmes and Policies to Reduce Re-offending*. Chichester: John Wiley and Sons.

McGuire, J. 2002b. 'Criminal sanctions versus psychologically based interventions with offenders: A comparative empirical analysis', *Psychology, Crime and Law*, 8(2), 183–208.

Miller, P. and Rose, N. 2009. *Governing the Present: Administering Economic, Social and Personal Life.* Cambridge: Polity Press.

Millie, A. 2008. 'Anti-social behaviour, behavioural expectations and an urban aesthetic', *British Journal of Criminology*, 48(3), 379–94.

Monture-Angus, P. 1999. 'Women and risk: Aboriginal women, colonialism, and correctional practice', *Canadian Women Studies*, 19(1/2), 24.

Moreton-Robinson, A. 2004. 'Whiteness, epistemology and indigenous representation', in *Whitening Race: Essays in Social and Cultural Criticism*, edited by A. Moreton-Robinson. Canberra: Aboriginal Studies Press.

Morrison, B. 2009. *Identifying and Responding to Bias in the Criminal Justice System: A Review of International and New Zealand Research.* Wellington: Ministry of Justice.

Moster, A., Wnuk, D. and Jeglic, E. 2008. 'Cognitive behavioural therapy interventions with sex offenders', *Journal of Correctional Health Care*, 14(2), 109–21.

Murumali. 2007. *Wingangali Marumali: To Put Back Together.* Available at: http://www.marumali.com.au/about_healing.htm [accessed: 11 December 2009].

Nathan, L., Wilson, N. and Hillman, D. 2003. *Te Whakakotahitango: An Evaluation of the Te Piriti Special Treatment Program for Child Sex Offenders in New Zealand.* Auckland: New Zealand Department of Corrections.

New South Wales Aboriginal Justice Advisory Council. 2003. *New South Wales Aboriginal Justice Plan: Beyond Justice 2004–2014.* Sydney: New South Wales Aboriginal Justice Advisory Council.

Newburn, T. 2007. *Criminology.* Cullompton: Willan Publishing.

Niceforo, A. 1901. *Italiani del Nord e Italiani del Sud.* Turin: Fratelli Bocca.

Ogloff, J. 2002. 'Offender rehabilitation: From "nothing works" to "what next?"', *Australian Psychologist*, 37(3), 245–52.

Ogloff, J. and Davis, M. 2004. 'Advances in offender assessment and rehabilitation: Contributions of the risk-needs-responsivity approach', *Psychology, Crime and Law*, 10(3), 229–42.

O'Malley, P. 1998. 'Indigenous governance', in *Governing Australia: Studies in Contemporary Rationalities of Government*, edited by D. Mitchell and B. Hindess. Cambridge: Cambridge University Press, 156–72.

One News. 2006. 'Warrior gene prevalent in Maori study', 9 August 2006. Available at: http://tvnz.co.nz/view/page/425826/810285 [accessed 12 March 2012].

Orange, C. 1987. *The Treaty of Waitangi.* Wellington: Allen and Unwin New Zealand Limited.

Patterson, J. 1992. 'A Maori concept of collective responsibility', in *Justice, Ethics and New Zealand Society*, edited by G. Oddie and R. Perret. Auckland: Oxford University Press, 11–26.

Pedersen, P. 1995. 'Culture-centred ethical guidelines for counsellors', in *Handbook of Multicultural Counselling*, edited by J. Ponterotto, J. Casas, L. Suzuki and C. Alexander. Thousand Oaks: SAGE.

Perreault, S. 2009. 'The incarceration of Aboriginal people in adult correctional services', *Juristat*, 29(3), 4–27.

Phillips, C. 2005. 'Facing inwards and outwards? Institutional racism, race equality and the role of Black and Asian professional associations', *Criminal Justice*, 5(4), 357–77.

Phillips, C. 2007. 'The re-emergence of the "black spectre": Minority professional associations in the post-Macpherson era', *Ethnic and Racial Studies*, 30(3), 375–96.

Phillips, C. and Bowling, B. 2003. 'Racism, ethnicity and criminology: Developing minority perspectives', *British Journal of Criminology*, 43(2), 269–90.

Poata-Smith, E. 1996. '*He pokeke uenuku, tu ai*: The evolution of contemporary Maori protest', in *Nga Patai: Racism and Ethnic Relations in Aotearoa/New Zealand*, edited by P. Spoonley, D. Pearson and C. Macpherson. Palmerston North: The Dunmore Press, 160–79.

Poata-Smith, E. 1997. 'The political economy of inequality between Maori and Pakeha', in *The Political Economy of New Zealand*, edited by C. Rudd and B. Roper. Auckland: Oxford University Press, 160–82.

Policy Strategy and Research Group. 2007. *Findings from the Evaluation of the Special Māori Cultural Assessment.* Wellington: New Zealand Department of Corrections.

Policy Strategy and Research Group. 2009. *Māori Focus Units and Māori Therapeutic Programmes: Evaluation Report.* Wellington: New Zealand Department of Corrections.

Pollack, S. 2005. 'Taming the shrew: Regulating prisoners through women-centred mental health programming', *Critical Criminology*, 15(3), 71–87.

Pollack, S. 2007. '"I'm just not good in relationships": Victimization discourses and the gendered regulation of criminalized women', *Feminist Criminology*, 2(2), 158–74.

Pollack, S. 2009. '"You can't have it both ways": Punishment and treatment of imprisoned women', *Journal of Progressive Human Services*, 20(2), 112–28.

Pratt, J., Brown, D., Brown, M., et al. 2005. *The New Punitiveness: Trends, Theories, Perspectives.* Oregon: Willan Publishing.

Public Works and Government Services Canada. 1996. *Commission of Inquiry Into Certain Events at the Prison for Women in Kingston.* Ottawa: Canada Communication Group Publishing.

Purvis, M., Ward, T. and Willis, G. 2011. 'The good lives model in practice: Offence pathways and case management', *European Journal of Probation*, 3(2), 4–28.

Roberts, J. and Melchers, R. 2003. 'The incarceration of aboriginal offenders: Trends from 1978 to 2001', *Canadian Journal of Criminology and Criminal Justice*, 45(2), 211–42.

Robertson, P., Larsen, J., Hillman, D. and Hudson, S. 1999. 'Conceptual issues in therapy with sexually abusive Maori men', in *Cultural Diversity in Sexual Abuser Treatment: Issues and Approaches*, edited by A. Lewis. Brandon: Safer Society Press.

Rose, N., O'Malley, P. and Valverde, M. 2006. 'Governmentality', *Annual Review of Law and Social Sciences*, 2, 83–104.

Ross, L. 1998. *Inventing the Savage: The Social Construction of Native American Criminality*. Texas: University of Texas.

Royal Commission into Aboriginal Deaths in Custody. 1991. *Royal Commission into Aboriginal Deaths in Custody Final Report*. Canberra: Australian Government Publishing Service.

Sergi, G. 1901. *The Mediterranean Race: A Study of the Origin of European Peoples*. New York: Charles Scribner's Sons.

Sheldon, W. 1949. *Varieties of Delinquent Youth*. New York: Harper.

Smith, L. 1999. *Decolonizing Methodologies: Research and Indigenous Peoples*. London: Zed Books Ltd.

Snowball, L. and Weatherburn, D. 2007. 'Does racial bias in sentencing contribute to Indigenous over-representation in prison?', *The Australian and New Zealand Journal of Criminology*, 40(3), 272–90.

Sorrenson, M. 1995. 'The Waitangi Tribunal and the resolution of Maori grievances', *British Journal of New Zealand Studies*, 8, 21–36.

Spivak, G. 1985. 'The Rani of Simur', in *Europe and Its Others: Proceedings of the Essex Conference on the Sociology of Literature July 1984*, Volume 1, edited by F. Barker, P. Hulme, M. Iversen and D. Loxley. Colchester: University of Essex.

Spivak, G. 1990. 'The intervention interview', in *The Post-Colonial Critic: Interviews, Strategies, Dialogues*, edited by S. Harasym. London: Routledge, 113–32.

Spivakovsky, C. 2007. 'Negotiations of space: The indigenous prisoner and discourse', *EnterText* [online], 6(3). Available at: http://arts.brunel.ac.uk/gate/entertext/issue_6_3.htm [accessed 5 December 2009].

Squires, P. 2008. *ASBO Nation: The Criminalisation of Nuisance*. Bristol: The Policy Press.

Task Force on Federally Sentenced Women. 1990. *Creating Choices: The Report of the Task Force on Federally Sentenced Women*. Ottawa: Ministry of the Solicitor General.

Tauri, J. 1998. 'Family group conferencing: A case-study of the indigenisation of New Zealand's justice system', *Current Issues in Criminal Justice*, 10(2), 168–82.

Tauri, J. 1999. 'Explaining recent innovations in New Zealand's criminal justice system: Empowering Maori or biculturalising the state?', *Australian and New Zealand Journal of Criminology*, 32(2), 153–67.

Tauri, J. and Webb, R. 2011. 'The Waitangi Tribunal and the regulation of Maori protest', *New Zealand Sociology*, 26(Special Issue), 21–41.

Turnbull, S. and Hannah-Moffat, K. 2009. 'Under these conditions: Gender, parole and the governance of reintegration', *British Journal of Criminology*, 49(4), 532–51.

Wacquant, L. 2001. 'Deadly symbiosis: When ghetto and prison meet and mesh', *Punishment and Society*, 3(1), 95–133.

Wacquant, L. 2009. *Punishing the Poor: Neoliberal Government of Social Insecurity*. Durham: Duke University Press.

Wacquant, L. 2010a. *Deadly Symbiosis: Race and the Rise of the Penal State*. Cambridge: Polity Press.

Wacquant, L. 2010b. 'Class, race and hyperincarceration in revanchist America', *Daedalus*, 139(3), 74–90.

Wacquant, L. 2010c. 'Crafting the neoliberal state: Workfare, prisonfare and social insecurity', *Sociological Forum*, 25(2), 197–220.

Waitangi Tribunal. 1991. *The Ngai Tahu Report*. Wellington: New Zealand Legislation Direct.

Waitangi Tribunal. 1995. *The Offender Assessment Policies Report*. Wellington: New Zealand Legislation Direct.

Waldram, J. 1997. 'The reification of Aboriginal culture in Canadian prison spirituality programs', in *Present is Past: Some Uses of Tradition in Native Societies*, edited by M. Mauze. Lanham: University Press of America.

Walker, J. and McDonald, D. 1995. 'The over-representation of indigenous people in custody in Australia', *Trends and Issues in Crime and Criminal Justice*, 47, 1–6.

Ward, T. 2002a. 'Good lives and the rehabilitation of offenders: Promises and problems', *Aggression and Violent Behaviour*, 7(5), 513–28.

Ward, T. 2002b. 'The management of risk and the design of good lives', *Australian Psychologist*, 37(3), 172–9.

Ward, T. and Brown, M. 2003. 'The risk-need model of offender rehabilitation: A critical analysis', in *Sexual Deviance: Issues and Controversies*, edited by T. Ward, D. Laws and S. Hudson. Thousand Oaks: SAGE, 338–54.

Ward, T. and Brown, M. 2004. 'The good lives model and conceptual issues in offender rehabilitation', *Psychology, Crime and Law*, 10(3), 243–57.

Ward, T. and Eccleston, L. 2004. 'Risk, responsivity, and the treatment of offenders: Introduction to the special issue', *Psychology, Crime and Law*, 10(3), 223–7.

Ward, T. and Gannon, T. 2005. 'Rehabilitation, aetiology, and self-regulation: The comprehensive good lives model of treatment for sexual offenders', *Aggression and Violent Behavior*, 11, 77–94.

Ward, T. and Maruna, S. 2007. *Rehabilitation: Beyond the Risk Paradigm*. London: Routledge.

Ward, T. and Stewart, C. 2003a. 'Criminogenic needs and human needs: A theoretical model', *Psychology, Crime and Law*, 9(2), 125–43.

Ward, T. and Stewart, C. 2003b. 'The treatment of sex offenders: Risk management and good lives', *Professional Psychology: Research and Practice*, 34(4), 353–60.

Ward, T., Day, A., Howells, K. and Birgden, A. 2004. 'The multifactor offender readiness model', *Aggression and Violent Behavior*, 9(6), 645–73.

Ward, T., Laws, D. and Hudson, S. 2003. *Sexual Deviance: Issues and Controversies*. Thousand Oaks: SAGE.

Ward, T., Mann, R. and Gannon, T. 2007. 'The good lives model of offender rehabilitation: Clinical implications', *Aggression and Violent Behavior*, 12(1), 87–107.

Weatherburn, D. 2006. *Disadvantage, Drugs and Gaol: Re-thinking Indigenous Over-representation in Prison*, proceedings from the Conference of the Australasian Society on Alcohol and other Drugs, Cairns, 5–8 November, 2006.

Weatherburn, D. and Fitzgerald, J. 2007. 'Reducing Aboriginal over-representation in prison: A rejoinder to Chris Cunneen', *Current Issues in Criminal Justice*, 18(2), 366–70.

Weatherburn, D., Fitzgerald, J. and Hua, J. 2003. 'Reducing aboriginal over-representation in prison', *Australian Journal of Public Administration*, 62(3), 65–73.

Weatherburn, D., Lind, B. and Hua, J. 2003. 'Contact with the New South Wales court and prison systems: The influence of age, Indigenous status and gender', *Crime and Justice Bulletin*, 78, Sydney: New South Wales Bureau of Crime Statistics and Research.

Weatherburn, D., Snowball, L. and Hunter, B. 2006. 'The economic and social factors underpinning Indigenous contact with the justice system: Results from the 2002 NATSISS survey', *Crime and Justice Bulletin*, 104, Sydney: New South Wales Bureau of Crime Statistics and Research.

Wijesekere, G. 2004. 'Incarceration of indigenous and non-indigenous adults, 1991–2001: Trends and differentials', *Australian Aboriginal Studies*, 2, 54–63.

Williamson, P., Day, A., Howells, K., et al. 2004. 'Assessing offender readiness to change: Problems with anger', *Psychology, Crime and Law*, 10(3), 295–307.

Wolfe, P. 1991. 'On being woken up: The dreamtime in anthropology and in Australian settler culture', *Comparative Studies in Society and History*, 33(2), 197–224.

Wolfe, P. 1994. 'Nation and miscegenation: Discursive continuity in the post-Mabo era', *Social Analysis*, 36, 93–152.

Wolfe, P. 1997. 'History and imperialism: A century of theory, from Marx to postcolonialism', *The American Historical Review*, 102(2), 388–420.

Wolfe, P. 1999. *Settler Colonialism and the Transformation of Anthropology: The Politics and Poetics of an Ethnographic Event*. London: Cassell.

Wolfe, P. 2002. 'Race and racialisation: Some thoughts', *Postcolonial Studies*, 15(1), 51–62.

Wyvill, L. 1990a. *Report of the Inquiry into the Death of the Young Man who Died at Wujal Wujal on 29 March 1987*. Canberra: Australian Government Publishing Service.

Wyvill, L. 1990b. *Report of the Inquiry into the Death of the Young Man who died at Aurukun on 11 April 1987.* Canberra: Australian Government Publishing Service.

Zellerer, E. 2003. 'Culturally competent programs: The first family violence program for aboriginal men in prison', *The Prison Journal*, 83(2), 171–90.

Index

Advances in Criminology

Full series list